Indomitable

B. G. "Bunny" Inge
Edited by Jon Inge

Edited and expanded from notes written by Bernard "Bunny" Inge on his life and adventures in England, Canada, Hungary and China.

Published 2024
Printed in the United States of America
Print ISBN: 979-8-8692-7645-2

For information, address:
  Jon Inge
  9301 236th Street SW
  Edmonds, WA 98020

Dedicated to my parents, Bunny and Joyce,
a truly remarkable couple.

Contents

Illustrations

Introduction

As we were growing up, our house was full of the many mementoes my father had brought back from his travels: model boats made from horn, "trees" of jade, a map of Beijing's Forbidden City, a Chinese sword hanging over the back door, a presentation plaque of the crest from a Royal Navy destroyer, and much, much more.

These prompted many a story from him, always entertaining, never boastful and often told against himself, such as the time he missed a soccer goal from two feet out because he was running too fast to take the shot! He had seen Bleriot's plane crossing the Channel, sung in the choir at St. Paul's Cathedral and worked as a teenage farm labourer in Canada. He had been to China on the Trans Siberian Railway, and home again on a freighter in wartime.

His energy was boundless. He was always taking us on long walks, hauling back tree limbs and sawing them up for firewood, driving a tractor to mow the grounds of the school where we lived and he was headmaster, feeding the school farm chickens and pigs during school holidays so that the staff could have a few days off. (I can still smell the feed in the storeroom!)

It wasn't just his physical energy that impressed everyone, but also his upbeat, enthusiastic approach to every task. Whatever the setback he would always find a solution, a way to move forward while motivating those around him and keeping spirits high. No wonder his friend Captain John Magruder of the USS *Augusta* paid tribute to his "indomitable spirit that will never die."

In 1977, when he was recovering from a medical issue and was looking for something to occupy his ever-restless nature, we badgered him into writing about his experiences. He took up fountain pen and paper and set to work, producing 191 handwritten pages of stories and memories. His own title for it was *"Bernard Gane Inge: His Life (or what may safely be revealed of it!)"*, but it was always known amongst the family as *"The Saga"*.

This is the transcribed result, illuminated and expanded with various documents from his and others' archives, from the Internet's most helpful resources and from my own memories. I hope you find it of interest.

Jon Inge, May 2024

Childhood

I was born on January 21st, 1903, in Wimbledon, where Father had a small school. I wasn't Christened until 1908 owing to Father going off on a balloon trip (see original certificate) at the time originally set for the Christening, January 1st, 1904.[1]

In 1905 the family moved to Walmer, near Deal, Kent, where Father started up another school, Belmont House, a small private school for boys (day and boarding) which the three of the family old enough to do so attended. I remember almost nothing of the lessons except one history lesson, when the master talked about the Sikhs as "Six" - singular "Sick" - thus provoking the usual small boy merriment. Oh yes, one other lesson when a boy was playing with a golf ball: the master seized this and put it on the open coke fire. This was memorable because once the cover was off the ball hopped all over the place as the tightly stretched rubber bands caught alight and snapped. Great fun.

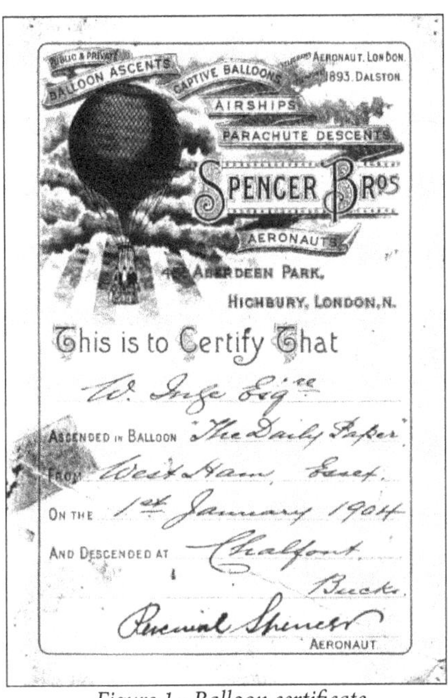

Figure 1 - Balloon certificate

Two other schoolroom memories: Father showing us how to get through the space of a small windowpane (first removing the glass) - roughly one arm and one shoulder first and then diagonally the rest of oneself, as astonishingly enough it was possible and was done. The other one was of singing lessons when we all gathered together and sang all the old songs - good fun as a rule. Father also

1   Percival Spencer, Aeronaut, was one of the leading balloonists in England at the time. The balloon flight from West Ham to Chalfont would have been about 30 miles, right across London – quite an adventure, and probably very cold in January!

had the horrifying habit not only of making us learn (to me, vast) poems but then making us stand up in front of the school and recite them. I have distinct memories of *"Othere, the old sea captain,"* who for some reason had a walrus tooth in his nut-brown hand.

Memories come crowding in, such as of Coronation Day 1911, when a master converted his bicycle into a submarine and got "submerged" in the steady rain as the procession went down Drum Hill opposite us. Also opposite were two things: a shop where they sold fruit, sweets, etc. (including rum toffee, which Father promptly banned as being possibly intoxicating) and a pub. I used to watch with fascination while barrels of beer were offloaded thunderously down to the cellars. As a result for years I was convinced that thunder was caused by beer barrels unloading in heaven!

On one occasion in 1910 Father took us all out to see Halley's Comet, a splendid thing to do seeing how seldom comets appear, and I can still see it as clearly now in my mind's eye in the east. We stood near the school garden, which also has its memories, amongst other things of blackcurrants. The boys at the school were pressed into picking them but had to whistle while doing so. Poor Ron couldn't whistle and was thereby somewhat under suspicion! In this garden were also a little thatched shelter, made by Father and the Scouts on Coronation Day, and outside gymnasium apparatus - ladders, bars, ropes, etc.

I have good reason to remember the latter because one day after I had shinned up the rope - a favorite hobby of mine - three of the boys came along and started swinging on the rope, which was suspended from a tripod of some height. Within minutes the inevitable happened - they swung too far and the whole thing came crashing down. I shot up one of the ladders and luckily escaped. Father was livid; swinging on the ropes was forbidden anyway, but when did that ever stop boys doing anything? He gave the boys the Homeric award of 1,000 lines for one boy and 500 each to the two others; I don't know why there was a difference.

We also had another small garden opposite the school, where I remember doing French with a French governess out of - so help us - *"French Without Tears"*. There was a small Victoria plum tree and a few apple trees. There were also some unfortunate worms. I had heard that if worms were (presumably by accident) cut into two they would join up. I was not prepared to wait for accidents, so I chopped

worms in two and put the two ends together. To my disappointment
nothing happened, and that was the end of my biological researches.
I remember playing a lot with Betty in this garden; Daphne was too
small and the older ones - Ron, Marnie and Norah - were presumably
immured in the classroom.

What else? "Baby" - Olga Ruth - died before she was a
year old, and flowers were brought up to the nursery for us to make
bunches and wreaths out of. To this day I cannot smell sweet peas
without thinking of that occasion. Olga was born the same day
Edward VII died, 6th May, 1910, and that was the end of the family,
as it were.

One winter there was a tremendous amount of snow and we
went tobogganing down the hill opposite the church. Ron took me
down once on a small two seater. The track was then like ice and I
was terrified - reasonably enough as Ron, I believe, lost control on
another run and tried to climb a tree. No damage to Ron, happily,
unlike another occasion on a Sunday school walk with Father, when
some enthusiast used a stick as a golf club and tried to drive a fir
cone. Unfortunately, and unwisely, Ron was standing behind and got
the full force of the downward swing on the top of his nose, which
didn't do him any good.

On another occasion Ron missed his direction with an axe
while camping with some scouts, and they brought him back to the
school on a trek cart, bugles blowing and all. Father was not amused,
which was a pity because it was all good fun.

Father was one of the pioneers of the Scouting movement
in England and got the Scout Medal of Merit for his services to
Scouting. Certainly his school troop was one of the earliest in the
county, and great were the preparations for camping. I can smell
those "billikins" (cooking utensils) now! It was always a grief to me
that I was too young to join, especially as Marnie and Norah became
two of the first Girl Scouts, before they became Girl Guides - or
"Good Girls", as we irreverent youngsters called them. There is a
wonderful family photo which shows all the family with the various
scouting members in full rig, truly one for the archives.

It was in many ways a nuisance being young and small and,
I suppose, fairly insignificant. I was even known as "Boy" for years
instead of by a proper name, though Mother always made great
attempts to get the family to call me Bernard - and did so herself,

Figure 2 - A Scouting Family
L-R: Marnie, Norah, Mother Edith with Daphne, Ron, Bunny.
Betty, Father Walter, A. N. Other (non-family)

especially when I was in trouble. The family quietly did nothing about it, and - thank heaven - avoiding the impossible Bernie (the name of one of my uncles) settled on Bunny. I don't think Mother ever got used to that!

I have digressed. Being small meant that I missed one big treat. Early one morning Father took all the bigger boys (and girls?) to see 24 (or was it 40?) aeroplanes crossing the channel at Dover. This was as spectacular sight then as if one were to see nowadays a series of moon men (little green ones if you like) walking up the High Street. Actually, we did see Bleriot on his second channel crossing; we were on the beach at Walmer and he came over at about 100 feet up. The plane we saw can be seen today in the Science Museum at South Kensington, all string, wire and bits of wood.

This reminds me that in 1913 an Uncle (Edgar, I think, Mary Ely's Father) took me to the cinema (where we saw "The Taming of The Shrew") and then said nonchalantly, "Let's go along here." So we went and came to two large factory doors. He pulled one open and there they were - men building airplanes with the aforesaid string, glue, wood, etc. It was an incredibly lucky thing to see and I made the most of it at school. I found out later that it was the Hawker factory at Kingston. I don't think I can convey the excitement and privilege it was to see this. After all, man had only flown for the first time the year I was born and that was only 10 years earlier.

Figure 3 - Bleriot monoplane

And while talking about films - inter alia - in 1912 or 1913 we went to Deal to see the Delhi Dunbar[2] on the screen; that was the crowning of the King (George V) as Emperor of India. Two things have impressed me always about that visit. One, that part of the film was in color, incredible in those days, and two, there was also a film of a rose growing and the bud opening up - all stuff years ahead of its time. Joyce and I sought out this cinema in the 1950s when we were staying at Deal, and, blow me down, there it still was, closed down, looking very small and dilapidated - but there it was.

Another entertainment we had was to walk down to the Royal Marine barracks at Deal after church and watch the band marching and playing. They have always been my favorite band since then and I still feel a thrill every time I hear *"A Life on the Ocean Wave"*. I always felt distinctly swindled when they had the drum and fife band out instead of the brass band. The Royal Marines - I think it was they - put on *"Ali Baba and the 40 Thieves"*, my first pantomime and my first disillusionment when I realized that the "forty" thieves were the same ten men going in and out of the scenery. Well, one has to learn sometime.

2   An Indian imperial-style mass assembly organized by the British at Coronation Park, Delhi, India, to mark the succession of an Emperor or Empress of India.

The great thrill really was not necessarily the show but the means of getting there - the horse and cab. Nostalgia, nostalgia, I know, but I can still smell the inside of the cab with its old leather, and the generally "horsey" smell of the whole outfit. And anyway, it was a tremendous luxury for us to go in a cab. I once went in a "brake" with Father and his cricket team, pulled by two horses, sitting on the box next to the driver - a wonderful experience for a small boy. Obviously progress, and, as always seems to be the case looking back, the sun was shining brilliantly - except on Coronation Day, 1911. I even thought it was hot all day until the evening.

In fact the sun overdid it once. I was walking down to the beach after having the compulsory "rest" after dinner, and had a bad headache. The next thing I knew was coming to in my bed, 24 hours later, very sick. Apparently I'd had a really bad attack of sunstroke and I was informed (how do "they" think these things up to tell a very sick little boy?) that "another little boy has just died of what you've had." Well, well! That was in 1911 or 1912, which was a phenomenally hot year, like 1921 when I was in Canada.

I had an odd experience one day. I was in the games field some way from the school on a summer evening with some of the family, when a wave of very warm air rolled across us. I thought that this was a "heat wave"! The day can almost be pinpointed because the news had just come through that a man named Burgess had just swum the channel[3], the only previous chap to do it being Captain Webb, I think about 36 years earlier.

There were so many exciting things being done then for the first time, and I often wonder whether boys nowadays have the same number of new discoveries and inventions to get thrilled about. There was no radio, no TV, practically no cars, very few aeroplanes, no central heating, no atomic power, very few gramophones and so on. Probably every generation feels this way about its own time.

Churchgoing was of course regular and boring. I can even now recall the taste of the pine pews one seemed to kneel endlessly against, as indeed I can see the dozen or so boys of another private school. Immaculate in Eton suits, they had been taught to bow their heads whenever the name of "Jesus" was said or sung. There was one hymn where the word comes in constantly, and I was fascinated by the Guards-like precision with which the heads all bowed solemnly - down, up, down, up, and so on. It was worth waiting for.

3   7 September, 1911, on his 16th attempt.

Mother had an "Infra" or "Instra", a silver object about four inches by two inches into which she put a glowing stick of charcoal. On went the top and into her muff went the whole thing, keeping her hands warm for the whole service. A similar "invention" is on the market now, and very efficient it is, but "there is nothing new under the sun."

In 1912 the school went broke, and we moved to Ye Olde Cottage in Kingsdown, two miles away. The cottage was in fact two

Figure 4 - Kent & London

small houses joined together; one (thatched?) was indeed an old cottage, with a vast chimney/fireplace, red brick floor and cool cellar, while the other was a more modern brick affair. There was running water in this one but no "loo" inside. All we had was the traditional earth closet, inside which building incidentally the Baker would leave the bread if no one was at home! We had to pump a lot of the water and the ceilings in the old cottage were very thin. Mother warned Ron and me not to scrap or gadabout in our own bedroom or we would come through. After the first few weeks of treading carefully we reverted to normal behavior, but never descended suddenly as warned. We had a smallish garden (where guinea pigs thrived for some time) and opposite the house was a large village green, extending to the Walmer cliffs with no houses in between. Alas, it is all now enclosed and solid with houses.

There was a great craze about 1912 to 1914 for little model aeroplanes flown by twisting a rubber band round and round into knots and then letting the whole propeller go. We had a French boy once with a splendid aluminium-framed monoplane and silk wings.

It was too successful, for on one of its early flights it streaked up onto a high roof and stayed there until the wind eventually dislodged it. This was at Kingsdown, where we were also shown the power of horse over steam. A traction engine got stuck some two feet down on a wet chalk road, so four large Shire horses were hitched on, and up she came - no mean feat but, as I discovered later in Canada, a horse can pull almost incredible loads.

Talking of horsepower, it was at Kingsdown that we had our first ride in a car. It was a Clement-Talbot owned by "Uncle" Edgar and I remember two rides. One, with 13 others on board plus a bulldog, careering along at 40 mph. Personally I was pretty scared, though it was thrilling, but not as scared as when Uncle took us over to Dover to see Kent play Hampshire. All I remember of the match was the immortal Frank Woolley[4] tearing to the boundary after a ball and collapsing in a lady's lap. He is now 90 so probably doesn't remember that. Anyway, as you may know the hill out of Dover is a very steep one and I simply could not imagine the car being able to get up it. I didn't see how it could, and I expected to disappear backwards down the hill. All went well, but it was all "unknown territory" being in a car, and so slightly scary as well as exciting.

At Kingsdown we frequently used to see planes coming across the Channel. We were the first bit of land they could see after leaving France, and the pilots were only too glad to find some terra firma to land on. We knew that if we ran in their direction we should probably see them land, and we often did. In fact Ron helped one French pilot out once when the latter knew no English and Ron produced what French he could to help. We also saw the planes on what was I think the first Round Britain Air Race; compared with present speeds they seem to be almost standing still. The sight of a plane was sufficient for us to leap up from the table, scattering food all over the place, and rush out to gaze in wonder and amazement. I wonder, again, what wonders surprise children nowadays in the same

---

4   Frank Woolley (1887 –1978) was one of cricket's greatest all-rounders. He played for Kent County Cricket Club between 1906 and 1938, and in 64 Test matches for England. A left-handed batsman and bowler, he was an outstanding fielder close to the wicket and is the only non wicket-keeper to have held over 1,000 catches in a first-class career. His total number of runs scored is the second highest of all time and his total number of wickets taken the 27th highest.

way.

We lived at the top of a hill and it was there that I had one of the most frightening and enjoyable experiences, that of sitting in a bath chair out of control with only a little wheel to control your direction at the end of a long-ish handle. Terrifying but, again, great fun. There was one shop at the top of the village and a few more by the beach where we used to repair before breakfast for "huffkins", a large sort of flat roll, and get them back to the house, still warm, for breakfast. I sometimes used to get a lift into Deal (three miles away) to do some shopping, in a motor tricycle affair

Figure 5 - Bath Chair

which the milkman used to convey his vast urns of milk. I had to walk back of course, but it was worth it.

Other excitements were the annual practice launching of a lifeline to ships in distress and the launching of the Walmer lifeboat.[5] This was particularly thrilling because the lifeboat rolled from side to

Figure 6 - The Walmer Lifeboat

side as it shot down the heavily greased planks to hit the water with an almighty splash and disappeared into clouds of spray. It always righted itself as soon as it hit the water but I always wondered (and do still) how the crew managed to stay put during this crazy rush down

5   Walmer and Deal were the closest ports to the Goodwin Sands, notoriously treacherous sandbanks where over two thousand ships have been wrecked, and their lifeboats were constantly in action.

to the sea.

And there were more thrills, for every year the Fleet anchored off Deal on their way to the Spithead Review. So we saw battleships, cruisers, TBD's (torpedo boat destroyers, as they were called then) and those wonderful ships, submarines. Occasionally, if we were very lucky, we would see a diver in his intriguing and fascinating headgear. All these things happened rarely, of course, and were all the more exciting for that! But there were other things, and no one who was alive at the time will ever forget the appalling shock in 1912 when news of the loss of the great and unsinkable *Titanic* was received, with about 1,100 lives lost. It was beyond belief.

The summer of 1913 was made more joyful for me in that I suddenly acquired an interest in the County Cricket Championship. As I was living in Kent (and for all I know didn't even realize I had been born in Surrey) I followed Kent avidly and have done so ever since. They won the championship in 1913 and Woolley became a lifelong hero of mine. It was just 50 years later that I was proud to shake his hand at Earley, Reading, where he had come to choose the Man of the Match in a Gillette Cup match. We all (I hope) have our heroes, and I'm certainly not ashamed to have had Woolley as mine, often described as a "a gentleman above all".

This has an amusing sequel. About 1932 I was invited to Lords by a member of the MCC to watch Kent play Middlesex. It was a typical English May day - bitingly cold - but we sat at the top of the pavilion to get a good view. In came Woolley and I settled down to watch and admire. He made zero. I watched him making his way back and borrowed my friend's binoculars to see how he (Woolley) was taking it. To my amazement there was a grin on his face, so I assume Woolley was showing his delight at getting back to the warmth of the pavilion. The man was human after all, not just a brilliant cricketer. He certainly endeared himself to me at that moment.

We had few games or amusements unless we made them ourselves, but once a year, having obtained permission from the owner, we went off over the way to some neighboring woods and picked primroses and bluebells in masses, sending them off to our friends. A picnic lunch made it a great day for us.

School – St. Paul's

In 1912 I got a scholarship to St. Paul's Cathedral Choir School (Ron was already at St. Paul's School) and had to travel there on my own from Kingsdown, at age 9. The long, 90-mile train journey was fun; I changed trains at Dover, and Mother gave me a postcard to post at Dover to say I had got that far successfully - 7 miles away! I can't see what she could have done if I hadn't got there successfully, not by the time she'd received the card. I traveled in the guard's van which had a fascinating seat level with the window at the top of the back end of the carriage, and I used to arrive in a shocking condition as regards cleanliness. Uncle Alan met me once and nearly disowned me, but rushed me to the Gents where I had a good wash and became presentable before he delivered me to the Choir School. It was at the entrance examination to the Choir School that I pointed out that someone had taken the clock out of one of the Cathedral clock towers, not realizing that it was the belfry. One learns. It was fun going on a horse drawn bus, too; motor buses were very few in 1912.

I had been told that for the "voice test" I had to sing a scale, and should not start too loud but keep plenty of breath for the top note. The result was an almost trumpet-blast at the top of the scale which even shook the Cathedral organist. However, in spite of that I got in, with four other boys.

Choir schools are not like other prep schools[6], in that timetables have to be adjusted to the times of Cathedral services. We worked until 9:45 AM, when the choristers went over for the 10 AM service; the cathedral was only two minutes walk away. Those boys not yet admitted to the choir and known as the Probationers, or Pros, did not go to this service but did attend the 4:00 PM one. From 11:00 AM to 1:00 PM were lessons, then 2:00 PM for an hour's choir practice. I believe we had from 3:00 PM to 4:00 PM off, then worked

---

6   Prep ("preparatory") schools were developed in England and Wales in the early 19th century as boarding schools to prepare boys for the Common Entrance Examination for the leading public schools, which included Eton College, Radley College, Harrow School, Charterhouse School, Oundle School, Rugby School, St Paul's School, Westminster School and Winchester College.

till 6:00 PM and had supper in time for prep afterwards. Because the boys were needed for services at weekends we only had ½ day off a week, on Thursdays, when we went by train from Blackfriar Station to Bellingham for games.

On Sundays we all went to 10:30 AM Matins, followed without a break by Holy Communion. We got back about 2:15 PM, a long, long time with far too much kneeling, which resulted in my being very sick right within Chancel on my first Sunday - an unfortunate start. On Sunday afternoons we had to go for one of two walks, either along Queen Victoria Street or along the Embankment. This was quite pleasant, and if you went at top speed you could just get to Westminster and back before going to afternoon service at 3:15 PM, until 4:15 PM. Back for tea. Incidentally, before 10:00 AM we all had to sit down and learn by heart the Collect for the day; how we hated Advent with its lengthy ones.

I might add that the Embankment walk was not as attractive on Sundays as it might have been, because with only one or two water biscuits inside one we had to walk to Waterloo Bridge and back before breakfast. That wasn't fun, though we did enjoy seeing the great trams with their bright green, white and red lamps coming over Blackfriars Bridge and charging along the Embankment. What <u>was</u> fun was going on training runs before Sports Day, before breakfast, but a master took us around the city streets where there was hardly a horse or a person at 7:00 AM. I wonder what it would be like now! Suicide, I imagine.

On Sunday evening the "Rev", as we called our pretty strict headmaster, had us all in a study and read to us - the Probationers, that is - and surprisingly sent a large bottle of sweets around the room once or twice. Some Probationers joined the choir on Sunday evenings and even then did not sit in the choir stalls proper, which were occupied by the "Sunday evening choir" men. I never knew where they came from. Talking of being read to, one splendid master - he really was the best schoolmaster I ever met - used to read to us at times, and he read Edgar Allan Poe!! I still remember the horror and thrill of "*The Pit and The Pendulum*," and another story where a man brought a mummy to life and was then promptly pursued by it down to the station. Strong meat for boys of nine and ten, as the Pros were, but it certainly never gave me a moments nightmare, nor anyone else as far as I know - and we would have known, because the boys were divided into 2 dormitories of 20 each with partitions separating the beds.

Being right in the city there was no playground, of course, so we played on the roof, which had been made into a flat area about the size of two cricket nets, and where we had to wear special "overalls" to avoid getting our Eton suits in a mess. Incidentally "The Roof", as it was known, adjoined the Deanery, and the Dean on more than one occasion had to get into the Deanery via The Roof and his own roof, having unhappily forgotten his keys. The Dean was Dean Inge[7], no relation though his signature underneath my name in three prizes I won my first term looks like a subtle bit of nepotism.

Figure 7 - Dean Inge

The teaching was undoubtedly good; it was the only time in my life I liked mathematics. "Chesty", alias Mr. Hugh Chesterman, the wonderful master I wrote of just now, taught us Latin and Greek. The Greek was particularly fascinating to us small boys as it dealt with the methods used by the Greeks in mummifying the dead, the removal of the brain being especially horrible! Unfortunately my voice deteriorated in the London air and I never was admitted as a chorister, but the training stood me in good stead when I went to Christ's Hospital. I was in the choir for five years - all my time there - and I have sung (to my delight if not necessarily to others') in church choirs here and abroad, and of course in Gilbert and Sullivan, so I have few regrets.

We had our times at St. Paul's, for this was the age of the great suffragette protests in their endeavors to get "Votes for Women". We read and heard with interest of these good ladies setting fire to letters in pillar boxes, of breaking massive shop windows, slashing pictures in the Royal Academy, pouring acid on golf greens (horror of horrors!), chaining themselves to Buckingham Palace and Parliament railings, one throwing herself (and killing herself) in front of the King's horse in the Derby, and so on. And we had our services in the Cathedral constantly interrupted by fanatical women chanting or

---

7   William Ralph Inge was Dean of St. Paul's from 1911-1934. He was a prolific author; in addition to scores of articles, lectures and sermons, he also wrote over 35 books and was a columnist for the Evening Standard for many years, until 1946. Due to his generally pessimistic views he was known as The Gloomy Dean.

screaming "God save Christabel Pankhurst" or whichever Pankhurst was the last one arrested. Women hanging on to the Chancel gates, clinging onto the lectern, having to be prised off, knees in back, by 6-foot Metropolitan policemen and carried out over their shoulders - all this in the middle of a service.

But worse was to come. "Chesty" came into the Pros one morning (7th May, 1913), put a paper on the grand piano and said, "Look at this." Headline: *"Bomb found in St. Paul's"*. A bomb had been placed under the Bishop's Throne, between the choir and the altar, due to go off at 10:00 AM when the morning service started. Luckily, an alert verger heard the ticking, investigated and got the bomb removed and defused, but this to us was the ultimate limit. A church was burned down near London as well.

The activities of the suffragettes had one odd effect. I got stirred up inside so much during one outburst that I decided I had to come out of the service. So I got to my feet, said to the next boy, "Stay in" and off I went. (I was Senior Pro then and had to lead the Pros in and out of the services.) To my horror I was followed by all nine Pros, and when I remonstrated with the next boy that I had told him to "Stay in" he said he thought I meant "Keep in close to the side". Clot. Anyway, I should imagine for the first and only time in the history of the Choir School and of the Cathedral the Probationers calmly walked slap out of the service after about half an hour. Authority was puzzled more than cross; why had I done it? As I didn't exactly know I couldn't say, and the affair died out. Just a little bit of history but it certainly shook everyone at the time. At least we all escaped another long sermon, and as we had a sermon every Saints Day in the week as well as two or three on Sundays, it could have been worse.

One other effort of the suffragettes thrilled us. They hired an airship – blimp-shaped - stuck "Votes for Women" on it in large letters, hung out a flag with their mauve, green and white colors on it, and sailed around the Dome of St. Paul's while we watched entranced from The Roof. To see an airship was really something.

We learned to roller skate in Canter Lane, where the school was, on Saturday afternoons when there were no horses about, the city was absolutely peaceful and quiet and we could fall down as we liked in the deserted street. It was different from Ludgate Hill on ordinary days where we went to spend our precious pocket money.

We seldom got further than Maynards, the sweet shop, though
Strakers the stationers had a fascinating shop too. Our total pocket
money was one small silver threepenny piece handed out to us with
ceremony once a week - little enough even though sweets could
be bought at two (or even, if you were lucky, four) ounces for one
penny, and small cakes cost a half penny or one penny at Bellingham.
"Ginger pop" cost one penny.

Once in a moment of (probably misplaced) generosity I gave
a threepenny bit - a whole weeks pocket money - to one of that now
nearly vanished army of pavement artists who drew both very good
(and sometimes awful) pictures on the pavement of ships at sea,
royalty and other subjects. I must have been overtaken by sympathy,
for he couldn't have been more broke than I was! This brings to mind
another occasion at Christ's Hospital one Sunday, when instead of the
usual penny in the collection I put in three pence; I was feeling flush
at the time as I had been given a half crown previously by a relative.
It was only after the service that I discovered I had put in the half
crown as one of the pennies, a shattering blow both of my finances
and my morale.

The choristers of course were very unlucky in one respect;
because of the primary cause of their existence - to sing at the
Cathedral services - not only were their school holidays shorter but
they could never have Christmas or Easter Day at home. This was
and is to some extent made up to them by extra trips to the theater,
cinema, exhibitions and similar entertainment. Not that we were
without our own frolics in term time; we were taken to the Oval to
watch cricket matches, to Mackelyne & Devants (the great magician
show near the site of the present BBC), and all new boys were
taken right up to the top of the cathedral, just under the huge bowl
supporting the cross. Quite a trip.

First there is the endless wooden spiral staircase, then a
series of steep iron ladders, culminating in a final vertical one of
eight feet, to reach which you have to step across a two-foot gap with
a deep, deep emptiness beneath you. At the top of this last ladder
you peer out over endless miles of London and the surrounding
counties. Beneath the "cross and ball" can be seen a gilded gallery.
We went out on this and I put my foot on a low nail which was part
of the enclosing railings, and nearly died of shock. The railings slope
slightly outwards and this gave me the immediate effect of being

about to hurtle down and down - a nasty moment.

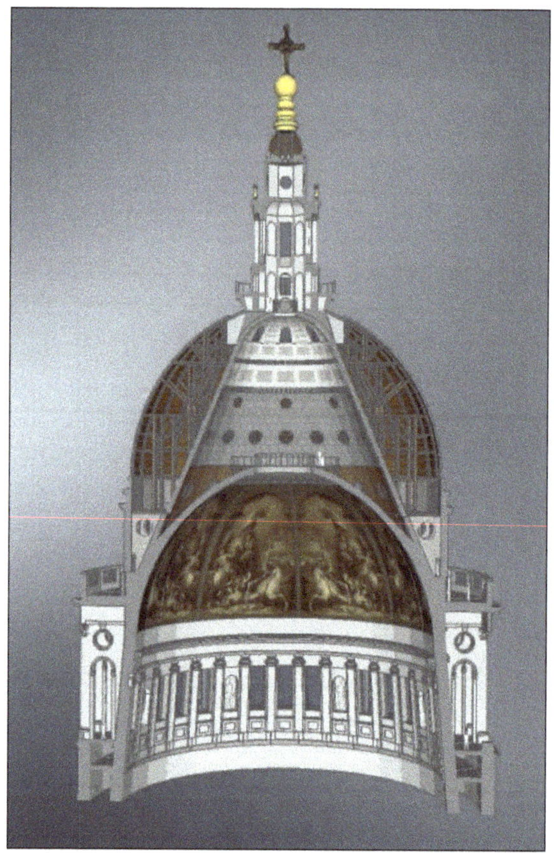

Figure 8 - The Dome of St. Paul's

Incidentally, when you look down on the Dome from the Golden Gallery you can see quite clearly that there are two domes: the one you see from below and an inside one. By way of contrast, there is the crypt, with Wellington's fantastic funeral carriage made from guns he had captured and which, drawn by 16 horses, went slap through the road during the funeral procession. This is not the place for a "Guide to St. Paul's", but while there is much to admire there what almost impressed me the most was the vast openness of the Cathedral, which is why Westminster Abbey has never appealed to me; it always seemed hopelessly over-ornate. (Greater maturity has helped me to appreciate the splendor of the Abbey, but you can't expect a small boy to approve of a building where lived and sang our

16

"mortal enemies" - Westminster Abbey Choir School! There was a
special cup for sports competitions between the two schools.)

Two services stand out, or three, to be exact. The first was the
memorial service for Scott of the Antarctic when the vast altar steps
were completely covered in black. The second was the funeral of Sir
Arthur Wellesley, when his coffin was lowered through the special
slab down into the crypt. The third was different; I was in the choir
for the St. Paul's School Confirmation Service and was processing
down the chancel singing a hymn when I looked up and right beside
me was Ron! I don't know which of us was more surprised.

They were happy days at the Choir School, I imagine. You
don't think about them being happy or unhappy at the time, you
just take life as you find it, but I was contented enough - until I had
to leave because my voice lost its top notes; they came back later,
happily. And on top of that I had to leave a few days before the end
of term because one of the family had some contagious illness; details
escape me.

Speaking of the family, in 1913 they'd moved back to London
from Kent, Father excepted as he was absent and Ron and I being
away at school. The family initially settled in with Father's sister -
Aunt Sissie, "much given to missionary and other good works," - who
presumably had a strong influence on Marnie, Norah and Daphne
as all three became missionaries! Aunt Sissie lived in Sinclair Road,
West Kensington, but in 1914 helped my family move about half a
mile away to a basement flat in Gordon Mansions, Addison Gardens.

Figure 9 - Gordon Mansions, Addison Gardens

It was pretty grim but all that could be afforded, Father being away most of the time and then joining up. A couple of years later (1915-16, date uncertain) they moved 200 yards away to 13 Dunsany Road, Brook Green, where they lived until 1924.

Figure 10 - 13 Dunsany Road

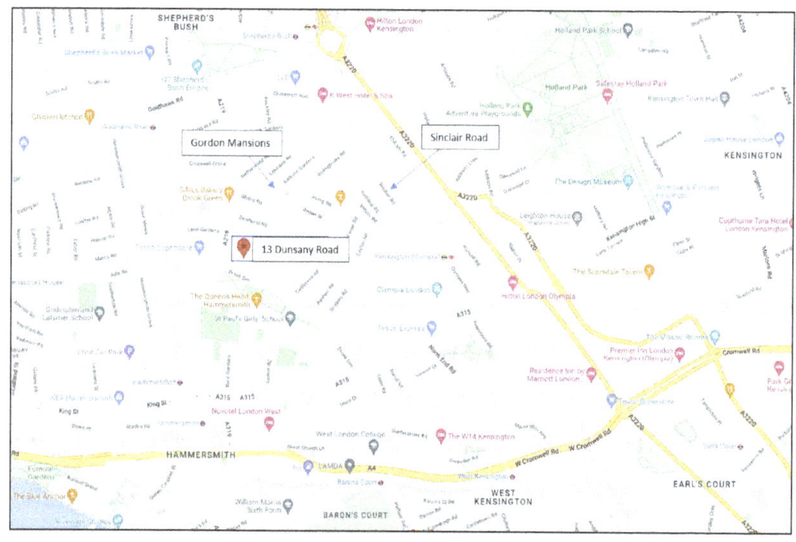

Figure 11 - Hammersmith/Kensington, London

School – Christ's Hospital

Anyway, in 1914 I left St. Paul's at 11+ and got into Christ's Hospital[8] on a scholarship, due undoubtedly to the splendid teaching at the Choir School and being made to use my brain, and also due to some extra coaching given me by a family friend in maths. Speculation is vain but interesting, for had I become a Chorister at St. Paul's and stayed on to 13 or 14 I should have been too old for admission to Christ's Hospital, and then what? We certainly could not afford fees for any other school. As I have found so often in my life, things turned out for the best anyway.

The next term was filled in at a rather deplorable small private boys' school near Shepherds Bush, near where the BBC is now. It was, be it said, at Shepherds Bush that I used occasionally to creep into a cinema for two pennies, though how I got that amount I cannot imagine. For that sum I had a plush tip-up seat, and a cup of tea and biscuits brought to me by a waitress (I was 11 at the time!) - all quite incredible but I assure you, very true. Going to the cinema then was as rare to us as flying by Concorde is now to most people, and Mother, fortunately, never knew of these efforts of mine.

So I went on being prepared for the Christ's Hospital exam, and eventually took it - Latin, French, English, Arithmetic (I'm not sure about algebra and geometry). I saw copies of the Christ's Hospital scholarship papers of the same period some years later and I just don't know how I passed. It certainly was an incredibly stiff exam designed to weed out vast numbers of examinees not quite up to standard. C. S. Forester (of "Hornblower" fame) said that 20 scholarships were awarded for competition between 20,000 boys. I don't know how accurate he was but this gives one a feeling of delight to have acquired one. Actually, every member of our family won scholarships to their schools; we had to, for there was no money for school fees and council schools were unthinkable to a family like us, and that's not (I hope) being snobbish. Ron got into St. Paul's,

8   Christ's Hospital is a public school (i.e. an English independent boarding school for pupils aged 11–18) located near Horsham, West Sussex. The school was founded by royal charter in 1552 as a charity funded by city businesses and the church, to offer children from humble backgrounds the chance of a better education.

Marnie, Norah, Betty and Daphne won theirs to St. Paul's Girls School, and Norah got one to Westfield College, London, later.

Anyway, one morning at breakfast Marnie said to me, "Aren't you feeling excited?" I said, "Why?" "Because of your scholarship." But, I said, I didn't know anything about it. "Well," said Marnie, "you were in bed when the news came so we came in and told you; you said "Good", or something like it." I had no recollection of hearing a word.

So in January 1915 down to Horsham I went with the other new boys, who arrived I think a day after the others. We went in our ordinary "civvies" and were put into the traditional uniform the next day. But the pinning of the "bands"- unlike those at RBCS- is so difficult that your "mentor" appointed to look after you and help you to settle down had to do them for you for the first three weeks. I don't remember being particularly homesick and slept like a log in the antique beds with boards under the mattress. Christ's Hospital is such a vast place that it took some time even to find your way about.

Figure 12 - Christ's Hospital, Horsham, today

I was soon drafted into the Choir which, apart from my enjoying it, had the added privilege with the Band of having rows of seats reserved up in front, just behind the staff, for all entertainment put on in Big School. We had Choir practice twice a week unless special concerts were looming, when of course the number was increased. Tuesday at 12:00 PM saw us all in Big School rehearsing music for the school concert; Friday evening we were all in Chapel rehearsing hymns, psalms and anthems for the next weeks services.

Figure 13 - Christ's Hospital school uniform, which had to be worn at all times; in BGI's day it was boys-only.

It would be impossible, useless and boring to give much detail about my time at Christ's Hospital. Authority soon found that I had a brain and pushed me along. I was going very well until 1917 when the school broke up half a term early owing to widespread illness. The "Sicker" (infirmary) holding about 90 beds was full; one of the boarding houses was taken over as further sick bay accommodation. 100 boys had conjunctivitis - better known as pink-eye - some seriously. One master and two boys died, and a halt was called.

I think probably this high incidence of illness was caused by the very poor food and small amounts of it that we endured, owing to the war period. The loaves of bread, for instance, were marked off with nails at small intervals, by a construction like a small rake which was pressed into the loaf. You cut the bread at the marks and that was your lot. We seemed permanently hungry, but as there was nothing we could do about it, we just put up with it. We were in fact short of sufficient food at meals and it has always surprised me that in general we had pretty good health, kept fit and grew.

I needed to, especially, for I was still very small and was continually unwell with nothing in particular for the first year. Of course, it might not be surprising for I was extremely weak for the first two years of my life with, again, nothing in particular. As Marnie said, "You just didn't seem to want to stay with us!" I was in fact told by my housemaster that in view of my size I need not join the OTC (Officers Training Corps) which was "voluntary/compulsory" for all boys.

I joined up anyway because the OTC chaps looked down on the non-Corps boys, and my first parade was nearly a disaster. We wore those abominable "putters" which you wound round and round your legs. Determined in my innocent pride in my uniform to look smart, I wound them beautifully tight and neat around my legs and off I set to the parade ground. By the time I got there I was suffering badly - putters should be wound <u>not</u> tight but comparatively loose. I had restricted the circulation in my legs so badly that I was in sheer agony all afternoon until I could get the things off. I honestly don't know how I survived that afternoon.

We had two OTC parades a week, square-bashing, rifle drill and the very occasional route march, which was a relief. My rifle was quite a weight for me, but practicing "fix bayonets" always had an exciting air about it because the odds were that some unfortunate fellow - never being allowed to look at the scabbard while sheathing his bayonet - would plunge it cheerfully into his thigh, which amused everyone except the victim. Still, I suppose it was all good for discipline - the drill, not the thigh plunging.

Other afternoons in the week were divided into: Mondays and Thursdays, cross country runs; Wednesday and Saturday, rugger or cricket, depending on the season. Running was one of the things I found I could do, when not being told to keep back by Seniors who weren't going to be shown up by a small boy getting ahead of them. This problem eased as I went up the school but I chased a friend of mine for five years without beating him into first place in house runs. At the end of the run he and I would put on 100-yard sprint and end up with heads spinning in the changing room. There were three runs of three or five miles for those up to 14, known as Big Tower and Little Tower (a name which is only just to come back to me after 60 years) and one called Southwater of seven miles.

How we did all this sport and games on the food we got passes my comprehension, though I must pay tribute to the authorities for feeding us even as well as they did in view of the terrible shortage of food in those war years, especially 1916 to 1918. There was an annual school steeplechase of about seven or eight miles for which boys were entered from every house. It ended with a wide water jump which only a very few ever tried to jump; the rest of us happily plunged in, hot as we were, and pushed our dripping bodies to the finishing tape. It was rather fun, though I only took part in it my last year.

Size was always a problem in games, and the fact that apart from my friend "Squire" Browne taking me a few times to the cricket nets I had no coaching at games. I was too small to be considered for the first XI or first XV house teams, and anyway there was practically no coaching for the ordinary run of folk. I did play for the house on occasions at cricket and rugger, being able to field and being the right size for fly-half, and I managed to swim the necessary 5 lengths required for one to climb out of the rather despised "non-swimmers" ranks and swim with the house.

Academically, I was doing pretty well until I met a "dug-out" wartime master, Mr. Coghlan. He imbued in me a great love of much of the English we did and was the most likable person. However, he didn't put much pressure on me and I imagine I was pretty lazy unless up against a strict master, whose intentions I acknowledged and therefore for whom I worked hard. I know that I read most of Taffrail's sea stories under the desk which I had claimed at the back of the class, during Mr. Coghlan's afternoon lessons.

The term after, we had broken up half a term early and our Form Master was missing. In strode the Headmaster - an awe-ful figure – who decided that the top four boys in the half term order (which was on the board) should go up to the next form, called Great Erasmus Latin; I was then in Little Erasmus A2. So off I went, being I think second on the list, to creep in amongst the collection of what seemed huge boys of advanced age whereas I... As it happened Mr. Coghlan was Form Master of both forms, and when he saw me in the Senior Form amongst the 16- and 17-year-olds he said, "What are you doing here?" Able to give the reply beloved of all boys, I said, "The Headmaster told me to come up, Sir." "Well," he replied, "if I had been here I wouldn't have allowed you to come up, you're much too young. But now that you are here, don't work too hard." What lovely words to hear - and I fear I obeyed them.

Oh yes, we did lots of work but I was never under any

pressure until the proper Form Master, Major Goodwin, came back from the war. Then there was a change - a rude shock to the system and we had to knuckle down to it. The older boys to my relief accepted me as one of the oddities of life, only objecting once when they thought Mr. Coghlan had been a bit lenient with me ("Just because he has got a squeaky little voice...") but life was peaceful in that class. After about three years came the time when I was allowed to "specialize" in the subjects I liked (or had to do) with permission from the master whose subject I was giving up and him to whom I was going to apply for extra lessons. It was all very easy; no prolonged discussions with parents, Form Masters, etc. You went your own sweet way, as long as your timetable was filled up. The net result was that I ended up doing eight lessons weekly in Science, Latin and English, with French and Maths filling in. The senior Science Master was leaving so he spent the last term mostly making organizational arrangements for his successor and for the new Headmaster, for the present one was leaving.

I can only imagine that I exhausted the energy of Headmasters and even of House Masters, or at least had some devastating effect on them. Both my Headmasters left the schools the term I did, doubtless exhausted, while the House I went into at Christ's Hospital (Barnes A) had four different Housemasters in my first four terms, which must have been a record. Anyway, the House, which was a crack one when I joined, went steadily downhill from that time on. I think this was not due to my influence this time, but rather to our ending up with a really useless Housemaster who seemed to have no influence on the House, who was universally mocked (and knew it), and also to the lack of really outstanding boys to lead the house. We had some good ones but I still feel the trouble lay in the Housemaster. RIP.

Reference to science reminds me that a few others and I used to make flares and fireworks, lacking often any supervision in the labs. Magnesium powder was the base; I forget the other ingredients except that added strontium produced a green effect and barium red (or is it the other way round?). We let off these "flare" mixtures behind the Fives courts, where they produced such an appalling volume of smoke that we never knew why we were never caught. The practice died when I made one of almost everything I could find, put it in a bottle, corked it and put it in my locker in the House for use

later on, to see what would happen. I found out. My locker backed
onto the wall of the Junior Housemaster's room and the heat from
his fire started some form of chemical reaction. When I opened the
locker I was nearly knocked out by a dense cloud of chlorine. This
caused some comment, so I hurriedly removed the bottle and flung
it in the dustbin outside, then strolled back to the day room with
an air of complete detachment. I was lucky the whole thing didn't
explode, but I think it must have been merely a matter of time. It
would certainly have provided a topic for discussion, as my neighbor,
one Neville, did once. Against all warning he held a liter flask of
hydrogen over a naked flame – though not for long. There was a bang
which brought everybody in from neighboring labs, while Neville
stood there looking slightly dazed holding all that was left - the cork
and two inches of the flask neck. This took place exactly one foot
behind my back and was undoubtedly useful as a warning!

A different type of excitement occurred the day when
a balloon (ye Gods, a balloon! Most of us had never seen one)
descended slowly on Sharpenhurst, a hill just outside the school
grounds. This could only be reached by crossing the main London to
Brighton railway line, which it was strictly forbidden to cross unless
on a Sunday one got permission to go for a walk up there. Anyway,
it was lovely summer afternoon, sunny and peaceful, but this balloon
was too much even for school discipline. About 200 of us of all
ages ran from our cricket games, poured over the railway lines and
scrambled up the hill where we watched the balloon gradually deflate
with a noisome smell of coal gas. We knew there would be trouble
but who cared when such vast numbers of us had transgressed? In
the end the offenders got two hours of drill the following Wednesday
afternoon. It was a hot day but that discomfort was considerably
allayed by seeing so many of the dignified Grecians (our Sixth
Form) and Monitors who had also been there having to parade with
us. They merely took charge of the drill, but there was dignity and
position reduced to our level - all rather splendid!

On another occasion, also another sunny afternoon, two Old
Boys came over in a small biplane, tottered with failing engine over
the school and sank ignobly in the school grounds behind some trees.
Great excitement! This was a Saturday. We heard that the plane was
being repaired and would take off from the enormous playing fields
after Sunday evening service. During the service we heard the plane

revving up; you have to remember that very, very few boys had even seen a plane nearby, let alone seen one takeoff. The service drew to an end but then came near disaster. The Headmaster suddenly got up and said what a lovely hymn we had been singing, and more, and more… He'd never done this before and we were frightened the plane would go up before we got out of Chapel. In the end he stopped talking, but if a man could have been killed by thought he would have gone up like an atomic bomb.

Not one boy ran out of Chapel; all 800 went out at the usual pace - and then tore madly to the plane. We were in time. Soon it took off, watched by the whole School and most of the Masters. It just cleared the big oak tree, swerved right - and crashed on some rough ground. Off went the whole school like rockets, despite shouts of protest from the Masters. Then someone had the *nous* to produce a whistle. Now you can pretend you don't hear a shout, but you can't pretend not to hear a whistle. The running rabble slowed down and came to a halt - it was the clever piece of thinking on someone's part. Happily, the two men were not hurt, but various parts of the plane, including the propellor, turned up in different parts of the school.

Apart from this we had our usual school amusements if we liked to join in; a particularly mad form of single wicket cricket played in the area between the Houses, roller skating, Natural History club outings and so on. In fact life was quite endurable except on Sundays. You might (if confirmed and felt like it) go to communion at 8:00 AM. Then, some years, followed about an hour's Bible reading, religious instruction or what have you about 10:00 AM, Chapel from 11 to 12, afternoon walk (the only occasion when - in summer - we are allowed to take off our coats and put on blazers), tea, Chapel, prep. The area for walks was limited but out of sheer boredom we occasionally went out of bounds just for a break on these appallingly monotonous Sundays. No games whatever were allowed on Sundays, and there were no gramophones, nor of course any radio or TV. The only concession to humanity lay in the fact that while we had prep every single night, on Saturdays and Sundays you could read a book or write letters, I think, in prep time; it was up to you to choose which night you would do your weekend prep. We were all of us, 12 to 18, living in the dayroom the whole time of one's existence in the school, apart from playing games and parading for the OTC. And we wore the whole uniform all day and every day, except for, again, games and OTC. On really hot days it became somewhat annoying, but it's surprising what you get used to. How things have changed, my word how they have changed, and rightly too.

As a footnote to my earlier notes on work and particularly Science, when I took London Matric I failed, not surprisingly, in Science. The next time I took it I failed in French, being convinced that I needn't work any more at my pet subject, and when I finally heard that the third attempt had been successful I was in the midst of cows, pigs, hens and horses in Canada, unable to see that the Matric was going to do me any good at all. Of course I was quite wrong - it became the only qualification I had to start teaching years later - but that's another story.

I should add that for London Matriculations you took five subjects and only five, and you had to pass in all five. Failure in one meant taking the whole lot again. In fairness to myself I should add that (like all boys) I did work hard at subjects I liked, such as English and French and even at maths which was mostly Greek to me. It was Mr. Coghlan's lessons only - and he the only master- which were concerned with my taking it fairly easy.

I remember little of the exam itself except that we had been doing "Othello", and in answering questions on the play I wrote - and I remember it with horror always – "This play is very true to life." In 1978 a boy of 15 might know enough to make that sort of remark, but 60 years ago it was sheer effrontery. What on earth did I know about the heartbreak of a married man, the machinations of Iago, etc.? What our examiners have to put up with.

Class distinctions between the boys didn't really arise at Christ's Hospital, but I went to see an uncle of mine in London Hospital in 1916, and in the course of conversation he made an odd remark; "You know, the pride of the Inges is a difficult thing to cope with." I had no idea what he meant. He had been wounded, in Italy I think, during World War One, and thereby, in those days, automatically acquired a certain aura of fame. I couldn't see what he was trying to say, which I think was, "Here am I, an officer, in a ward of wounded soldiers of <u>all ranks</u>, and few officers!" Well, that was the way it was in those days, but it took me years and years to find out. When I did I thought it was rank snobbery, but it wasn't really. Officers had, by King's Regulations, to keep themselves apart from Other Ranks, having for instance to travel always First Class in trains.

School was really a state of life through which one had to pass. One made a few friends but never (officially) with any boy outside your own House of 50 boys from 12 to 18. You were never allowed to be friendly with boys from other Houses, even if you sat next to them in class for day after day or sang next to them in the choir for years on end. It was the old Victorian suspicion of immorality which merely produced clandestine and totally innocent meetings in illegal and often ridiculous places in greater number. But that was life.

There <u>was</u> immorality in the school of course, though I never contacted it personally. On one occasion the Headmaster addressed the whole school on this topic in two age groups, 11 to 14 and 15 to 18. I was in the younger group, and he might have more profitably addressed himself to the school clock; I hadn't a clue what he was talking about, but it made a bit of a break. Anything to break the monotony.

Thus we quite enjoyed (some of us) the "pink-eye" epidemic. Some boys were so bad they were not allowed to use their eyes for working. This was too good an opportunity to miss, so some of us who had it told Mr. Coghlan that we were not allowed to work. Instead of checking up on us, he said that he was sorry but even so we should still have to come to class. The next day, tired of the sight of us sitting there doing nothing, he told us to go for a short walk. The next day he told us that we had better bring in chess or draughts to play, which we did with delight while our wretched and envious fellows had to go on working. At the end of the week we thought it might be getting dangerous, so we pronounced ourselves cured. What luck that Mr. Coghlan hadn't mentioned the matter to other Masters in the Common Room, Masters for whom we were wisely doing normal work. Fortune favors the brave - or foolhardy, perhaps.

I really did enjoy singing in the choirs, though I could never get used to what I considered the awful and huge murals by Frank Brangwyn in the Chapel; many people like them, even so. I remember one occasion in particular which was harrowing in the extreme: the funeral service of a boy of 15 from the next House to mine at school. There is something terribly heart-pulling about this sort of tragedy, and funeral music - especially Chopin's Funeral March - takes you down to depths you didn't know existed. Selected members of the choir would sing part songs at school concerts or go to funerals of past members of the staff and so on, and I was usually in these parties.

But appearing on platforms to perform, especially singing (unless with numbers of other people) has one most unfortunate effect on me - I always want to giggle. Once in Big School I had to commit the awful sin of holding the copy of my music in front of my face so that people couldn't see I was grinning. But the worst occasion was when a small choir of eight of us went to sing at the funeral of the late school Medical Officer. We stood right by the open grave and it was all I could do not to laugh out loud - appalling but true. I just managed it and went home with an enormous feeling of relief, because if I had laughed I could never have explained it. Nobody would have understood and I should never have been allowed to forget it. I should also unquestionably have been thrown out of the choir, which would have been a tragedy to me - if not to the choir.

These "outings" of whatever sort were a great relief, for we were firmly immured in the school. Usually we would see none of our family or friends for the whole of term - there was no half-term break back in those days. We could go out occasionally for an afternoon (Saturday or Wednesday) with a relative if they could find the time (and the fare!) to come down, but these were rare occasions. Ascension Day was the glorious exception; it was a whole holiday from after Chapel (8:30 AM) until the evening, and we could go out for the day on such excursions as Natural History Society expeditions (merely a happy excuse to get out into the countryside - we went to Box Hill one year). It was sheer heaven to wear "civvies" for a whole day, especially in hot weather. If it rained, alas, the whole holiday was cancelled, normal lessons took place, and we were given two extra half-holidays later in the term instead, but this wasn't the same thing at all.

Talking of half-holidays there was one purple patch in 1918. While we were playing a House rugger match in the afternoon one Monday, news came through that the Armistice had been signed - no radio to flash the news - and that the next day would be a half-holiday, i.e. no more lessons. Then followed the award of two more half-holidays given (one can only presume) in a moment of euphoria by "The Butch" as Headmaster was amiably (and I think unfairly) known. Then some old boys cabled from Egypt requesting a half-holiday for the school to celebrate the event. This too was given, and as Wednesday and Saturday were already half-holidays we had a week of them.

The only other occasion that I remember the rigid routine being relaxed in any way like this was in the winter of 1917 to 1918. It was so bitterly cold and the earth so frost-bound that games and even "runs" were utterly impossible, so we were given permission to go out skating to get some badly needed exercise. There was a choice of some small lakes or large ponds just near the school, or there was a vast millpond at Warnham, a mile or two the other side of Horsham. That meant about a four to five mile walk each way but lots of us went, and drawing heavily on my remaining pocket money I bought a pair of new skates for half a crown - 12½ p in modern money. These were fixed (illegally but no one seemed to mind) to our OTC Corps boots, and a splendid time was had.

I remember this for another reason. Each year, by tradition, every boy was given some money by the Lord Mayor of London, varying from 1 pound for the most senior boys down to one shilling (5p) for the hoi polloi, and a shilling was a shilling. Each year I tried to keep mine and each year I failed. I remember a sweet shop tempted me beyond bearing on the long walk back from Warnham and bang went the shilling on masses of sweets. I still have the last shilling given me, with the date and my name engraved on it.

Then someone had a brilliant idea. There were lots of cold and flu cases about; surely this must be due to inefficient nose-blowing? So every morning we had to stand at the end of our beds and (1) raise your arm with handkerchief held in the right hand, (2) put handkerchief to nose, and (3) blow!! What an excuse for boys to mock the whole thing; the whole school must have rocked to its foundations at the almost simultaneous trumpeting of 800 boys. I simply cannot imagine who thought this up, but it soon faded out, as did the morning and evening taking of temperatures of all boys by the Monitors (Prefects). The casualties amongst thermometers was frightful, as can well be imagined. There seemed to be a special committee for thinking up comic ideas, but as I've remarked elsewhere, anything to break the monotony.

Canada

At last, in July 1919 and at age 16, I left "Housey", as Christ's Hospital was and is known to past and present members of the House (school). So, what was I going to do? Or more specifically, perhaps, what was going to be done with me? I'd failed Matric[9] so I worked at home for a bit, failing it again as explained elsewhere. So off to Battersea Polytechnic to swot up for Matric again, which I eventually passed - although I didn't hear about it until I'd left the country. I had had thoughts for some reason of market gardening but there seemed to be no openings, so Father got me into the Gravesend Sea School, a training place for boys to enter the Merchant Navy. It was a tough place, but my time there didn't last long. They had a training ship, the *Triton*, moored in the Thames between Tilbury and Gravesend (which are on opposite sides of the river). After a few days someone discovered that I hadn't had my eyes tested. This was done and I was found to be slightly color-blind. In spite of a further and more stringent test, authority decided my eyes weren't good enough and there was I, out on my ear, after five days!

What next? Well, it turned out to be Canada. Father, who must have been home more than usual for once, got the Salvation Army (!!) to find me a job in Canada on a farm. So at the end of July 1920, now 17, off I went. Poor Mother was terribly distressed when I left, while as far as I was concerned it just seemed another step in some direction. Having been away at boarding school since I was nine I wasn't much of a "home bird", and I used to spend much of my holidays exploring London on my own. I embarked at Tilbury and without any regret watched the *Triton* fade away in the distance.

There was nothing remarkable about the journey, which was pretty rough and ready travelling "steerage". I remember being fascinated by the lovely journey up the Saint Lawrence, when it seemed at times as though one could almost talk to the people on shore so close to land were we on either side. Eventually I was directed to the train from Quebec to Toronto, and from Toronto to Milton, where I was met by my future employer, Jimmy Turnbull, who took me in the buggy back to the farm to meet Mrs. Annie Turnbull.

---

9   Matriculation – common entrance exams for universities.

Figure 14 - Milton, Ontario

What do I say about the Turnbulls? He was pleasant enough but a hard task-master; she was much more tricky but could be pleasant, though she would hardly (when he came into her orbit) allow you to stop to say hello to the traveling postman - mirthless. Jimmy was Scotch, she was Irish, I was English - the mixture just didn't work, but I did. Lord, how I worked. It was survive or die!

The first day I was told to follow the binder (the old machine which used to cut the corn, tie it in sheaves and then throw them out) and put the sheaves into "shocks" - 6 sheaves to a shock, leaning against each other like an inverted V. I thought I was supposed to keep up with the machine, in my blessed ignorance. I couldn't, of course - in fact, two men working together couldn't - but I did my best and staggered on. The next day I was utterly incapable of doing more than put a few sheaves together and then sitting down, exhausted. In short, I soon started developing some muscles. I was neither big nor strong, but the three years on the farms gave me a constitution for which I feel grateful ever since. It's odd how things turn out.

Hours were 5:00 am (5:30 in winter) to 9:00 at night, winter and summer, with plenty to do on Sundays, though not so bad in the summer when the cattle were out. But as cows had to be milked, horses and cattle and pigs all fed, eggs collected, hens fed, stable "mucked out" and so on, a great deal of Sunday work was quite inevitable and one accepted that. But every evening I dropped into bed in a blissful state of exhaustion - and it is a heavenly thing to lie there in the pitch dark knowing you have hours of sleep ahead of you, relaxed and at peace. I still like the feeling of great physical weariness - once I have stopped doing whatever it is! Learning to milk was difficult and I never came to like it. Driving horses was sheer delight, much more enjoyable to me always than driving a tractor (not that there <u>were</u> any tractors about then), and some jobs I reveled in, such as pitching sheaves. More details, perhaps, later.

It was a small 125-acre farm. Contrary to the usual impression, farms in the east, especially in Ontario and I believe Quebec were (and many still are) not vast empires of thousands of acres – that's for the wheat-growing prairies - but farms of 100 to 200 acres. This means that everything goes on - grain growing, corn (maize) growing, haymaking, clover seed production - and you deal with horses, cows, calves, pigs, hens, and get a wonderful all-round experience, much of it pleasant though not all. Take threshing, for example.

On American and Canadian threshing machines, there is a "blower" installed with a fan at the bottom. This blower is a vast metal tube of about 1 foot to 18 inches across, up which all the straw, etc. is blasted after being separated from the grain. At the end of the blower is a hood which can be moved in various directions, so that some unfortunate chap, usually the most junior worker (me), could build up a proper straw stack (like a haystack) as the straw came through. Endlessly the straw came through, plus any stones the binder had picked up, at a speed which was almost murderous - and would have been if some of the stones had hit you. That was the most unpleasant chore, made even worse when the straw was blown inside the barn.

It was worse still when you were thrashing "black" clover to get the seed out (the seed being used for dying in industry), for the clover had gone almost black while ripening. You were not only unrecognizable when you came out of a barn after half a day of this (and it went on perhaps for a whole day) but your lungs were almost choked with the dust and chaff. Oh, for a bath!

But there were no baths; in fact I had no hot baths for three years, until I got back to Liverpool in 1923. One had to strip and do one's best with the cold water tub in the woodshed, with sometimes a little hot water thrown in. On the Turnbull farm there wasn't even any soap available, unless I had a surreptitious wash on a Sunday when they weren't looking. On threshing days, at home or on other people's farms, there was no chance of a good wash. Neither were there any "loos", except for the lady of the house. It was largely an animal existence, sleeping in the shirt you worked in all day, but you came to accept most of it, although not all. At the Prossers, my second farm, Billy and I went for a swim in a neighboring creek twice: most refreshing, though not necessarily cleansing!

Happily, life had its occasional moments, such as when we took Pat - a half-jersey cow - over to the bull. Pat was one of twin cows, most rare because twin heifers - called "martins" - are usually sterile. Pat disliked intensely being separated from her twin, Mike, and we had the devil's own job getting her through the bush over to the next farm. On the way back Jimmy Turnbull stopped to talk to the farmer, and I went on with Pat at the end of a 40-foot rope. Gradually Pat increased her pace as we went along a lane, which was solid ice for 100 yards. I lost control and - still hanging onto the rope - was towed on my stomach for 100 yards, shooting along on the ice like a demented toboggan. I dared not risk losing Pat in the bush. Eventually I did let go as we got to the bush full of pine roots half-buried in the snow, which would have ripped me from stem to stem. Pat, of course, ambled off straight home.

The full horror came to light a little later. Before we set off I had found a hidden nest of hens eggs, very old, and had put some in my coat pocket preparatory to burying them. So when I next put my hand in my pocket I shoved it straight into a mash of scrambled - and revolting-smelling - eggs. Ugh!! Hens are odd creatures. One used to leave the warmth of the hen house in the depth of winter and hop step by step up a ladder leaning against the straw stack. Once at the top she hopped off and laid eggs in a nest she'd made. By the time we found her at it she had several solid frozen eggs up there. On another occasion I put my hand underneath a hen to collect any eggs there and my horror found a rat there - dead but limp, so it hadn't been dead long. Anything less probable than a hen sitting amiably over a dead rat I find difficult to imagine.

Then there were the occasions when we had an ice storm or when the snow started to thaw, and then everything froze up. You could quite literally have skated miles and miles along the roads and

could see nothing but ice. We usually watered the cattle daily at the
creek, chopping the ice with an axe to make water holes, but when
it was like this, all ice, the creatures simply couldn't stand, and their
legs spread out in all directions as their bodies crashed to the ground.
With calves you pushed their front legs up straight and then went
around to the back to lift up the hind legs. Down with the front ones
- and so on. So we had to give this up and carry all the water from
our pump to all the cattle and horses. And this wasn't funny because
a strong wind was blowing, and whatever sorts of boots you had -
wellingtons or leather - you were absolutely powerless when the wind
caught you on the slippery surface and carried you straight past the
barn towards the vast manure pile in the yard.

It was a tiresome business, only made bearable by seeing
one's more dignified elders whistling past the doors completely out
of control slap into a fence. But when the sun was rising or setting,
then came scenes of supreme magnificence - the sun shining on these
endless fields of ice, with gold and blue and red against the crystal
background of trees, branches and little things all covered in ice.
In fact, the most remarkable thing I saw was a bunch of horse hair
caught on a fence and which had been blown into a sort of question
mark, with each individual hair encased in its own sheath of ice. We
used to see the Northern Lights sometimes, but I never saw them any
other color than white, shimmering away. They were supposed to
forecast bad weather.

I referred earlier to the horrible job of straw-stack making
during threshing. There was one other task which was physically
even more exhausting. The grain came out almost at floor level into
"bushel boxes" - round metal and wood containers. When full these
boxes had to be picked up, carried to the granary about 10 feet away,
then rushed back for the next one. The flow is constant and unless
the threshing machine (through the mercy of Allah) broke down as it
did occasionally, there was absolutely no respite for four or five hours.
The pace varied with the crop; oats poured out, and barley came
steadily enough, and wheat was slower, but oats were light-ish, barley
heavier and wheat heaviest of all. I think the weights were something
like, per bushel, oats 28 pounds, barley 34, wheat 50. It was murder,
but one survived. You couldn't slack off because grain just piled up
on the floor.

Threshing went from 7 to 12, one hour's break for dinner

during which one ate a prodigious amount for half an hour, and eased
up for the other half hour, and then one to six; two spells of usually
nonstop work. Pitching sheaves towards the machine wasn't too bad;
there was a limit to the amount that the machine could take, and you
could chat a bit to your fellow workers. On top of this of course you
had to do your chores and milking and have breakfast and get to the
farm - wherever it was - by 7:00 am, and after a full day threshing
get back to your own farm and more chores and milking, though
sometimes this was done before you got back. There was of course
no end to "mucking out". All farmers helped towards each other's
threshing on a mutual aid agreement, but I don't think Jimmy T liked
going to threshings. I did it only to get away from the farm, and I
knew by that time I could hold my own with anyone.

There were some astonishing arrangements for filling the
barn, methods by which the corn or hay was unloaded by means of
slings or hay forks, held up by a rope to the top of the barn where
it ran along a little girder, and when it was where you wanted it you
pulled a trip rope and the lot came down. Ingenious. The most
awful thing (to me) was when the entire wagon was hauled up to the
roof by the horses, leaving only the wheels and chassis on the barn
floor. Frankly, the whole thing terrified me. I always hated heights,
and there are few things more slippery than leather soles on straw;
there was I, perched in the infinite, pitching sheaves off the wagon to
Jimmy and expecting to shoot off at any moment and break my neck.

I must admit that I got so mad about it that in a raging
temper I hauled off the sheaves at an incredible speed, even too fast
for the experienced Jimmy to deal with. "You'll kill yourself if you
don't slow down," he called out. I couldn't have cared less. Happily,
no disaster occurred, and the wagon was let down again with an
exhausted me the sole person in it. I wonder whether it wasn't
necessary to use it again in this way - it was only needed for the very
top of the mow – or whether it was my fury which stopped Jimmy
doing this to me once more! Not too creditable to me, I fear, but
I threw off about 150-160 sheaves and as I felt with each one that
one slip could send me hurtling into the floor, I think I had some
justification for being scared! Not a pleasant experience.

There were other bits of ingenious farm equipment, such as
the "stonebolt" and the ditch clearer. The former was a flat sheet of
iron or steel, with the ends slightly sloping and little ridge along each

side. It was a most sensible thing and was used for moving large stones, tree roots and other objects out of the way, or whatever you wanted them. No lifting was necessary - you just rolled the objects on and off - and incidentally you had a nice free ride standing on it when empty.

The ditch clearer saved us much labor when clearing out the foot-wide ditches across the fields. It consisted of a 5 ft. long round center log, with two side wings and a sloping nose. You stood on the wings, hitched up the horse and off you went. The horse walked along the ditch followed by the contraption, and the nose pushed any soil out and up onto the soil each side of the furrow. You had to clean out the crossroads where ditches met, of course, but that was a very minor job.

I really loved driving horses. There were two big ones, a Shire (Cora) and a Percheron (Prince), each weighing about a ton. Prince once stepped on my foot when I was leading him pulling a scuffler (a harrow about two feet wide used for weeding between rows of small fruit, etc.). I had the devil's own job getting him off as I was right beneath his head, couldn't lead him and could get no purchase, but eventually he moved; perhaps he just got bored. Happily, the ground was soft from the harrowing, and there was no damage.

Once I was bringing in a load of corn (maize), which we sometimes left in the field stocked up in the winter, and was using the sleigh - a superb feeling, driving a sleigh. As we came to the farm gate we were trotting along merrily and started to slow up, which you must do well in advance of where you want to stop because of the difficulties of stopping a moving load on ice. We got to the gate and I wheeled the horses sharp left. They went left, the sleigh went left, I went left - but the load went straight on, shooting off the sleigh. It struck me as extremely comic and I nearly died laughing. The Turnbulls couldn't see anything funny in it. I also remember the date; it was January 21st, 1922, my 19th birthday. All was well in the end; I reloaded the sleigh and proceeded barn-wards.

We kept the stable very clean (my job usually) but when I look back at the milking I am filled with horror. The cows were never cleaned down or washed before milking; you brushed off the more obvious bits of dirt, etc., and what fell into the bucket as you milked fell into the bucket. The milk was emptied into the separator and the cream "spun off". I can't remember whether the milk was strained into another bucket first, but we came in just as we were from the fields or mucking out stables or what have you; no one thought of putting on clean overalls or getting oneself clean in any way. I've often wondered just how pure the cream was. The skimmed milk was used for pigs and hens, and for washing your arms to prevent too bad sunburn - for me, that is. The others were hardened to the sun. Talking of sunburn, each January we had the Chinook winds; this was a terribly mild and relaxing wind which made you almost incapable of work, and oddly enough gave you a delightful tan. A few days later you were back to freezing solid, but with a nice tan layer ready for improvement in the summer.

It was the summer of 1921 which I will never forget; I believe it was almost a record summer for heat all over the world. It got so hot that farmers just gave up working in the hot day time and worked all possible hours early and late. All of course except Jimmy Turnbull, and that meant me as well. We never stopped. By 8:00 o'clock in the morning I was just about done, but we had to go on until 9:00 pm. That really was tough and I think pretty merciless, but I suppose his line would have been, "If I can do it, so can you." In winter it was the other end of the scale of course, when you dared not touch the metal parts of the harness or chains or any metal outdoors, or you would lose your skin; it was gloves or else. One way or another there was plenty of variety.

I spent two years with the Turnbulls and then went to the farm next door, to the Prossers, a Welsh family who had emigrated from Merthyr Tydfil. It was sheer and utter bliss after the Turnbulls; they treated me as a human being, as one of the family, and I was really happy. I couldn't believe it when my first afternoon we all went off to a sale; it was heaven. With the Turnbulls work wasn't the main thing, it was the only thing, and I left my unheated attic room with no regrets. The work was just as hard of course at the Prossers, but there was someone to talk to, and a family. I can't properly express the contrast; it was bliss.

By this time I was, I say it diffidently but it was true, a very good farmhand. I was enthusiastic, strong, worked like a beaver (physical work has always appealed to me) and could do pretty well anything anyone else could in the normal laboring line. Before that it was Mrs. Prosser (where I was threshing at the time) who told me one day to get my arm seen too or "You won't have anyone to work for in the morning". I had a badly poisoned wrist and arm. So I told Mrs. Turnbull, and though Jimmy was going into town that evening with the cream he didn't take me to the doctor. Mrs. Turnbull rang him up and he advised hot poultices every two hours during the night. Meantime I had to milk with one hand. Unbelievable but true.

That night I set the alarm every two hours, put on a new poultice, then went back to the sofa in the kitchen for two hours. This went on until the morning, when the whole thing burst and the poison gradually came out. The great line up my arm faded out and all was well, but it was a near thing, and to put it mildly was not helped by what I had best call the unfeeling attitude of the Turnbulls. I must have been pretty fit otherwise to have taken that one, for it was really serious and Charles Prosser was desperately worried. By way of contrast, when I developed a great boil on my chin, Billy Prosser took me in to the doctor on a Sunday morning and the whole thing cleaned up in no time after freezing and opening. Dear, dear, what a contrast.

I am by nature a gregarious person who likes the company of his fellow man, and this is what I missed so much at the Turnbulls. The one thing which made all the difference at the Prossers was that I was no longer lonely, and had someone to talk to. Both Mr. and Mrs. Prosser were most likable people, and their son, Billy, was 16 and a splendid companion. There was also Maudi, aged 14, but I didn't see much of her. I suppose she spent a good deal of time at school, but even in holiday times she spent most of her time around the house, with her friends elsewhere, or helping around the farm on occasions. Even so it was a family home I was in, and I was one of the family. Billy and I had a lot in common and the whole lot of us got on well.

There are always occasions when one has to work on one's own. At the Prossers they were rare, but at the Turnbulls I got so terribly lonely, working on my own in the fields or stables, or sawing wood for days on end, with no one to talk to except at meal and milking times. The "Loneliness of the Long Distance Runner" has nothing on the loneliness of a 17 year old in the fields. And the Prossers were human; they didn't jump on you if you stopped for a short breather, or to pass the time of day with someone going by. The Turnbulls did, Jimmy seldom but Mrs. Turnbull constantly. I was genuinely, desperately, lonely - no conversation at the end of the day - while at the Prossers we sat around chatting, playing euchre, mending bikes and so on. But it had one good effect; I was continually being stretched beyond what I thought was my physical limit. I came to realize in the end that one could always do just that little bit more in anything, a most valuable lesson to me in the future. But I'd had enough of the Turnbulls, and of being 3,000 miles away from anyone I knew, family or friends.

I'm reminded of another "purple" moment. Charles Prosser was splitting logs and tree trunks; he held the wedges and gave me the sledgehammer. I was standing on the log and brought down the hammer with all the speed and force I could muster - and I nearly killed the man, for the sledge whistled past his head, hitting the peak of his hat on route. I'd never before seen a man really turn white - and, of course, I thought it was terribly funny and could hardly stop from bursting out laughing. Why he didn't lay me out on the spot I shall never know, but it <u>was</u> funny. The narrowness of the escape, I suppose, got all my nerves jangling with the usual result - I just wanted to laugh. He said practically nothing and we proceeded with the work - me still with the sledge. What a man!

Fencing was not very popular with me. Each posthole had to be 3 1/2 feet deep and about 18 inches square. Most of the earth and stones were removed by an auger, which you turned endlessly to bite into the earth. Anchor posts had to go in four and a half feet, into holes that were two feet square. That wasn't too bad in summer, but in winter there was two feet of frost in the ground and the auger couldn't be used. So you had an 8 or 9 foot iron bar with a sharpish end and had to chip away at the frozen earth. It was a long, long business, very hard work and made more difficult in that you had to wear thick gloves in the bitter weather or the iron bar would have taken the skin off your fingers. I bet that particular post is still there today; so is much of my sweat.

The winter really brought some most unpleasant conditions, especially clearing out ditches and furrows before they all froze up solid, with the water coming over your boots. I had no wellingtons then; it was so cold that your feet were entirely numb and you couldn't feel them even when walking home. One thing I did enjoy each winter was seeing the muskrats' great domed "houses" in the creek. Like the "frail bridges" at Niagara they were swept away each year by the spring floods and new ones appeared, each summer for Niagara and fall for the muskrats!

I did have one day's holiday a year when I was with the Turnbulls. Jimmy took me to the station about 4:30 am where I caught the Toronto train, and then I spent the whole day at the annual Canadian National Exhibition. At the end of the day I caught a late train back to Milton and walked home, about 5 miles; I got home about 4 am so, rising at 5 I was little short of sleep on those days! Once when Jimmy was ill, apart from help from Mrs. T. with the milking and hens I had all the work on the farm on my shoulders - getting down the hay and straw, oats and general feed for the livestock, clearing out the stables, getting all the feed ready for the midday and evening feeds, sawing up wood in the intervals with a bucksaw (now known over here as a bush saw). I sawed wood endlessly for the kitchen stove and the central heating stove, and always swore I would never saw another log in my life. (Rash words in view of what have I have done since at Sonning and Pewsey!)

Apparently all duties were carried out to Mrs. T's satisfaction, because one day they said I could have a day off as a reward and go to Niagara, which I did. I found the outward appearance of Niagara uninspiring, so I decided to go over to the American side after a trip in the little steamer (the *Maid of The Mist*) up to the foot of the Canadian Horseshoe falls - quite exciting, but I had heard that you could go down to the bottom of the American falls. So over the bridge I went, only to be stopped by an American customs official who refused to let me pass. The US was being particularly fussy about immigration at the time, and they wouldn't believe I had just come down for the day and was returning to the farm next day. So the fellow handed me an "Aliens Deportation Ticket" and sent me back.

I was furious at being so categorized, but next morning stole my way over another bridge. There too I was stopped, but this time was allowed to go on. On Goat Island, on the edge of the falls, you were literally only feet from the water, and the smooth running of this mass of water over the edge gently drew one mentally nearer. I suddenly stepped back, or I might well have gone over after the water. I can quite understand now the hypnotic effect of this smooth-running water; it seemed to pull you with it.

After that I went down below the falls, changing completely into waterproof clothing and going down in an enclosed lift. Then you walked along fragile bridges amongst the rocks at the bottom

Figure 15 - Horseshoe Falls, Niagara, from Goat Island

of the falls, coming into spray which at one point made it almost impossible to breathe! Somewhat panic stricken, I pushed on through into lots more spray. It was a little frightening, some of it, but great fun.

The year I was with the Prossers there was no suggestion of a day off for the Canadian National Exhibition, but I got there all the same. A great family friend of ours, Humphrey Playford, who rowed four times for Cambridge, had come out to Canada with a Leander crew (the Cambridge second Eight) to row against other universities (US and Canadian) on Lake Ontario, and he drove down from Toronto to see me one Sunday. The Prossers let me go off with him to spend the night in Toronto.

I went out in the coaches' boat and watched Leander practice, and then Humphrey and I went back to the great arena show at the Exhibition in the evening. It was a splendid evening, and the first time that I had ever seen a three-ring circus, amongst other things. But there was an after-effect; seeing Humphrey again made me very homesick, and I determined thereupon to go home, if only for a visit. So I got in touch with various shipping companies, having very little cash for I was earning about £35-40 a year (board-free of course). I eventually found one which provided free passage on a cattle boat leaving in August 1923, in return for looking after the cattle. I had at the time every intention of returning to Canada, and was indeed offered a job at another farm if I returned, as the Prossers would presumably have found someone to replace me as soon as I left.

But I didn't commit myself. I had had three years of farming with no break and was happy to leave it for a while, while I went back to what was invariably referred to in Canada as "The Old Country". I had been fortunate in that comparatively brief time to have learned a great deal about so many sides of farming. Horses, cows, pigs, hens, crops, hay, fencing, tree felling, weather conditions - I could tell the time to within 5 minutes without a watch, sun or no sun after two years, and had been able to develop physically into a pretty strong youngster. You had to, there was no option.

Cattle Boats

Doubtless other things will occur to me about Canada as I go on with this saga, but meantime, dear reader, let's go on to cattle boats. These, which sailed from Montreal, were merely ordinary cargo boats which were hired from the old White Star company for the cattle shipping seasons. Pens were put up on every deck where they could find room, and then the fun began. These were no ordinary 2-year-olds but 3-year-old steers from the West, much bigger and full of horns!

Before they came on board some brave souls had put a rope around the horns of each beast, the end of the rope dangling only about a foot in a special knot. Once you had the required number of cattle in any pen you went in amongst them - a risky business - grabbed the end of the rope, pulled it out into its full length, and tied it through a hole in a 2 inch plank about four feet above the ground - and there they stayed for the trip. Except that all cows and steers believe the "grass is greener" in front of the next or next but one animal, and if that beast was lying down then he or she walked over him - hence the tether ropes got crossed. Simple to sort out?

Certainly, in theory, but, and especially when it's dark, you have to untie both ropes, hold a lantern in one hand, hold the spare rope, and tie the other one in its proper hole. If you are Houdini and can manage this, then tying up the other beast is simple. It takes two hands to tie up a beast; you try it with one. And we dare not have any stray beasts strolling around the pens; they created havoc. We did have one stray, and I had to go in and tie it up. The animal was uncooperative and I just made it to the outside of the pen before its horns got me in a place I shouldn't have liked at all.

Well, there they are, all mostly installed. What did we have to do? It wasn't hard work, not after the farm. I did the trip twice; on the first one we got up at 6-6:30 am but on the second at 4:30 am - and 4:30 am in the middle of winter in the middle of the Atlantic is not my favorite time for doing anything. We brought hay up from the holds and had to break the bales, quite simple but energetic at the time, and we had to carry simply endless pails of water. Animals are infuriating; you put a lovely pail of water in front of the beast, he looks at it, decides that the next animal has a better one, tries to get at it and knocks over his own. If you are particularly unlucky, he knocks them both over. There's nothing you can do about it except to go and get some more. The second feed was about 4:00 pm, and the rest of the day was ours to do with as we felt.

I don't remember what we did except that I had acquired a cheap gramophone and used to put records on, challenging the needle to stay on while the ship corkscrewed and dipped its happy way along. One day a huge stoker suddenly appeared out of the depths, blacker than the ace of spades. He looked threatening but apparently all he wanted was to hear the *Blue Danube*. In view of his size he got it, both then and later, and proved most amiable.

It was an 11-day trip, and for seven of those days across the Atlantic we never saw sight of another ship, which really taught us what a tremendous area the Atlantic covers. That was trip number one. Trip number two is very different - of that more later. I had my clothes and other items stolen on the second trip; we got them back because the silly fellow had stolen a silver spoon I had bought for Mama in Montreal, and this was found in his luggage. Two or three were involved and were convicted at Bristol; this is all by the way.

Back to the first trip! When we got to Birkenhead, all we cattlemen, from every calling under the sun, were taken over in a tug to Liverpool and there I had my first hot bath for three years. I cannot describe the sheer luxury I felt! Unfortunately, I also had my traveling money stolen, so I wired the family asking them to send me some money at Liverpool so that I could get home. Now, I had made this difficult, because I was coming home unexpectedly early, and to keep up the surprise I had sent a postcard from Milton the day I left the farm saying that I would see them at Christmas - and this was September.

Nevertheless Mama, bless her, sent the money to the police station where I had gone for advice as to how to get home - we were not on the phone - and a policeman solemnly escorted me round to the Post Office to cash the money order. Fine. Off I go to London, nobody to meet me and I didn't expect it, but on the Underground I sat near somebody who might have been Mama - but I wasn't sure. Sounds incredible but true, after only three years.

As I watched, she got out at Hammersmith; I got out at Hammersmith. We got on the same tram and got off at the same place. I followed her and let her go around the corner into Dunsany Road first. Then I belted around the corner, dashed up to the door as she disappeared into the house and was warmly welcomed by Mama who was just explaining that she was afraid all the time it was a hoax because they had received my card saying I wasn't coming till Christmas! Quite extraordinary, my not definitely recognizing Mama , and a bit odd that she didn't recognize me, but I had grown a lot and changed considerably. I didn't recognize Betty or Daphne but assumed they were who they were, and none of them could properly understand what I was saying with my strong agricultural Canadian accent.

So, three weeks at home creeping back into civilization, then back to Avonmouth for the free trip back to Montreal. Incidentally, after the cattlemen had been dropped at Birkenhead the cattle were unloaded. They were then fattened up for a few weeks, killed and sold as home-killed beef, a subtle way of fooling the housewife into thinking that they were home-grown beef. After that the ship made its way down to Avonmouth, cleaning out all the muck from the pens and flinging it into the sea! Do you want to go bathing?

I tried to get some sort of a job in England but there was nothing doing, so it was off to Canada again on this empty ship, with three other cattlemen (American students, actually) and the most revolting food, much of it the worst I've ever tasted. The ship was empty, that is, except for one racehorse and some tin plate – boy, did we bounce en route! No jobs seemed to be available in Montreal, so I wangled (with a small bribe from my almost non-existent funds) passage home in November on another cattle boat, which would be the last to leave Montreal before the Saint Lawrence froze up.

I was almost broke, and found digs in the dock area, wandering about the place in the daytime. I could not afford a midday meal so got over the feeling of hunger for the time being by going to a small cinema which cost only $0.10, which wouldn't have bought enough food even to swallow. The films (long before "talkies") had all the story put onto the screen divided into two - in English on the left, in French on the right. Good for one's French, if nothing else.

Finally we left, and having done the trip before I was put in charge of one of the gangs, simultaneously wangling a berth in a four-berth cabin hut on the deck. I remember that place particularly because we used to "turn out the light" by leaning out of the bunk and extracting the bulb. Replacing it one morning I put my finger in the socket - that woke me up! It was from this hut that my clothes were stolen one day, as already mentioned. All went well, apparently, for a few days, and then one became aware that all was not well.

The exact order of events is not now clear, but in short this is it. We had amongst the cattleman two Irishmen - reputed "gun-runners" - who amongst other things didn't like the food, which was passable though no more. They broke into the hold where the hay was kept (as well as other supplies) and took a case of 30 dozen eggs; there was nothing smaller. They then, Heaven help us, set a fire on the <u>wooden</u> deck of the foc'sle, later transferring their cooking to the galley when there was no one about.

However, the Captain got to know of this, and one evening the First and Second Mates went smoothly along to the galley and blocked each end of it while the egg enthusiasts were blithely frying eggs. There was some scrapping and the First Mate came out with a beautiful shiner, but as he was really big 6-footer and the other Mate was also big, the issue was soon resolved and the miscreants were put in irons. Incidentally, a day or two before this climax the two Irishmen had produced a gun, and threatened anyone who gave away their nefarious actions with the customary bullet. There was naturally no enthusiastic betrayal to the authorities.

The sequel was, for me, annoying. Both men were in my gang and I, who had worked a nice little number for myself as a foreman, found myself with the rest of my gang working harder than all the other guys, being two men short! Such is life. I felt that the culprits in question might perhaps have been treated as one of the steers, which died, was hoisted up from below by derrick and disappeared overboard into the Mersey. Most of the cattle, though they lost weight, stood the long, rough trip much better than some of the men, but these two other chaps had been so lazy and so offensive that we almost preferred to work without them. The captain, after the two had been immured down below, got us all together; "You all know what you signed," he said. But of course none of us had read the long document, and he threatened us with all the pains of hell if there was any further trouble - which there wasn't.

Teaching – Early Appointments

Shirley House School, Blackheath, London

So back to Birkenhead, Liverpool, London and home. I tried to get all sorts of jobs, and then one day Ron said, "Why don't you try the family curse?" (teaching). So, with no more qualifications than a London Matriculation Certificate, I got in touch with those erstwhile twin pillars of independent education, Gabbitas and Thring[10], and Truman Knightley[11]. The latter eventually sent me notice of a job as a Junior Assistant Master at a school at Charlton, on the edge of Blackheath in Kent, two miles from Woolwich, where I started in January, 1924.

It was a bit odd. The school was called Shirley House School, the Masters lived in the same building as were the classrooms, and the Headmaster and Boarders lived in a house called Cherry Orchard - all very confusing to a novice. There were masses of Day Boys as well, and it was a Prep School, one of masses in the country. It is now defunct, the Headmaster, one Colonel C. J. T. Robertson, eventually selling the whole place to the former London County Council for, I believe, £75,000 in the days when money was money. Wise man. I went down there to look long ago, and found a large, new housing estate. The school had been wiped off the face of the earth as though it had never existed, which still hurts because I had a very happy time there.

I fell in love with the job and with teaching the moment I started. But I must admit it was a pretty poor place academically. As far as I remember the staff consisted of a man with a degree (age 38) for Classics, a retired Major of 40 (aged, to me!) who knew nothing; he took elementary Latin and even then had all the translations of sentences, etc. penciled into his book. He also loved Raggett's Stout and would periodically kick the bottle over as he sat by the gas fire, whereupon he would say, "Great Scott, we do live like pigs here!"

---

10   The first known private employment agency, Gabbitas and Thring was founded in London in 1873 to recruit schoolmasters for private schools.

11   Truman Knightley Ltd., Educational Consultants, founded 1901.

Then there was an odd character for Maths, another one called Boris Maschinski - I don't know what he took - a very pleasant youngster about my age, and me.

I wonder if whoever reads this has ever been so paralyzed as I was, at age 21, standing in front of my first class, which, so help us, included boys from 7 to 11? French was the subject. What does one do? How does one teach? Then suddenly came help. I saw that the title of the French book they had out was that old friend of my childhood, "*French Without Tears*" - and we were off. I also taught Latin.

But that wasn't the main problem of life, and I don't know whether I can convey what it was, exactly. In brief it was that during those vital years of growing up and learning all about life and people, from 17½ to 21, I had been entirely cut off from civilization, and was constantly finding myself in awkward spots. Such as, does one take off one's hat? Who shakes hands with whom? What clothes does one wear for this or that? All small talk and forms of politeness were temporarily unknown to me, and I had to work hard at catching up. I don't think anyone knew the agonies I went through at times, but fortunately I had a few weeks at home to become comparatively civilized again. Farming was such a simple if animal life (no pun intended) in Canada then.

Life was good. Not a care in the world, tennis on the lawn outside the house at school, dancing lessons with the Kentish's (whose cousins became my lifelong friends) earning the then (to me) princely salary of 100 pounds a year, and completely independent. In games all I had to do was to supervise the game of the master who was off for the afternoon. We all had one afternoon off a week; mine was Thursday, and although Blackheath was 12 miles from London, by dint of sprinting after morning school I got a bus to the station, a train to London, Underground to Aldwych and was one of the first in a gallery queue to see the Gilbert and Sullivan "*Iolanthe.*" We had done this at Christ's Hospital, when I (with a much-reduced part) <u>was</u> *Iolanthe* – sung, not acted, in our ordinary clothes.

Sunday duty was taken in rotation, and I remember one Sunday afternoon when a boy, quite legitimately driving a golf ball, got another harmless youth right in the back of the skull with what sounded like the crack of doom. I was terrified that the boy would have concussion and I should be blamed and probably fired, but in the event nothing happened.

What fun we had with very little. Dances in a small room, the furniture having been moved elsewhere, music supplied by a portable gramophone which had to be wound up for each record, drinking nothing but lemonade - and we still managed to have some pretty riotous evenings. Anyway, I was a rabid teetotaler (why is it spelled "tee"?) until I was 27 - and no comments needed!

The Kentish's often invited me to spend a week or two with them on holiday and I went gladly, for they were all splendid company. There were five children, Margaret and John the elder ones, about 17 and 14 when I first knew them, then Helen at 10, Elizabeth 6, and David 1. John and I hit it off from the first – we even shared a birthday; he was exactly seven years younger than me - and I used to go round and play tennis a lot with the parents and John and Margaret. [12]

I had been to Studland with the family. We spent one holiday in what was then a popular novelty, converted railway carriages parked at various seaside stations, in this case Bridport. And then one holiday we all went to Hythe; John would have been about 18 then. We went of course to the miniature railway, we roller-skated on a special concrete rink (at sixpence a time), and then we went on the Grand Military Canal. This had been dug to hinder Napoleon's march inland should he ever invade the country and get past the Martello Towers, many of which still stand.

We hired a canoe and presently John sat on the bow for a change while I paddled along. "That's an idea, John," I said, "I'll do the same," and I got up to sit <u>on</u> the other end of the canoe. What I failed to realize was that my move took away every trace of weight or ballast from the bottom of the canoe, with the inevitable result. In two seconds dead the whole thing turned over, and John and I were in the water, which was fortunately quite warm even at Easter that year.

We surfaced (I remember distinctly that my pipe was still in my mouth in spite of my ducking) and struggled with the canoe to the bank, where we emptied out all the water we could. Then we got in again, feeling chilly by now, and paddled madly home, picking up

12   John Kentish remained a lifelong friend of Dad's. He attended Rugby School and Oriel College, Oxford, became a renowned operatic tenor with Sadler's Wells Opera, and was later Director of Opera at the Royal College.

my tobacco pouch which was making its way slowly along the canal. I'd taken my coat off before the accident and was most relieved to find it still wedged under the seat when we righted the canoe. Once back at the landing stage we ran about two miles in what was now bright sunlight, dripping all the way home, hoping we could neither of us catch pneumonia.

We didn't, but that isn't quite the end of the story. John had been anxiously waiting for a new suit of plus-fours; eventually they'd arrived and he'd put them on just before we embarked on the fatal trip. It was bad enough getting a brand new suit soaked through and through - and John's Mother was hardly enthusiastic about it - but there was still more to come. When John stripped off, he was a beautiful brown color all over; the dye had come out of the suit and he looked as though he had spent a month on the Costa Bravo rather than five minutes in the canal. It was quite a day, ending up with us walking miles in the hot sun in the afternoon looking for a dry cleaners, a day of which we remind each other regularly even now, and even now we haven't stopped laughing.

Ardvreck, Crieff

Since a degree was an essential qualification for more remunerative posts, at different times I made abortive efforts to obtain one by correspondence course through the famous University Correspondence College. I have never forgotten getting back one of my French tests, duly corrected with a shattering comment, "Did you really pass in French at Matriculation? It is difficult to believe." I finally managed it during the war, but in the meantime continued working my way through the education landscape.

After two years at Shirley House I got a job as Senior French Master at another prep school, Ardvreck, at Crieff in Perthshire, starting in January 1926 – a Senior at age 23! This was another pretty low-standard place academically (or they probably wouldn't have taken me! Perhaps other men didn't want to go so far away; I didn't mind where I went as long as I could get a job), Boarders only, about 40 of them, Scottish and English. The only visible difference was on Sunday, when the English boys were in Eton suits (horrible) and went to the Episcopalian church, known as "The Circus", while the Scottish lads, resplendent in many-hued kilts, were escorted to the Presbyterian Church, known (to the staff) as "The Roundabout."

I can't think how Mr. English, the Headmaster (known to us

as Pongo), ever became a schoolmaster. I can only imagine he liked
the idea of being a Headmaster and had the money to buy the school.
The staff all had to wear gowns; "You see, Inge, if boys are ragging
about and they happen to touch a gown, they respectfully fall apart."
I ask you! The work standard was, I think, pretty low. For instance,
I had to teach geography (of which I knew nothing) to two classes in
adjoining rooms with just a door in between. So I just stood in the
doorway, facing the two rooms alternately, spraying out geographical
facts ad lib and ad nauseum. I also took the shooting (with BSA air
rifles) of which I also knew nothing, but became pretty expert and
dented endless threepenny bits.

You see, it has long been a joke in the teaching profession
that if you are qualified in, say, Latin and Greek, you are then asked to
teach - and do teach - Maths and Science. So when you are asked by
the Headmaster to do something, you say in self defense, "Sir, I know
nothing about it." You invariably get the same answer; "That's alright,
my boy (or old chap), you'll soon pick it up." And the astonishing
thing is that you do! It was the old principle of "keeping one page
ahead of your pupils", though not necessarily literally. But it did
mean a good deal of private studying at times; there was no option.

My education had finished at Matric level (until I took
my degree at Oxford from 1942-45), and with Matric as my only
qualification (and that in 1920, followed by a three year gap in which
I forgot nearly everything) it seemed I found myself teaching at one
time or another every subject in the prep school syllabus, and English
and some French up to school certificate level. No wonder I had to
do some catching up! I'm not sure which surprises me most; my
nerve at applying for jobs to teach subjects I hadn't taught before,
or my Headmasters' quiet acceptance of my ability to do so. But I
digress.

There were some odd things about Ardvreck, which was
a pleasant enough school. The Headmaster strongly disliked the
Masters having any contact with the boys outside lesson/games time,
and if he saw you passing the time of day with any boys he always
reacted, expressing his displeasure. As the company of boys is one of
the things which has always appealed to me in "teaching" I didn't like
it much, apart from thinking the man must be out of his tiny mind.
He was obviously afraid of any boys and masters getting too fond of
each other, and he had his quite unexpected "reward" when the two

Figure 16 - Teaching positions in the UK

senior Masters I knew were both thrown out suddenly for the type of offense he was so scared of happening in his school.

More pleasant were other things, including the free time I enjoyed because I took no games and the two masters concerned above neither invited nor welcomed assistance in running the games. So I used to play golf a great deal on the Crieff course, where a round cost the princely sum of 1 shilling (5p today). Occasionally, however, three of us Masters - including the two already mentioned, whose other activities were not then suspected - used to hire a car to go the ten miles over to Gleneagles, that splendid place so famous nowadays. I can't remember which course we played on, but the scenery was magnificent and it was an afternoon out of school. We ended up having a massive high tea in the excellent restaurant of this famous hotel, while music was played (as was usual in those days at tea time) by no less a man than Henry Hall, who became nationally famous with his dance band.

There was another particularly pleasant tradition. On days when there was a rugger international at Murrayfield the Masters were allowed to go off to the match for the day, leaving the entire school - 40 boys - in the hands of the Headmaster. This was grand. We left at 8:30 am, took the train for Edinburgh, a few hours away, had a stroll around the city, got some food, went to the match and returned home about 8:30 pm. I have a vague idea that one Master was left behind, because there were only four Masters and I cannot remember more than three going, but I'm not sure.

What I do remember is being shaken by the sight of hundreds of schoolboys strolling down Prince's St. in Edinburgh in their (rugger) school Honors Caps - frightfully un-English! I don't know if they still do it, or even whether Honors Caps are still made or awarded, for those were the days even in Prep Schools (as well as Public Schools, Colleges, etc.) when there were different caps for earning one's Colors in different sports, as well as different blazers and ties.

When bored, and if I had any money, I would occasionally hire an Austin 12 and drive around the glorious scenery; the Trossachs were not far away. However, the job was rather dull, so I looked elsewhere - after losing my appendix in April 1926. I was staying with the McNeils (parents of one of the boys) in a large country house (Shennanton, at Kirkcowan near Newton Stewart); a charming family, parents and both boys. One day I developed appendicitis, and Mr. McNeil fixed me up in a nursing home in Dumfries, 60 miles away. They took me back for convalescence and I missed a few weeks of the term, being welcomed back by a cheering crowd of boys as my taxi arrived at the school. I'm sure the HM put them up to it; very sporting of him.

The year was 1926, the year and the time of the General Strike. All young men were driving buses, trains, lorries, etc. I was longing to be in it, but instead had to lie in bed listening to the times of all the trains in and out of London being announced on the wireless which the matron very kindly fixed up for me. The McNeills had one of the first wireless sets, with a large horn-shaped speaker, a change from scratching about on a "cat's whisker" set which I had used at Shirley House. One Master there had bought a receiver (for five shillings!) and with the aid of a 50-foot aerial gave us the thrill of listening to the wireless. I know the first thing I ever heard over the air was "Softly Awakes My Heart", that magnificent aria from *Samson and Delilah*, broadcast from Covent Garden.

It was about this time that the first "unbreakable" records came out, at a cost of 1 shilling. John Kentish and I hurled one discus-fashion at each other in his garden until it flew over the fence. We were naturally convulsed in giggles and laughter as we had solemnly to approach our neighbor with "Please may we have our record back?" "Your what?" "Our gramophone record; it came over the fence." We got it back, but our insanity was confirmed.

South Lodge, Lowestoft

So, in May 1927 it was off to South Lodge, a Prep School at Lowestoft, right on the promenade. Lowestoft is the most easterly point in England, and the wind leaves you in no doubt about it. Coming off the sea it would go slap through the house irrespective of tightly shut windows. Very healthy, of course, but... I was taking Senior French and some Senior Latin, and the Headmaster - Major T. J. E. Sewell, CMA - asked me as soon as I arrived if I had a "key" to "*North and Hillard*", a standard Latin book much in vogue for years and years. He obviously wasn't too sure my capabilities, for I hadn't touched Latin for six or seven years. I, equally doubtful as to my capabilities, was able to reassure him that I <u>had</u> got one. Relief all round.

I also took the cricket, though not with conspicuous success. No games for me to supervise except in the summer, so I had the occasional hockey game (new to me) with the boys and joined the Kirkley Soccer Club in Lowestoft. The Club, alas, is no more. I knew no soccer and had to learn as I went along. Having good ball sense and being able to sprint pretty fast, I was put on the wing. It was all very pleasant. I only played in the first XI when they were short, and I can't quite think why they played me even then. The reason for being short of players was that many of the team worked on the fishing smacks and trawlers, which of course being all sail could not always get back into port on time against adverse weather. They were a good crowd and I particularly liked going to play Norwich way, because instead of coming straight home we would stop off for a meal, a musical or the cinema, then fill up with fish and chips from a stall and leave about midnight. A nice break.

At South Lodge we had this abominable business of Early School from 7 to 7:30 - or was it 7:30 to 8? Anyway, it was barbarous, before breakfast. In view of that, what follows will seem even more absurd. The headmaster had a Standard car; he also bought a large motor mower for the school playing field, which was half an hour's walk away. I wanted to drive the mower, and said I would go up before Early School to do some mowing, whereupon he said I could go up in his car. To cut a long and incredible story short, I would get up at 3:20 or 4:00 am (sometimes sleeping on the floor to make sure I woke up in time), go down for the car, race up to the field, mow, mow and mow, rush back, take the car back down to its garage, wash, shave and go into early school. For food I used to get bars of chocolate out of automatic machines.

I did this for weeks until I had the whole vast field leveled down; most of it had never been cut before, and I could only go two or three feet at a time. Incredibly hard work, but I had (and always had) vast stores of energy, and it kept me fit - apart from nearly killing me towards the end. But I was determined to finish off the field. The HM used to protest, saying "You'll kill yourself," and I had a job getting the car key out of him, but he always gave in.

We had one odd warning from "The Beak", as we called Major Sewell; "When taking fielding practice, for goodness sake don't break the fingers of one boy." The boy? Benjamin Britten, who even at 12 had composed music and was already an excellent pianist. Ben was a delightful boy, with no "side" at all, and used to play for me when I tried out new songs - until The Beak expressed his non-approval. It was the usual sort of nonsense; "There mustn't appear to be more attention paid to one boy than to another," sort of thing. It was quite stupid. I would have got any one of the 60 or 70 boys to play for me if they could. I don't remember Ben much as a cricketer, but it was a pleasure to have him on the team. His Father was my dentist and he had an elder brother, Bobby, with whom I passed some working hours over holidays, and some non-working ones.

Periodically, I was still making some sort of an effort to get a degree, knowing and having seen so many men who were unqualified and realizing that the future without one was hopeless. At this time, I had a spasm of wanting to write articles for the newspapers. I got a typewriter, became pretty proficient at it, joined a correspondence course in journalism, but never got anything published. I don't think my heart was in it.

One holiday I took two boys on the Broads for a week, and that was a saga in itself. The motor boat was called the "*Patience*" and by gosh we needed it. We set sail from just north of Lowestoft harbor, where I used to go sometimes very early in the morning (about 6:00 am) on a fine day to watch the fishing trawlers and drifters sailing majestically into the harbor. This was no easy job with cross-currents; sometimes ships would take three or four attempts before they got through the narrow entrance. Sometimes on a relatively calm morning I would stand on one of the docks and a hail would come from the incoming boat; I would wave back and a rope would come hurtling across. This I hitched to a bollard and the ship was able to swing around the jetty in a U turn. Very neat and I enjoyed it.

I also used to go to watch the men unloading the fish and sorting them out, fish of every variety, from dogfish to cod and eels. It was wonderful. From the "tray" onto which the craws were emptied the men flung each fish sideways - and <u>behind</u> them - into the right box without looking; I never saw them either miss the box or put a fish in the wrong box. You may wonder why I had this mania for getting up so early in the morning; even at Blackheath I used to go for morning runs for "training", to the horror of the other Masters. I had then started to play rugger for one of the Old Blues (Christ's Hospital) teams and was a bit more successful than I had been at soccer, though this eventually improved very considerably.

I have never forgotten once when we had been playing the Norwich YMCA and the "Pink 'un" (the Saturday evening sports paper) in an account of our match contained the immortal sentence "Inge unaccountably missed from two feet!" Not at all unaccountable; I was steaming towards the goal so fast that I couldn't change feet to push the ball into the net, but pushed it outside the right hand post with my left foot!

But back to the "*Patience*", which did everything but sink. I had Michael and John, both 13 year olds, with me and we duly pop-popped away from the bank, heading for Beccles. Suddenly one of the boys said, "Sir, sparks are coming out of the side of the boat!" Quite right, they were. The water pump had apparently jammed, and while I was looking at it, holding onto the tiller with one hand, the handle came out of the tiller and we were heading straight for the bank. Leaping onto the stern I grabbed the rudder with my hands and straightened her out and, fine, we breathed again. We eventually moored for the night.

The next day the brute wouldn't start. I primed the engine, and after interminably swinging the engine there was a colossal bang and one of the sparking plugs, complete with seating, shot straight up into the air and fell back into the sump. The plug was duly replaced and we pottered on towards Yarmouth, but on only one cylinder - she only had two - pop popping like some early motor car. However, we could still steer her, so on we went.

Then we did meet trouble. Before we got to Yarmouth we had to cross a vast expanse of open water, I think called Breedon. There was a strong current, for here the water was tidal, and the engine was not producing enough power to give us control over the boat. There was only one thing for it; I made for one of the large posts which marked the channel, and hung on to the post while the boys hung on to me as we waited for someone to come by. Eventually they did and gave us a tow into the outskirts of Yarmouth, where we asked a garage to fix the engine. They did - for a few hours, when it died again.

We were all quite determined to go on with the trip, so made for Potter Heigham. About our third night out (or rather the following morning), I woke up feeling rather a lot of weight on me, and found that one of the boys, who were sleeping on the seats/bunks (I slept on the deck) had rolled over and fallen on me, waking neither of us up at the time! The next event came at Potter Heigham bridge, where there is only room for one craft to pass at a time. I saw another boat coming towards us, so I waved it on and pushed my engine into reverse. It didn't have the slightest effect as one cylinder was useless, so I did the only thing and steered straight for the bridge. Fortunately, owing to the aforementioned lack of power we were only going slowly - and we hit the bridge head on, with the firm bump. We spent a few nights at Potter Heigham, and then the engine passed out completely.

It was there that I tried water skiing, on a flat board towed behind a motorboat. I crawled up on to the board and was just beginning to enjoy myself when the inevitable happened – and then I knew what it felt like to hit the water at speed, just like hitting concrete. We bathed and ate and enjoyed ourselves, while I sent messages via John's Father (who had come to look us up) to the owner of the boat asking him to come and do something about the boat and expressing my annoyance that the boat was in such a bad condition as regards the engine. No useful reply, so I told him that we were going to leave the boat where it was and that he would have to fetch it or pay for it to be fetched. A furious reply came, saying that he would sue me for damage to the boat and for the cost of getting it back. This was where I played my ace: I told John's Father about it. He was a solicitor, and dictated a letter for me to write, the gist of which was that far from him suing me I would, if there was any trouble, sue <u>him</u> for hiring out a boat in such bad condition. No further word was received.

Lowestoft has its memories indeed for me. I was once driving a car down the Main Street when for some reason I stopped to unscrew the radiator cap. No one had ever warned me about that, and a passing tram driver was more than a little astonished to find a jet of boiling water whistling past his nose. I merely scalded my wrist a little, but I never forgot the lesson.

It was at Yarmouth, next up from Lowestoft, that on one afternoon two of our party had cars and I climbed from one to the other while the drivers steered their cars accurately along the Main Street - stupid but fun. Once wasn't enough, as they and I did it several times.

I was put in charge of a House of 12 boys as the school grew, and in many ways I was happy, but the HM and I were too alike and had some healthy clashes with no holds barred but no hard feelings either. So I decided to move on, and we parted with, I think, mutual relief and mutual respect. Alas, when Joyce and I went for a brief holiday at Suffolk once the South Lodge school had completely disappeared, its place taken by ornamental gardens, and the playing field had been taken over by the council as public playing fields. In fact, Tim played hockey in a tournament some years later over the grass I had mown so lovingly years before. South Lodge was quite a good school, certainly a slight improvement on my two earlier ones, as well as being bigger, and I was slowly going up into more senior posts.

South Lodge itself, which had already been moved to Lowestoft from elsewhere, was moved to Norfolk at the beginning of the war in 1939. It was then burned down in its new home and was moved again (it has a different name now, which escapes me) to Suffolk, but there was another fire. Happily, the school survived and is going strong under The Beak's son, who was born when I was at the school! So time flies.

Downsend, Surrey

The next one was Downsend, at Leatherhead, which I joined in September 1929, and this is really where life started in good schools. At age 26 I was put in charge of French, Common Entrance Latin, some English, all games, and the Scouts. For the record I taught every single lesson (as in my last two jobs), had one afternoon off a week (Wednesday, useful for the Derby if I had been able to avoid making a cricket fixture), established a Prefect system, looked after the 15 to 20 Boarders first thing in the morning, and so on. A very, very busy and hard life, but I thoroughly enjoyed it. My jobs so far had lasted two years, four terms, two years and one term; this one was to last six years.

I went off for the Downsend interview on a Saturday, and had all the interviews on Sunday. That over, I delayed my return to Lowestoft in order to see a "Bulldog Drummond" film. This resulted in my catching the milk train to Yarmouth - the only train left - and getting a lift in a Post Office van to Lowestoft, arriving back at the school about 5:00 am. As I had to get up again at 6:30 am, I imagine my lessons were somewhat uninspired that day.

I got the job. C. T. Linford (the Headmaster's son, who was in effect joint Headmaster and became a very good friend) always said that his Father offered me the job because, being teetotal at the time, I didn't drink any of the wine he always produced for Sunday lunch! His luck was not to last as I gradually abandoned some foolish ideas and partook of wine, beer, etc. with the best.

Downsend had about 70 boys then, including about 20 Boarders. The total went up to about 150 while I was there (it's now over 300) but no Boarders, which wouldn't have suited me at all; I would never want to teach in any school where there were no Boarders. I just like having them around all the time, which is one reason why I never liked holidays coming at Holme Park. The school became so empty and lonely, though fortunately of course one can see more of one's own family in the holidays.

This was, as CT admits, a Golden Age for Downsend, but

Figure 17 – Downsend, in 1939

not because I had joined the staff! I became unofficially the Senior Assistant Master and officially the Games Master. Goodness me, we did work. Lessons all morning until 12:15, then games, practice nets, shooting at goal, hockey, dribbling, passing - the lot. Rushed back to lunch; after lunch, games and lessons. Matches most Wednesdays and Saturdays, tea and then duty prep in rotation until 6:30-ish. You were free after about 7:00 pm, when we had our final meal. A. H. Linford – AHL, the "old man", the school founder and Headmaster - had a passion for jugged hare, and its welcome odor warned us well in advance of what was coming. He also insisted on mixing the French dressing for salads himself. We were well fed, and I have unfading memories of vast Bel Paese cheeses, and a very solid cake known as "The Bomb", which appeared regularly at the time.

Figure 18 - CT and Nell Linford

      The reason why it was a "Golden Age" is chiefly that during the six years I was there the school had a collection of really outstanding boys, both academic and sporting. One year we had three Winchester scholarships, which is almost as rare as winning the pools three times. As regards games, we had season after season of football, hockey and cricket hardly losing a game - the cricket team went for over three seasons without defeat - and on top of that the boys were an extraordinarily nice lot. Names which one can never forget (in the games line) include Lomas, Hughes, Harding and Conliffe. With tremendous and untiring energy, for I enjoyed it all, we had both success and enjoyment at the school.

I also (and all this is merely a matter of fact, not of blowing one's own trumpet) got the school Scout troop going into a larger and successful troop, started up Cubs with the help of girls on the staff, worked for and got my "Wood Badge" for Scouting[13], and went to the Scout Jamboree in Hungary in 1933. No wonder I couldn't find the time to work out for a degree until 1933, when I abjured other pleasures, including bridge (except on Friday nights), and started working three hours nightly after supper. I also had to give up my greatly-loved Gilbert and Sullivan singing and acting.

A year later in June 1934, having passed my inter-BA exams at London, I embarked on trying to get my BA itself in one further year. Quite mad, of course, considering what else I was doing, but worth trying. It really needed two more years but I wanted to get it out of the way, so I pressed on. Failure, alas. I had to take three subjects, French: passed, Latin: borderline, History: failed. By the time I heard the result I had got another job as Headmaster of a small school in China, so that put an end to studying for a bit.

There was nothing really striking about the six years at Downsend in themselves, but my whole life was changed through Downsend. One term a small boy called John Roberts turned up. His Father - head of West Park Hospital in Epsom[14] - used to pick him up from school and would often give me a lift into Epsom. On the way home we'd pick up John's two sisters, Bunty and Joyce, at their school, Parsons Mead. This school at one point was short of someone to teach Latin; CT went round to do it, and shortly after I took over. Amongst my pupils was one Joyce Roberts, who as I write this is sitting in her favorite place on the rug by the fire - and that is a good example of potted history.

There were some outstanding events and happy memories of the Downsend period, 1929-35. A parent lent me - without my asking - her baby Austin for a week in the summer holidays one year.

13   A leadership qualification.
14   The last of a cluster of five mental hospitals built outside Epsom, it opened in 1924 and housed 2,000 patients.

So, being footloose and fancy free, off I went to the South Coast and crossed over to Hayling Island to see the Roberts family, who I knew were on holiday there as they were every year. Dr. Roberts, bless him, invited me to stay with them for a few days and I had a lovely time, even being buried in the sand up to my neck by Joyce and Bunty, and probably John. I suppose Joyce was about 14 then, and I have distinct and pleasing memories of carrying her up to her room when she went off to bed one night - a feat I have never attempted to repeat. When I left I drove over to Dover and indulged in one of my favorite occupations, watching Kent play cricket, as I had done on the same ground nearly 20 years before.

Dr. Roberts was also responsible for one of the outstanding nights of my life. He very kindly invited me to the Annual Ball at the Hospital, where, before dinner, he plied me generously with a concoction the contents of which were a closely guarded medical secret - and I'm not surprised. It was insidious dynamite. So, by the time dinner was over with its further supply of wine and brandy, I was in a pretty euphoric state. At this point Joyce and Bunty appeared, and I asked Joyce for a dance. Total disaster nearly followed. Somewhat uncertain of balance for reasons already stated, I found myself launched onto a superb dance floor polished to degree of unprecedented slipperiness, while my feet behaved as if I had roller skates on. Why we didn't crash I shall never know.

The night wore on, and my memories of the rest of the evening are hazy. But I do know that at 3:00 am I was sitting on the floor of my room (I was staying with the Roberts overnight) giggling insanely while I tried to take the studs out of my shirt. They were of the screw-in type, and kept eluding my fingers. I had always wondered what it was like to be like that, and I found out. I found out even more the next morning with a head in which half a dozen pile-drivers were competing with each other. I was driven off to school for the usual day's work. Still, it had all been worth it, though I didn't think so for the rest of that day. (And <u>still</u> the girl married me!)

I was, as I have mentioned, possessed to my surprise with intense and probably superfluous energy, and this brought disaster once when getting ready for a knock-up game on a parent's tennis court. I hurtled across the court straight into the tennis post, which snapped off promptly at the base. As the afternoon's tennis hadn't started, I was not very popular. Previously, at Shirley House School,

I once turned off the tap on the hot water geyser so thoroughly that it broke clean off and stopped anyone at all having a bath.

But the most astonishing tour de force - I tell the story for amusement and not through pride - came later in Tsingtao when I was playing a terrific game of tennis in a match. The courts were on different levels there, and chasing a difficult ball I tore across the court like a demented hippopotamus, went slap through the wire netting - which couldn't have been all that strong - and arrived on the court below, to the astonishment and regret of the four people there who were in the middle of a game. Rather shamefacedly I climbed back and was not surprised to hear that I had lost the point.

Downsend also saw the beginning of my car-owning days. A parent (again) sold me their no-longer-used car, a Citroën, for 10 pounds. I took it out for a test run and found it smelled a little hot when I got back, which wasn't surprising for I had not checked the water and the radiator was empty. However, the car was none the worse, apparently, and served me well for a year or two.

Then I traded it in in part for a 350cc OK Supreme motorbike. I had never ridden one in my life, and this one was in a garage in Hampstead in South London. Even today I shudder at my temerity, for I went to Hampstead, got the bike, started it up through luck more than judgment, and rode straight through London and 19 miles the other side to the school at Leatherhead - all in the pouring rain. The engine kept stopping and I had no idea exactly where the ignition and petrol levers should be for starting, so every time the engine stopped I had to kick and kick until I got the thing right.

For some extraordinary reason I got down to the School in one piece with only one slight mishap. After an hour or so of getting used to the machine I saw that the road ahead took a sharp left-hand turn. Well, I'd obviously been around lots of corners by then, but for some reason or other I did the fatal thing; I started to think. "What do I do to get around the corner?" I was simply paralyzed, so cut out the engine and wobbled across the road, where I subsided gratefully onto a heap of gravel. It was just like the centipede who starved to death where he was, because he couldn't remember which foot to put forward first. I arrived very late at the concert in which I was due to be singing, rushed in to explain to the O/C, tore off my rain-soaked clothes, changed and whizzed back again to sing lustily about "*The Fishermen of England*", a suitably wet subject.

Inevitably connected with Downsend are my bridge evenings. CT and I used to play twice a week until I went all exam-conscious, when I cut it down to one. But whenever we played "away" we would greet the night with what we called a "three-pint cheer" as we rounded the final corner. Not that we drank much (this was obviously after my TT days – and I don't mean Tourist Trophy) but we always felt exhilarated. Sometimes at school in the summer after bridge, we would have a glass of port after swimming at midnight, and found to our astonishment that <u>one</u> glass of port could make us quite tiddly after a swim, an interesting piece of social discovery.

It was also while at Downsend that I taught myself to bowl leg-breaks, for the benefit of the brilliant boy, John Lomas[15], who was weak in that direction. I also played my first hockey games for one of the Epsom teams, learned squash from one of the staff (Hugh Abbot) and, with another master ("Bruin" Lewis), started up rugger at Downsend. In holiday time I had quite a few cricket matches with Ashstead. That's one handicap to being a Games Master in a prep school; you can't join a local club for any regular games in any sport because you are always busy umpiring or refereeing school matches.

However, one way and another one came to pick up a lot of knowledge and skill about a very wide range of games. I only wish I had had at school the sort of, and amount of, coaching boys get nowadays. As it was, one had to watch, practice, study books by the skilled sportsmen, and so on. I discovered that I was very fast, and this, plus apparently unending energy, made up for the inevitable lack of certain skills to start with. I would never have been a brilliant player but could have been pretty good. As it was I found myself able to cope and to be chosen for the First or Second XIs of clubs I joined, and games have always been a very important part of my life. Further, I enjoyed the company and the social side of things (as indeed I do now at the Bowls Club in Pewsey) and have played golf all over the place from Singapore and Tsingtao to Gleneagles, Blackheath and Epsom - not very successfully, but enjoyably as far as I am concerned!

In the summer holidays, Mr. Lomas would be largely responsible for organizing tennis tournaments and county cricket matches for schoolboys, and I spent a great deal of my time helping, <u>umpiring and generally enjoying</u> myself with the young all around. I

15   John Lomas was a renowned schoolboy cricketer, who shone at Charterhouse (1936) and Oxford University (1938)

also ran a Scout camp for about 10 days each year, a most exhausting process but which gave the boys much pleasure. The staff were an exceedingly pleasant lot and there was none or very little of the bickering which takes place in so many school Common Rooms.

Scout Jamboree, Hungary

While I was at Downsend I went to the Scout Jamboree in Hungary in 1933. Three great special trains took us from London to Gödöllő, near Budapest, and the whole time was spent in a heat wave. When we could, we got away to the swimming baths in the Hotel Gelbut, with its artificial waves! It was an astonishing show. Thousands upon thousands of Scouts, Rovers (do they still exist?) and Scoutmasters from I suppose practically every country in the world, in hundreds of separate campsites, each distinctive of its particular owners: French, African, Russian, Indian, etc.[16]

I was extremely lucky as I went out as an individual, not attached to any group, so I had all my time to myself except for two days when I took my turn cooking for the group where I was told to pitch my tent, a very friendly bunch. Displays in the main arena were unending; all we Wood Badge holders were addressed by the great Baden Powell, and we explored both the camp and Budapest. But it _was_ hot:102 in the shade, if you could find any. It really was something from the moment we met.

The Wood Badge training session beforehand (at Gilwell Park, the official scout training camp) was quite difficult. We were all divided into Patrols, like Scouts, and took turns at being Patrol Leader. We scrubbed our tents and duckboards, attended parades, lectures, tests of all sorts and so on, and in twelve days the powers that be reduced what had been a healthy strong bunch of fellows into a mob who were too tired even to protest. However, we really took the Mickey out of the officers during the last evening's "concert and entertainment". They roared with approval and we tottered home, very pleased with ourselves all the same at having passed.

Our particular group of Scouts met, hundreds of us, near Victoria Station in London, most of us complete strangers. I have little recollection of any details except that every single person, man and boy, was given a given a tin of Andrews Liver Salts, to ensure

---

16   This was the Fourth World Scout Jamboree, 2-13 August, 1933, attended by 25,792 Scouts representing 46 different nations and additional territories. They camped around the Royal Palace in the Royal Forest of Gödöllő, about 11 miles from Budapest.

that our innards kept on working properly. For it is a well-known fact that if you go to any other country you will be subject (and probably fall victim) to some internal disorder, known by different names according to the particular country you find yourself in. Thus in Egypt it's "gippy tummy" or something similar, in Tsingtao it was Tsingtao tummy, while Shanghai and other ports had their own varieties with appropriate nomenclature.

So, Andrews and all, off we went across to Ostend where three vast trains known officially as Red, White and Blue proceeded to take us right down to Gödöllő, just outside Budapest. It was long journey but had its moments. For one thing this was 1933, when Hitler was really starting up, and many of us amused ourselves by waving and giving Hitler salutes to men and women working in the fields. One unfortunate chap failed to realize how much closer to the train signal gantries are on the continent, leant out of the window with arm outstretched and crashed it into a signal post, losing nearly half his hand and being knocked unconscious into the bargain. Very bad luck, and that was the end of the Jamboree for him.

In Berlin we were met by a large detachment of Hitler Youth, swastikas, flags, badges and all. They gave us a very warm welcome. We exchanged our badges for theirs in ever-increasing numbers. In fact, "change" (i.e. exchange of badges) became the most internationally used of all words amongst all nations, and the amount of "swapping" that went on was really prodigious. It was a wonder that we retained any of our official badges at all!

After we had "de-trained" we were entertained by the Hitler Youth singing patriotic and other German songs, and magnificently they sang. All that over we said goodbye to our delightful and very smart young hosts, who included many men up to about 25 as well as lots of teenagers, and went to get back on the train. It had gone - not on to Budapest, just disappeared. After about half an hour it was tracked down in a remote, and to us unexplored, part of the station, and in we got.

Much of the journey I have forgotten. We spent the night on the train, but I have happy memories of a long haul down beside the Rhine in gorgeous weather, a beautiful trip, while the more romantic or musical (or bored) hummed or sang "*Lorelei*". Perhaps one of the most memorable sights to those who hadn't seen them before (or who were used to the Thames barges) were the simply enormous barges seen on the Rhine (and also, for example, in Holland); they really are stupendous. The scenery was grand, and we had our full share of "schlosses".

Before I leave the journey, I must mention the great Hungarian plain. I'd often heard of it, but it was an awesome sight, mile upon mile upon mile of flat, flat terrain, covered with golden corn waving and moving in the breeze. Even going across Russia I don't remember anything which seems so endless, though doubtless the Prairies could easily cope!

So, on to Budapest and Gödöllő. Rather creaky from sitting down for so long, we soon got straightened out by marching some considerable distance to the camp, which was on the grounds of the Royal Palace. And even this had its humorous side. Somehow Lord Rothermere of the Daily Mail had found great favor with the Hungarians for supporting Hungary in its efforts (alas, abortive) to

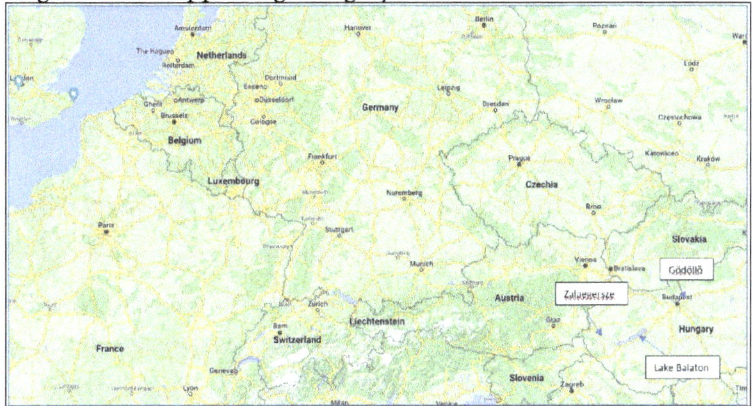

Figure 19 - Hungary

regain some of the territory of which it had been ruthlessly stripped by the Allies (that's us) at the end of the First World War, when the mighty Austro-Hungarian empire was split up and reduced horribly in size. Anyway, as a token a cage containing two doves (of peace, i.e. peaceful intentions to England) was solemnly handed to two of the more prominent Scouters who were asked to take them back to Lord Rothermere in England after the Jamboree. Poor fellows, they had to march all the way to the camp carrying these wretched birds in their cage.

For the rest of us the March was rather splendid. Bunches of flowers were thrown to us and we had a tremendous welcome. We

were escorted
by bands all the
way to camp,
and met for the
first time the
curious custom
of someone
towing the
big drum on a
little cart, while
the drummer,
free from the
weight of the
thing, simply

Figure 20 - The Royal Palace

walked behind and belted it as he went.

So, into camp. We found our site and I pitched my tent; we were there. It was an enormous camp, and of course had various shops and so on. The number of separate campsites was remarkable, and most of them had brought special signs and materials to give the

Figure 21 - Jamboree Badge

site its own individuality. We had a vast white hart (the Hungarian emblem, used as a Jamboree motif); one of the Scandinavian sites had three huge, magnificent reindeer made entirely out of silver birch logs and branches. The variety was wonderful.

The day's program was roughly: mornings, free; afternoons, displays in the huge arena; the rest of the day, free – i.e. free from any Jamboree duties.

Each detachment did what it liked, nothing, or preparing some display. We had two especially memorable events. One, when all Wood Badge holders (including this writer) were addressed by Baden Powell himself. We were all struck by the extreme firmness and youthfulness of his voice, as we were able at last to satisfy a lifelong ambition to meet him. I don't remember how old he was but as he

Figure 22 - Lord Baden Powell

was such a prominent general in the Boer War I suppose he must have been about 75.

The other occasion was when Admiral Houthy (then Regent of Hungary). together with BP, asked all who could to come into the main arena. The two figures, on horseback, sat quietly on their horses in the middle of the arena while we all lined up around the four sides of the arena. At a given signal we all rushed into the center as a way of saying Thank You to Admiral Houthy and the Hungarians for having us in their country. It was a wonderful and almost frightening experience as this vast mass of people surged forward, cheering, roaring on, until fortunately they stopped. It must have frightened the life out of the two men.

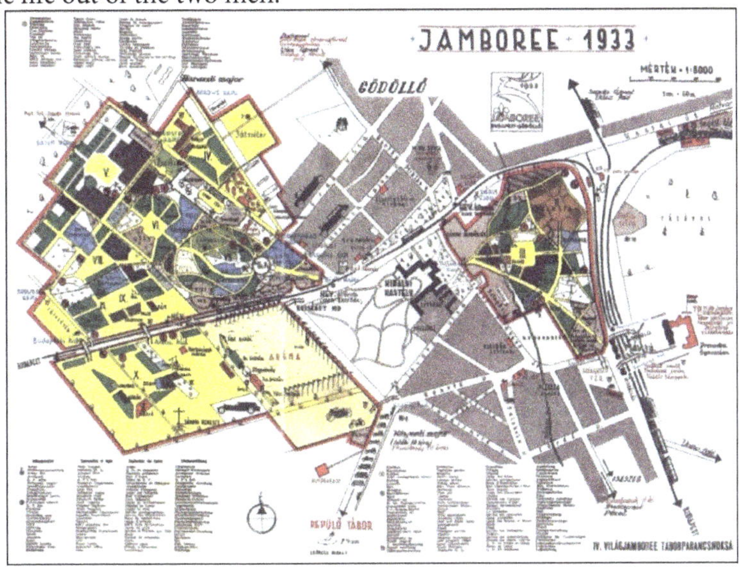

Figure 23 - Jamboree Camp

As I have said elsewhere I had practically no duties whatever, so I wandered around camp after camp, making friends and chatting away. To be helpful we wore little name tapes which said "English", or "parle Francais", or something which informed the other chap what language you both might find mutually available. It is true but extraordinary that I only found one camp where I couldn't get by on French or English, and that was a Hungarian one, where a delightful Padre and I tried in vain to communicate. Eventually I tried elementary Latin; his face brightened up, we exchanged a few happy if ungrammatical sentences, and left each other in a happy mood.

73

The Hungarian language is impossible, the only people of the same linguistic origin in Europe being the Finns, so direct communication in Hungarian was out of the question.

The weather was superb and in fact we had a heat wave, so I spent some very pleasant afternoons in Budapest itself where we found the St. Gellert hotel had a swimming pool with artificial waves. These "came on" every 15 minutes or so, preceded by a hooter to stop you going down the chute and finding little or no water below you at the critical moment. We consumed unknown quantities of iced coffee, a splendid drink. I was still TT then, and so drank no beer at all the whole time - except once. That was when I was taken to hear a German band playing in some gardens beside the Danube, surrounded by masses of people with tankards. I tried a beer, and enjoyed it; after all you simply couldn't listen to a German band pumping out its splendid military music without having a tankard in your hand, especially on a beautiful evening. But I digress.

I knew that Ron was at the Jamboree and I eventually tracked him down, so we had a drink together; it was good to see him. On the way to find his site I passed an American scout site, where to our astonishment and hilarity we found they had not only brought refrigerators, but mattresses as well. This, to us raised on the tough English principle of needing to be uncomfortable in order to be camping properly, clearly showed us that the Americans were "soft". Actually, of course, they were being sensible, but our minds couldn't take all that in at once.

Just before the end the Hungarians extended an invitation for someone to stay a fortnight elsewhere in Hungary with the son of the "County" Lieutenant Governor. As a Schoolmaster I was the only one who could stay on, so I accepted, and of this more in a minute. Meantime we had been taken to visit the great Lake Balaton, which is not only very warm but which had a bottom which seemed to consist of very soft mud. Still, it was most pleasant. We were also taken to a real sulphur springs "lake", where you couldn't sink in the very warm water and just lay on wooden frames idly floating about the lake - but, of course, the smell...

At one place we were entertained royally by the Mayor, with an enormous meal, plenty of wine and a large cigar, all preceded by an extraordinary tune being played by the band and which, halfway through, we decided it was the best they could do with "God Save

the King", so we leapt to our feet. This was <u>before</u> the meal. <u>After</u> the
meal came near disaster. We had agreed to play them at football, but
were given no respite - straight from this vast meal, into our football
things and into the game. How we stood up, let alone ran, I shall
never know, but we did. I believe we lost 0-2, in the circumstances a
highly credible result.

In the evening we visited some of the local "cafés" where
we drank the local wine (I was no longer TT, you see) and listened
to beautiful and haunting Hungarian gypsy music. This is really so
moving in its beauty and simplicity: wonderful, wonderful music.
And that about winds up the Jamboree itself, apart from some
delightful and colorful dancing displays by local village maidens and
men.

Just before we left the Jamboree entirely, about 15 of us made
an overnight trip by train to Vienna, sitting up all night or sleeping on
the floor, or - for a few of the lucky ones - even sleeping in the luggage
racks, where we spent a pleasant night despite the despairing and
finally unsuccessful efforts of the guards to turn us out of them.

Vienna left a deep impression on us, but not because of its
glory or magnificence. On the contrary, the splendor which had once
been the pride of the great capital of Austria-Hungary had gone. Its
vast, wide streets were almost empty; the whole place seemed empty.
The great empire had been carved up by the Allies after the war, and
the capital and its buildings and roads and streets - which had been
built for and filled with all the traffic of an internationally famous
and popular city, like Paris for example, with a vast population in
the country – now were occupied thinly by a sadly much-reduced
population. There was a distressing air of sadness and emptiness,
only broken on one occasion by detachment of what appeared to be
the up-and-coming German Nazis, or an Austrian branch of them.

Eventually we found our way to the splendid Schönbrunn
- the former imperial palace in Vienna - and though I am not one
who enjoys going around palaces and famous houses, this really was
a marvelous place. It had been kept in pretty good order, as indeed
are many of the Russian and Chinese buildings and palaces of ancient
days despite the present people being completely "anti" the old
Imperial days of royal extravagance beyond belief. They all, happily,
have got around to preserving much that is beautiful and even more
that is priceless in their inheritance, and by an odd quirk of fate take a

great pride in these treasures - which is as it should be.

Figure 24 - Schönbrunn Palace

We went through many of the rooms at the Schönbrunn and I remember being particularly struck by the Hall of Mirrors (an immense room with brilliant decorations reflected endlessly in multi-mirrored walls) and the Chinese room. The gardens on ascending levels were kept immaculate. The palace itself had (part of it) been used for a very popular film at the time called, I think, "*Waltzes in Vienna*", and a huge peace conference was beautifully sited in the vast mirrored halls. And then back to the Jamboree we went.

So off to Zalaegerszeg to stay in a vast, nay enormous, house, the home of the Lieutenant Governor whose son Zoltan was my host. I had difficulties, for my host, a charming man and perhaps a little older than I, spoke practically no English; I spoke no Hungarian. He spoke no French. Stalemate. He had learned a little English from a "fairy tale" by Oscar Wilde (if not a fairy tale then a children's story, but I cannot remember its full name; it was "*The Prince and ...*"), so we sat solemnly opposite each other at mealtimes, smiling amiably at one another, then he went about his business and I went about mine. He took me out to some relations of his on a large farm, where we saw *inter alia* an old English traction engine (dated about 1880) being used for threshing, just as we had used them in Canada.

The whole of my visit with Zoltan was saved by some Hungarian Rover Scouts who spoke English, bless them. Every morning after breakfast they would come around, pick me up, about five of them, and we would explore the little town, or go to neighboring villages where we played skittles and drank the local wine, which was both good and cheap, about a shilling (1 pengö) a bottle. Which reminds me that Budapest was unquestionably the cleanest and tidiest city, town or village I have ever seen, and why? Because if you dropped anything, even a small piece of paper, you were pounced on and fined 1 pengö on the spot. Happily, we didn't offend in that way. This reminds me that the Hungarians, who were most generous hosts, allowed us to travel on their buses free during the Jamboree.

But to return to my Rover Scout friends. During one skittles game we were all playing hopelessly, so, feeling rather full of myself I said, "We can't any of us knock down the skittles today; I'll show you how to do it!" Full of unjustifiable pride, I decided to throw the ball instead of using the proper underarm delivery, confident that I could knock the skittles down as I was a pretty good (sorry, but I was) fielder at cricket. So I took careful aim and hurled the ball down the track. Something must have been wrong with my aim, because there was a resounding crash and the lights <u>over</u> the alley came hurtling to the ground! That was bad enough and I felt (and was) an awful fool. But the worst thing was that the landlord wouldn't take a penny to pay for the damage. No, he was only too delighted to have me there, he said, and treated the whole thing as a joke. So, feeling about knee high to bee, I crept out, pride certainly coming before a fall.

Meals were vast, so walking to the various villages provided much needed exercise. I was invited to "tea" at the house of one Scout, and have never seen so much food on the table. Course after course, ending up (as it did with lunch everyday with Zoltan) with a massive and very rich cake covered with even more rich cream concoctions; one had to eat <u>some</u> to avoid offending one's host. They were determined to treat us well, so we had to do violence to our insides.

There's little left to record. I remember being very cold all night as the train took us back through Switzerland. We had no coats as it had been good, hot summer weather, and Scouts didn't carry coats anyway. And on the cross-Channel ferry back I was thrilled (being still a hero worshipper!) to see Les Ames, the England and Kent wicketkeeper and batsman. Just before that I had had the pleasure, the supreme pleasure, of seeing Ames and the immortal Frank Woolley bat against the New Zealanders; Woolley made over

200 and Ames over 100. As I write this New Zealand have just dismissed England for 64 runs, so I must have been luckier than I knew!

We had a few get-togethers in town after the Jamboree was over, exchanging photographs and memories, and four of us had dinner – goulash, of course, with plenty of paprika - at a Hungarian restaurant in London, and we did the Hungarian national dish proud. And so that particular chapter of my life was closed - until I was talking to Sam McClatchie in the Bull at Sonning one day, he being a friend of mine, when I found that he too had been at the Jamboree. The world is its usual size.

Teaching – China

The Journey Out

Much as I enjoyed life at Downsend, despite the workload, like the rest of my family I had itchy feet. I looked around for jobs in other schools, but "no degree, no job" was the usual situation. However, along came this one in China, at St. Giles British School in Tsingtao. The man they wanted to appoint turned it down (I discovered later) and so I got it, I think partly because there didn't seem to be anyone else willing to go so far for so small a salary (about £350 a year), and partly on the optimistic hope (alas, false) that I would have passed my Degree examinations. I was a bit nervous about that when I was greeted by the Chairman of the Trustees in Tsingtao, but he waved my apologies away, thank goodness.

So, after a farewell tea with the Roberts family, Bunty, Joyce and John, I left Victoria Station on August 5th, 1935, and got to Tsingtao on August 20th, fifteen days later. For the return trip six years later, I left Tsingtao on September 9th, 1941 and got back to England on January 20th, 1942 - over four months!

The route was through Berlin, then on the Trans-Siberian Railway to Manchuria and Port Arthur (now renamed Dalian), and a boat to Tsingtao, which was a 24 hour and very pleasant trip.

In Berlin I was met by an ex-Downsend boy, Philip Marrack, who looked after me and took me to a performance, in German, of *"The Life of Henry VIII"*. I knew no German but had seen the film before, so I quite enjoyed it. At midnight we left Berlin. The porter protested that I couldn't take all my luggage into the compartment with me; that invaluable asset, an American dollar, changed hands and the compartment suddenly became large enough. The next stop I remember was Warsaw, and later we came to the Russian frontier.

Now here the railway gauge changed to a much wider one, so one of two things happened. Either you got into a fresh train, or they lifted your entire carriage - without the wheels on it - onto a wider chassis on the other line. I'm hanged if I can remember which they did! What they (the Russians customs) <u>did</u> do was to seal up most comprehensively a small attaché case I had with me because it had

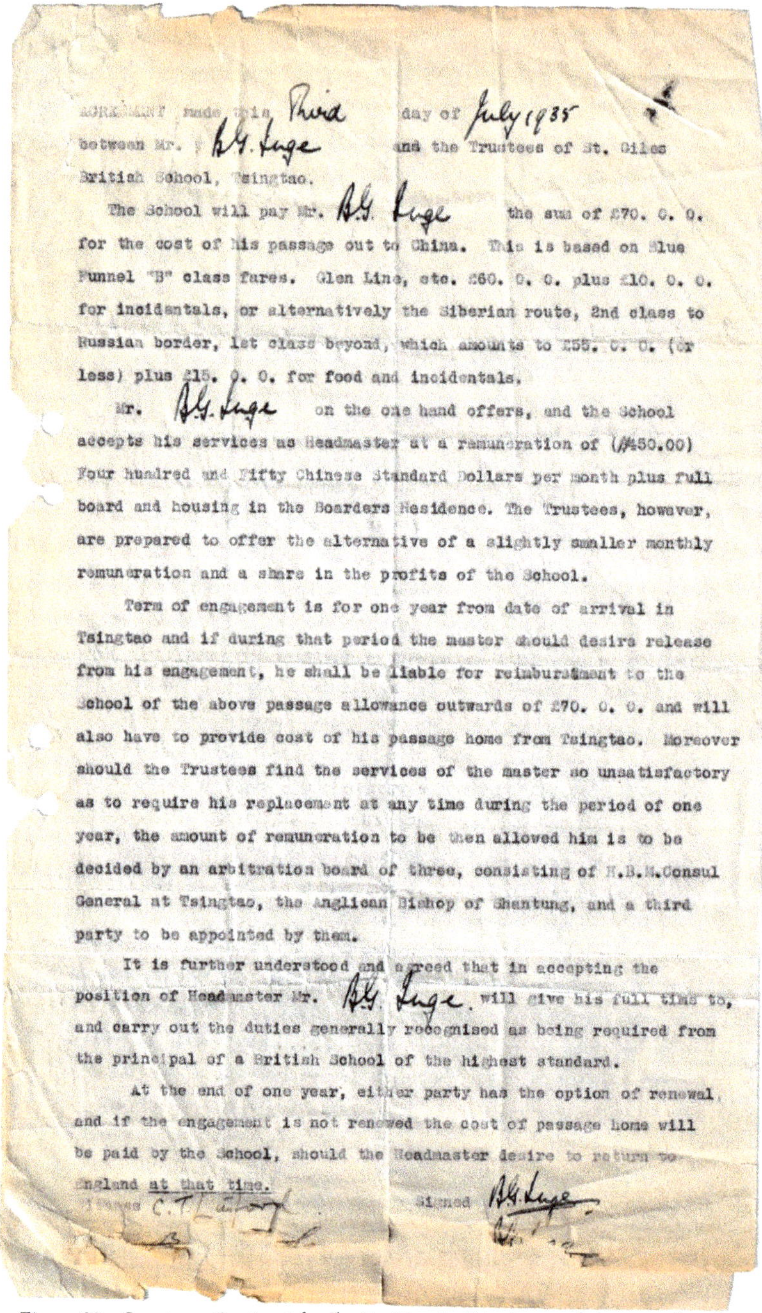

AGREEMENT made this *Third* day of *July 1935*
between Mr. *A.G. Luge* and the Trustees of St. Giles
British School, Tsingtao.

The School will pay Mr. *A.G. Luge* the sum of £70. 0. 0.
for the cost of his passage out to China. This is based on Blue
Funnel "B" class fares. Glen Line, etc. £60. 0. 0. plus £10. 0. 0.
for incidentals, or alternatively the Siberian route, 2nd class to
Russian border, 1st class beyond, which amounts to £55. 0. 0. (or
less) plus £15. 0. 0. for food and incidentals.

Mr. *A.G. Luge* on the one hand offers, and the School
accepts his services as Headmaster at a remuneration of (/#450.00)
Four hundred and Fifty Chinese Standard Dollars per month plus full
board and housing in the Boarders Residence. The Trustees, however,
are prepared to offer the alternative of a slightly smaller monthly
remuneration and a share in the profits of the School.

Term of engagement is for one year from date of arrival in
Tsingtao and if during that period the master should desire release
from his engagement, he shall be liable for reimbursement to the
School of the above passage allowance outwards of £70. 0. 0. and will
also have to provide cost of his passage home from Tsingtao. Moreover
should the Trustees find the services of the master so unsatisfactory
as to require his replacement at any time during the period of one
year, the amount of remuneration to be then allowed him is to be
decided by an arbitration board of three, consisting of H.B.M.Consul
General at Tsingtao, the Anglican Bishop of Shantung, and a third
party to be appointed by them.

It is further understood and agreed that in accepting the
position of Headmaster Mr. *A.G. Luge* will give his full time to,
and carry out the duties generally recognised as being required from
the principal of a British School of the highest standard.

At the end of one year, either party has the option of renewal,
and if the engagement is not renewed the cost of passage home will
be paid by the School, should the Headmaster desire to return to
England at that time.

Witness *C.T. ...*   Signed *A.G. Luge*

Figure 25 - One-page Contract for the Position in Tsingtao, and the cost of getting
there

"papers" and "documents" in it - consisting in fact of a few details about my new school, odd papers and correspondence. But the suspicious Russian mind wasn't taking any risks and the case had to remain sealed until we left Russian territory some 10 days later. And then the Japanese - we were then on the Manchurian border – went through it again as though it was stacked with letter bombs and anti-Russian/Japanese literature. All rather stupid.

So we settled down to the great trip - and it <u>was</u> a great trip. Remember that I am talking about the railway as it was in 1935, only about 18 years after the Russian Revolution, and it really was a relic of the Czar's days and of Imperial Russia. The Trans-Siberian Railway was a single track nearly all the way (though there were frequent sidings, of which more later, if I remember), and the track was of a far wider gauge than in England, or even elsewhere on the continent. Further, the rails themselves were only half the thickness of ours, which is why the train went so slowly as it made its dignified but leisurely way across the thousands of miles to Vladivostok on the Pacific Ocean, with a branch in Manchuria down to Harbin and Port Arthur.

Figure 26 - Trans-Siberian Railway

There were several classes but my ticket was fortunately First Class. I know little about the Second Class, but Third Class merely consisted of bunks; the passengers had to provide both blankets and all their food. It was quite a cheap way of traveling and I know that many English Schoolmasters out East used to come home to England during the three-month summer holidays "traveling hard", i.e. third class.

The First Class compartments held two people. At night the seat was turned into a bed (and a very comfortable one it was), while on the same level as the luggage rack but at right angles to it another bed came down, hinged at the end of the carriage. This second bed was about five feet off the floor. One of the charms of traveling, they say, is the unknown and that certainly applied here, for the authorities simply allocated compartments and therefore beds to passengers by name, without paying any attention to sex! So you might at anytime have a man and a woman in the same carriage. It didn't happen to me, fortunately.

First of all I had a man of uncertain nationality. He left somewhere along the route, and his place was taken by a high-ranking Russian Army officer. I tried English, I tried French; no luck, so we just sat and grinned cheerfully at each other. I have a very clear picture of him in my mind, as he sat on the edge of his bed - the upper transverse one - in army tunic top and brilliant blue baggy pants (and I mean underpants), while out of a paper bag he devoured quantities of shrimp!

Washing was well organized. Each pair of compartments had a washbasin and loo in a small compartment between them. Once inside you locked the door, which prevented people coming in from either side. I had been given the tip by an ex-Consul General (who sang with me in the Gilbert and Sullivan chorus), which was to take a large bottle of surgical spirit, with plenty of cotton wool. With this I could give myself a most pleasant wash down every day, and it was most refreshing. Another tip was to take some muslin and drawing pins; the muslin was pinned over the open window, still allowing us plenty of air in the heat but keeping out the sand and the dust.

As soon as I got on board I collected a four for bridge: a Scotsman, a Dutchman, a Frenchman and myself. We played bridge with several sessions a day right across Russia, admiring the scenery as we went, and knew everybody's play pretty well by the time we got to the other side. I made 10 shillings (50p) after all that, off the Frenchman, which, as we were crossing Russia and the number on the side of the restaurant car was 1812, seemed both just and relevant. I trust the allusion has not escaped you. We had breaks, of course, for meals, reading and in my case for typing an account of the journey; I think it was a Frenchman who lent me the typewriter.

The restaurant car had a menu the size of the Eiffel Tower but only a few items were either available or desirable. Borscht (that solid Russian soup of vegetables, beetroot and cream), eggs and red caviar were our staple diet - with the odd drink. In fact, I was introduced to vodka for the first time and, following instructions, I downed the vodka in one. There was a colossal explosion and the top of my head came down sometime afterward.

We stopped off early in the trip at Moscow and were escorted round by the inevitable official Intourist guide, a girl. The Russians were inordinately proud of their newly opened underground railway and it was well indeed worth seeing, although on the moving stairway you might well have been in England. It was such a perfect copy of Piccadilly Station, even down to the lights, with one splendid exception - no advertisements either on the elevators or on the platforms. The latter were wide, clean and most attractive, as they were made of different colors of marble for each station. All you had to do was to look up, see the colors of the station, and there you were; no bothering with names. I received a large rocket from a smart soldier, fully armed, who conveyed to me quite unmistakably that smoking was not allowed - and this was even in the entrance hall to the station. I did find the train a trifle noisy.

We saw Lenin's Tomb, Red Square, the Kremlin and the tremendous spires of - is it Saint Sophia? – anyway, of some of the churches. I went for a drive around. A remarkable feature of Moscow (whose female inhabitants had obviously won first prize for the drabbest-dressed nation) was that good roads and good houses suddenly stopped, as though the city had mathematically drawn lines all around it, and that was all that mattered. At that point it was as though you had left the large "square of civilization"; roads and houses all were suddenly on a far lower standard. Very odd. So, on we pressed to the East. At the Manchurian border the Japanese examined every mortal thing in our luggage, and we left our railway home of about nine days and took a train down to Port Arthur.

The train's maximum speed seemed to be about 25 miles an hour, or 30 miles an hour downhill, but it was enough to cause disaster when it took a left curve over some points. The train went left but someone's soup went straight on into the owner's lap. We would get out occasionally when the train stopped, and lie on the bank in the sun until a little whistle went; it was all very pastoral. After the first few days we had given up being healthy and vigorous men dashing up and down the platform for exercise at the many stations at which we stopped.

The scenery was interesting and often superb, with vast forests of giant trees contrasting with deep red earth, mountains, great rivers and lakes. We shall not likely forget Lake Baikal; in former days the railway line in winter was put onto the ice and the trains took a shortcut across, but now the train goes right round with seemingly hundreds of little bridges and tunnels. I should add that during the whole of this train journey Russian propaganda and gypsy music were broadcast more or less non-stop through loudspeakers in the roof of the corridors. It was, by the way, interesting to see how the people became more and more Mongol as we moved further and further east.

I see that I have forgotten to mention the sidings again. Russia is such a vast country that in order to cope with the thousands and thousands of acres of wheat and other crops, laborers are moved in large trucks to different points, and shunted into sidings where they live in the carriages overnight. When that area is cleared, off they go to another siding; quite a reasonable way to cope with a vast area with some very sparse areas of population.

It was very noticeable that near almost every big town or city there were great hydroelectric works, and many airfields as we neared the far frontier. There was no doubt of Russia's great expansion going on at the time. I mentioned this in my account of the trip and was told later that I was regarded as almost a "Red" by some people because, I assume, I had said something favorable about Russia, and in 1935 that was almost treason. People reacted almost with hysteria about Russia at that time. Anyway, I was not concerned about that, though it shook me when I heard it; I was merely reporting facts.

So into Japan-administered Manchuria[17]. Now in this period trains in Manchuria were being stopped by bandits, the passengers robbed and occasionally killed, but in spite of that I had no fears until

---

17   The much-disputed area in Northeast Asia encompassing the present-day Northeast China and parts of the Russian Far East. Controlled by China until 1860 when Russia annexed it, then ceded back to various Chinese groups in 1905. Invaded by Japan in 1932; briefly controlled by the USSR in 1945, then divided with China.

they placed armed guards at each end of the carriage. Fortunately, nothing happened and we arrived safely at Port Arthur, where we spent the night in a pleasant enough hotel - with large black beetles crawling up the walls. We killed as many as we could and went to sleep hopefully, after dinner on the roof where I heard played, for the first time, Ravel's *Bolero*. It was most impressive as it throbbed out its melody in the warm still air; I must beware of becoming poetical. The next day we caught the boat to Tsingtao, a very comfortable 3,500 tonner of the Japanese DKK line, which I used frequently in the coming years between Tsingtao and Shanghai. One night at sea and there I was, in Tsingtao.

Tsingtao

So began six years there, and how I'm going to sum it up I simply cannot imagine. Landing on August 20th, I stayed in private houses until September 1st (oddly enough St. Giles' Day) when I took up residence at St. Giles School. St. Giles I discovered to be the Patron Saint of Beggars, and seeing the financial state of the school then and later no more appropriate Saint could have been chosen!

The school consisted of about 60 pupils, made up of boys and girls, Day Pupils and Boarders, aged from 4 to 17. All the Boarders were in one house, where I lived; the other house was for classrooms only. I had two weeks before term started, and had my first surprise when swimming. I had been told that the water was warm, which in England means that you can stay in without freezing for 10 minutes instead of two. Here, though, it actually was too warm to be refreshing, and you had to swim out some 50 yards to find any water cold enough to be pleasing. When term started I met the staff, six ladies of varying ages and of whom a photograph exists among my China photos, to witness if I lie!

Figure 27 - Tsingtao

Tsingtao itself is one of the most beautiful places on this earth, as indeed I was assured before I left. Originally belonging of course to the Chinese, the Germans occupied it from 1898-1914 and made it the base of the German Far East fleet. The Japanese invaded it in 1914, but it was restored to Chinese rule in 1922. It remained an international port, one of the famous "treaty ports" (with, I might add, duty-free tobacco and drinks) where foreigners – mostly the British, French and Americans, though there were also many Russians and Japanese - had considerable independence under very nominal Chinese control.

This was bad luck on the Germans because they had developed the port tremendously, built first class houses for their top businessmen, put in excellent services - water, electricity, sewage - built up trade, put in first class roads, planted thousands of acacia trees on the hills (which were a rare sight in the spring and summer), and then they lost the lot. Under German control it had the highest school density in China, and even today it remains one of China's "most livable" cities.

Tsingtao was in fact an ideal place in which to live, a good port, with all the advantages of western civilization together with endless servants at ridiculous rates - and very good servants and cooks the "boys" (servants) were. The school was built on the side of a hill and looked over the vast racecourse area to a huge stadium and the sea. In the distance you could see the mountains of Laoshan, where we went occasionally on picnics, as well as the Pearl Mountains.

The population of Tsingtao was about 750,000 Chinese and perhaps 500 "foreigners"; that name included English, Americans, French, German, Russian and odd other nationalities. Consequently, the pupils at the school - who were preponderantly English - also included a few of the other nationalities, except (normally) Americans and Germans, who had their own small schools in Tsingtao. The Russians were of course "White" Russians, who had left Russia only too willingly after the revolution of 1917 and are also to be found in very large numbers in Shanghai. It might be worth mentioning that from the time that Hitler started up his activities hundreds and hundreds of Jews, German in chief, came flooding out to Shanghai also.

Everyone lived together in reasonable amenity and as far as the school was concerned no one was interested particularly in what nationality anyone was, except perhaps when the 1939 war started up; having no Germans or Japanese (or Chinese) in the school we all found ourselves on the same side. In this connection I must record that the Mayor of Tsingtao was Chinese Admiral Shen, DSO - he'd apparently served somewhere with the British during the First War with enough distinction to earn a medal - while the Head of the Police was a Russian, Mr. Antoshowicz. Oddly enough, my three senior Boy Prefects were all Russian, and splendid they were; in fact I found the whole school delightful.

Figure 28 - St. Giles' British School, Tsingtao, 1937
BGI in the center of the front row, hands crossed in his lap.

The school we ran on normal lines, as far as possible. The unusual was the distance some pupils lived from school. It took one family of three girls <u>two weeks</u> to get home, and most of the Boarders came from Shanghai, 350 miles away, or Hong Kong, 1,500 miles off, a week's travel by boat. There was no air service to speak of and no roads down the coast, and train journeys meant going inland for hundreds of miles to join the railway going South. Consequently, the only sensible thing to do was to take the direct route by boat, and for me to lengthen some of the holidays so that all children could have some time at home after getting there. I enjoyed many holidays in Shanghai and Hong Kong by acting as escort to the young.

School proceeded as normal. I had to learn to use chopsticks as the Boarders were particularly fond of the Chinese food which we had occasionally. Most having been at least partly brought up by Amahs (Chinese servants/nannies) and in China, they were perfectly at home with chopsticks, as they were with Chinese itself, an incredible language. I did start to learn it, but when I discovered that all the "boys" and shops spoke Pidgin English I gave up.

Pidgin English is an extremely useful "language", varying only with the language and people of the country where it is used as a sort of lingua franca, but you have to get used to it. For instance, shortly after I got to China the No. 1 boy said, "Master, two piece Missy have got top-side." This left me blank, but it turned out to be "Two ladies are waiting to see you upstairs." And there is the famous example of misused English, of the tailor shop in Bubbling Well Road in Shanghai; "Gentlemen's bespoke suits. Ladies have fits upstairs." Which speaks for itself.

I mentioned picnics in the hills. Once I went out with four youngsters, two boys and two girls, for a picnic, and the car broke down miles from anywhere. I simply had no idea of what to do; I could neither leave the children nor send them off to walk back to Tsingtao. Fortunately, a car headed for Tsingtao eventually came along. On another occasion I was not so lucky. I had then a vast Fiat open tourer, and we were headed for Tala Kuan. We crossed the odd small creek, then came to a flooded one. With considerable trepidation we crossed there, over 100 yards with the water up to the running boards. Splendid.

Then we came across another one, about 200 yards across. The water seemed the same depth, so over we went - or tried to. It was just too deep, and the car came to a halt with the fan spraying water like a fire engine. So there we were, five of us, two boys and two girls (all about 15) and me, in a car stuck in the middle of this river, which was flowing strongly and threatening to carry us down it. And not a soul in sight.

Suddenly, Chinese coolies appeared in numbers, apparently out of the earth. Roaring with laughter, as is the habit of the Northern Shantung Chinamen, about 20 of them waded into the water, and not only pushed the car out onto dry land but further some quarter of a mile to an Inn. Here we met some Navy Americans who offered to take the children back to Tsingtao, but it seemed a pity to spoil the adventure for the young. So I declined, with thanks, and we all spent the night at the Inn, which was well known and popular.

During the night the engine happily dried out sufficiently for me to start it up in the morning, but the brakes were still utterly soaked. So I had to drive through the passes and over and down the mountain brakeless, using my gears to slow down, and all this

in blazing heat. We got back safely to School - not having enjoyed
the trip back – to find the Consul-General inquiring as to our
whereabouts. However, all was well, and the young had enjoyed the
whole thing - except for the drive back.

Of course, we'd often use rickshaws, and the first ride I
had gave me an extraordinarily comic feeling, with resulting self-
conscious grins. I got used to them, but not to the tremendous blasts
of garlic which the rickshaw men puffed out behind them as they ran.

Japanese Invasion

Life was going along peacefully until January 1937 when the
Sino-Japanese war broke out, leading to the complete desertion of
Tsingtao by the Mayor, Police, all Chinese soldiers and any form of
control. To keep order, all the foreigners – English, French, German,
American, Russian, every faction - organized themselves into the TSP
(Tsingtao Special Police), about 200 strong, and the school was made
one of five substations. We were on duty (those in charge) for as
nearly 24 hours out of 24 as could be managed.

Figure 29 - Tsingtao Special Police armband

Our principal duty was to patrol (and control) Tsingtao,
where the Chinese, loathing the Japanese and fearing their imminent
invasion, were looting, burning and breaking up the Japanese shops.
Actually a few Chinese troops had remained at first to try and keep
order, shooting the odd looter, but as soon as the Japanese got near
off they went.

There is a full account of this time of the TSP and what went
on in Tsingtao before the Japanese came in in *"Oriental Affairs"*[18].
Prominent are the photos of millions and millions of dollars-worth
of Japanese cotton mills blown up by the Chinese before they left.
The Chinese had also blockaded the port by sinking some of their

18   see Appendix 6. Appendix 7 gives another report with a more
personal bearing on St. Giles' and BGI's participation in the TSP.

very few naval and customs ships right across the entrance. So, there
we were at school, with about 14 children who'd been unable to get
away to their homes in Shanghai and Hong Kong for the Christmas
holidays. And in the school we could hear violent explosions with
great rolling clouds of smoke as the cotton mills went up. Very
worrying - and what next?

Then we heard that the Japanese were landing a few miles
along the coast, and I drove a few youngsters to a hill to watch
the landings. It was all very peaceful. Presently along marched a
detachment of the Japanese Navy. Flanked by a large Union Jack
we waved amiably to them, and they waved amiably back. No
complaints about the Japanese Navy, and we all said to each other that
was because most of the leading Japanese top brass had been trained
in England and on British ships.

When the army came it was a totally different matter. From
the smart, clean and cheerful appearance of the Navy men we had
the opposite; you would have thought that the prisons had all been
opened. They were most unpleasant, especially in the way they threw
their weight about. We had to walk off the pavement when passing
a sentry, one had to bow to some sentries, and bowing to a dumpy,
scruffy little man doesn't go down at all well. Still, it was that or
risking a bayonet in one's tummy; which would you prefer?

A rather sad glimpse of the unreality of the whole affair was
the sight of Chinese soldiers, before the actual invasion, practicing
with weird but lusty cries the use of their large, heavy and unwieldy
swords. They were, of course, utterly useless against modern weapons
and bullets, though one sweep of the blade would decapitate anyone
with no effort at all. But it was totally unrealistic and so a very
pathetic sight. I have one of these swords hanging over the inside of
our front door at Pewsey.

There was one remarkable distinction between the Chinese
and Japanese, and rather a curious one. About 900 AD the Japanese
(and how like them) sent over to China, then an almost unknown
country, an Embassy, deputation, call it what you will, to take back
to Japan not prisoners, not gold, not material wealth, but as much
culture as they could; hardly, one would have thought, an exportable
item! However, they did take back a lot, hence, for instance, their
language, which when written shows a simplified version of Chinese
characters. There is no vocabulary as such in either country; it's

all the matter of "characters", which depict everything from men to monkeys to houses and back again.

But the odd difference is this. In all eastern and mid-eastern countries it is a part of life that no one should ever pay the price demanded for any item. Bargaining is essential to the enjoyment of the seller (and the buyer too), and to pay at once the first price demanded is not merely evidence of what a fool you are but, more important, a sad deprivation to a seller of his fun!

Now this holds good in China, but not amongst the Japanese. You could – and did - always get a reduction in the first quoted price from the Chinese, but in the Japanese markets, for instance in Tsingtao itself, you couldn't get a brass farthing – or a yen - off anything. They were quite nice about it, but a firm "No" was your inevitable answer. Odd.

Navy Friendships

Life under the Japanese soon settled down to being reasonably normal. The British government kept a ship - cruiser, destroyer or even an aircraft carrier, or submarine depot ship, frigate, sloop and/or submarines - in the harbor or conveniently offshore during this time for several years, until they knew what was going to happen. There was usually only one ship at a time with us, so we came to know a wide circle of people over the years. Occasionally an Italian, French or other naval vessel would come along on a courtesy visit to "Show the flag", throw a vast cocktail party and disappear again, leaving behind a euphoric atmosphere of cocktails and gin.

But these were few and far between. The schools (and my) immediate contact came through hockey. As soon as a Royal Navy ship anchored I would call on the Captain and the Wardroom, offer them a hockey match versus the school, and we were off. They enjoyed the games, as we did, and the adults resumed friendly relations and cemented friendships at the bar in the Club and at different restaurants after.

The Royal Navy was very good to us. Once I had to go to Hong Kong on urgent business to reassure parents that all was well and all were well at the school, not just out of concern for their families but because the school was totally dependent on the parents paying their children's school fees. The harbor was still blockaded by the ships the Chinese had scuttled, so I travelled the 1,500 miles there

Figure 30 - HMS Dorsetshire

on the "Grey Funnel Line" (i.e. the Royal Navy), in this case the heavy cruiser HMS *Dorsetshire*![19] It was a delightful trip.

The Wardroom always made you an honorary member so that you could pay your whack when it came to drinks, and they always made one very welcome. On another occasion they put me up at the Navy Club at Wei-hai-wei (the Royal Navy's HQ in North China, NE of Tsingtao), where I stayed in most pleasant surroundings. Thanks to their kindness I saw a great deal of the Navy and was entertained by them frequently, staying on board for a week or two sometimes. [20]

While in Hong Kong they couldn't do enough for me, offering a trip out submerging in a submarine, firing dummy torpedoes, in a destroyer on another occasion picking up the dummies as they surfaced, and so on. I was invited onto the bridge of the aircraft carrier HMS *Eagle*[21], watched planes catapulted off, and came across a plane in the water which had by radio "Requested permission to ditch, engine failure"- a nice request, that.

19   The *Dorsetshire* was transferred to the Atlantic in 1940, and in May 1941 fired the torpedoes that finally sank the crippled German battleship *Bismarck*. She was sunk on 5 April 1942 in the Indian Ocean, along with her sister ship HMS *Cornwall*, in an attack by 57 Japanese dive bombers.

20   BGI never mentioned it, but the Navy probably also appreciated having regular contact with an observant and reliable source of local information about events in Tsingtao.

21   Originally intended to be a battleship for the Chilean navy, HMS Eagle was bought by the Royal Navy in 1918 and converted to an aircraft carrier. Transferred to the Mediterranean in 1940, she was sunk on 11 August 1942 by torpedoes from a U-boat.

Figure 31 - HMS Eagle

The trip picking up dummy torpedoes was quite a day. As it was all practice, the Captain of the destroyer picking them up had a time schedule, so that he knew exactly when to expect the "fish" to pass under his ship. After each torpedo had sped on its way watched by us on the bridge, he would look at his watch and say, "Time for a gin before the next one." So down below, down with the gin, and up on the bridge again. A pretty wet day it turned out to be internally, though glorious without.

It was when watching one torpedo pass under us that I discovered that its rudder is not fixed but has a little play each way; this, I was given to understand, ensured greater accuracy of direction. The reason that we could see the torpedoes at all was that the water was fantastically clear; I have never seen anything like it at that depth.

There was more to come that day. When young Submarine Officers are learning the submarine business and practicing submerging and coming up, they're only allowed to go down a short way, totally submerging the submarine except for the periscope which was kept up and had a red flag attached to it to warn the skippers of other ships that a submarine was not very far below the surface.

One enthusiastic "learner" had his day; we suddenly saw the submarine emerging from the sea at about 45 degrees, an impossible angle. "Good God," said our skipper, "he's taking off!" Things were sorted out the other end, but the crew must have had an unpleasant few minutes.

Being rather claustrophobic I was a bit scared as to what I

should feel like when submerged, but there was no difference at all. Only one exciting moment occurred; the skipper had said to me on the bridge, "When the klaxon goes for submerging don't go down at once; watch the tanks being blown, the spray is tremendous." So I obeyed; the klaxon went, the tanks blew, and I stood there fascinated. Suddenly a yell behind me: "Come on down, Sir, we're submerging!" - and we were. Never a dull moment.

During lunch that day on board HMS *Eagle*, a Naval Air pilot came to me and said, "Care for a flip this afternoon?" Being scared of flying at the time I declined, with thanks. Later, a friendly N/O (Naval Officer) said to me, "You were pretty wise not to take that offer up; Dick was practicing dive bombing." I regard that as a most fortunate escape!

Back in Tsingtao the Navy were indeed good to us. They almost invariably invited the School on board for afternoon tea, and the pupils, and particularly the girls, managed to come ashore with souvenirs of all sorts, the most remarkable being a hard-boiled egg and a piece of lavatory paper! We had at the school a collection of over 24 cap ribbons (all legally obtained) from different HM ships, with some ships badges, cast plaques about 8 inches by 4 inches - splendid things. I imagine the whole lot went when the Japanese eventually took over Tsingtao.

Life in Tsingtao

Much of my own traveling was due to my getting no home leave (because there was no one to take over for me) or to illness, also due to no home leave. A tour of duty out East should not exceed four years without home leave; I had six, with a nervous breakdown as the final result as well as several periods of excessive stress. I also ended up in the splendid Fabenkrankenhaus (the German hospital - the <u>only</u> hospital) with pneumonia, and managed to lay myself out occasionally at games. Only once was serious, when I messed up my ankle horribly (tearing tendons, etc.) when trying to tackle a French sailor in a soccer match. A plaster cast and several weeks in bed resulted, but no harm was done permanently. I also broke my right collarbone, having already broken the other one at a Scout camp in England, but this was a minor affair.

Once we had settled down to having the Japanese running

the town, life proceeded fairly normally. It must be said that they
did not interfere with us at the school except to gain possession of
the boarding house (owned by the Chinese) and force us to go to
another house nearby. The boys had been put into a separate house
by this time under a Master I got from England, but after two years
he married the Kindergarten Mistress and went to Malaya. So I lost
two staff at once, but somehow managed to find someone to take over
their jobs, not satisfactorily but to get anyone was a triumph because
there were no spare people out there. You didn't go to China unless
you had a job already.

From 50/60 pupils in 1935, we had got the numbers up to
about 100 in 1937 when the Sino-Japanese war cut numbers down
badly, to about 60. We were building them up once more towards
the 100 mark when the European war started, and down went the
numbers again. Most frustrating and disappointing. Still, we carried
on, while various parents either sent their children away or more
usually went with them (Mothers and children - the Fathers stayed at
their jobs) from Tsingtao and Shanghai to Australia and elsewhere.
In spite of urgent pressure many parents refused to leave Hong
Kong with their children, and were imprisoned for 3½ years when
the Japanese finally invaded. It was understandable to have such
confidence in Hong Kong, but it was tragically misplaced confidence.

In 1939 I had a holiday with the Navy in Wei-hai-wei, their
base to the north-east of Tsingtao. It was a lovely place, and it was
there I saw my first mirage. Looking back at the hills after we left
harbor on the deck of a minelayer, I was astonished to see apparently
half His Majesty's ships more than halfway up the mountains - very
odd. Talking of minelayers, this one was towing a target for cruisers,
destroyers and submarines to aim at, and for airplanes to bomb – in
turn, of course. The target was towed half a mile behind the ship,
which seemed a long way until you translated it into 880 yards, and
saw the splash of shells far too near to be comfortable - for a land-
lubber, anyway.

Coming back from the cinema one Sunday evening in 1939,
September 3rd to be exact, I switched on London on the radio to hear
Chamberlain announcing that we were at war with Germany. This
was at 7:00 pm (11 am in London). I told the staff, who flatly refused
to believe it! I of course resigned in order to come home and join up,
but such a course was not allowed by His Majesty's Government at

home without an adequate substitute being available.

Everyone wondered what was going to happen next and life became worried and anxious, because of the unknown rather than for any other reason or effect. A British Residents Association had been set up a year or two earlier, and social life stopped with a bang. Things gradually got back to normal as we were not, happily, at war with the Japanese yet. After all you can't live on the edge of your seat forever; unfamiliarity with danger did not so much breed contempt as remove anxiety.

1940 saw me staying with some parents near Kobe, in Japan. My memories of Japan are not very exciting. I stayed the night in Tokyo at the Frank Lloyd Wright-designed Imperial Hotel, which was built on a vast mud raft to counteract the innumerable earthquakes that occur, and which was the only building of any size to remain standing on one occasion in the central area.[22] I noticed that my room and luggage had been not-very-carefully searched, however; a suspicious lot, the Japanese, and they didn't like us anyway.

Figure 32 - Imperial Hotel, Tokyo

In Japan I visited Lake Chuzenji, up in the hills north of Tokyo, where I was desperately cold at night having forgotten I was going into the mountains; the temperature down below in Kobe was very high and exhausting, with great humidity. I went to the ancient temples at Nikko (in the same area), where the famous "three-monkeys" motif was much in evidence; did that start in India, or Japan?

---

22   The great Kwanto earthquake of 1923

Figure 33 - Japanese temples at Nikko

Actually, I didn't stay in Kobe itself but in a little place called Shioya, a few miles away. This was a completely British settlement, just developed by the British bang in the middle of the surrounding Japanese area, with its own British Club, swimming pool and so on. Very odd. Odder still was to find a brass plate on the gate of the house near us, bearing the name of a chap I was at school with and who lived two roads away from us in London! It seemed to me typical of the British overseas; as they say, put two Englishmen together anywhere and they will form a Club.

The other remarkable thing in Japan was caused by the lack of petrol; taxis, lorries, and some cars were propelled by gas from wood burning stoves. Wood was the fuel needed, and the vehicles went well except up hills when they were apt to come to a stop. Talking of wood, you could buy cheap sports and other shirts made, as you discovered later, largely of wood pulp. You found this out because when they were washed holes developed all over the place. This wood fibre was a distinct loss, but there was of course a desperate shortage of everything.

On the journey back I was plainly told (without speech!) by a Japanese sentry that I had to go below and not watch the cargo being loaded. This was cargo I had already seen on the docks, with guns, ammo, etc. All rather childish, but at least more peaceful than the terrifying cyclone we hit on the way over. It was the only time I

99

have ever been scared of the sea, and I repeatedly thought the ship was never coming up again after its wild plunges down the horrible valleys. At any rate I wasn't seasick, and as the only white man on this Japanese ship I jolly well wasn't going to be!

Oh yes, and in September 1940 Joyce and I became engaged! We had visions of her coming out to Tsingtao (despite the huge challenges and dangers of wartime travel) and then honeymooning in Japan during the incredibly romantic cherry-blossom time, but it was not to be. More on this effort later.

At Christmas 1940, while Tsingtao was occupied by the Japanese with trigger- and bayonet-happy sentries all around the place, Ian McGillchrist and I, having spied out the land before, took saws and cut down two live Christmas trees at night. The noise of the sawing seemed deafening in the utter silence but the dreaded soldiers did not appear, and so two places had good Christmas trees, the least we could do for the children who could not get home.

In 1941 I was ordered to go away on sick leave, and so I went off to stay with a friend in Peking, which is really indescribable in the beauty of its ancient buildings, particularly in the Forbidden City. I have some tourist souvenir photos which will give some idea of what it was like. I did not unfortunately get to the Great Wall, which was forbidden territory owing to the civil war which was still going on

Figure 34 - Peking palaces:Tai-hai-tien

as well as the Sino-Japanese one. I remember drinking "gimlets" while listening to guns going off the other side of the hill! A very odd country.

Figure 35 - Peking palaces: Pei-hei Park, Nine Dragons Wall

Peking's Imperial Palaces are superb examples of magnificent splendor, and of how you can create something beautiful by "embezzling" funds; the old Empress had used the vast funds which were intended to build up the Chinese Navy. One memory holds fast; the sight of hundreds of little boats, each with a candle on it, sailing *en masse* slowly into the dark on one of the lakes, placating the "Spirit of the Lake".

It was on this trip to Peking that I received permission to go home, someone finally having been found to take over the school for me.

The Voyage Home

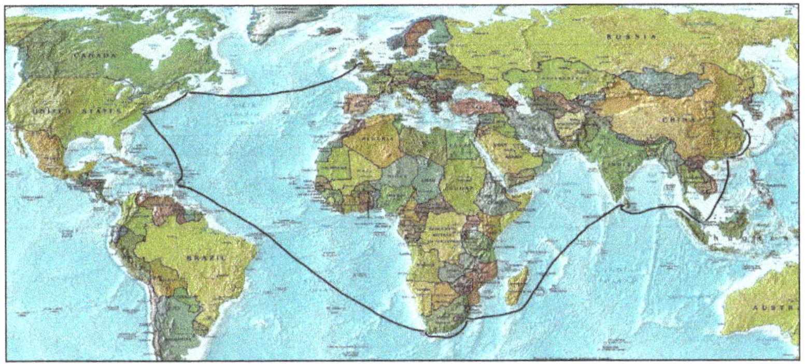

Figure 36 - The Voyage Home
Tsingtao – Shanghai – Hong Kong – Singapore – Penang – Ceylon – Durban –
Cape Town – St. Lucia – Norfolk – Halifax - Liverpool

I left Tsingtao on I think the 9th of September, 1941, on a long, long trip. That I was allowed to leave Tsingtao with all my "luggage" was pure "joss" (luck); in addition to my suitcases I had three massive cases of personal belongings, records and books! To get out of Tsingtao at all I had to get permission from three parties: the Japanese occupying forces, the Japanese Navy, and Japanese customs, and in true official style no one would give permission until the others had done so – a hopeless situation, which somehow was eventually broken.

The Japanese, although we were not then (September 1941) at war with them, would not allow the British to leave the port, so I had to swear black and blue that I was only going to Hong Kong to see the parents of some of my Boarders, and would be coming back in a month. That was the $64,000 question; would the Japanese believe it? I had some unpleasant moments until they finally stamped my exit visa and that was that, or nearly.

Because what about luggage? I was going down on a British ship but the Japanese authorities were in charge of the harbor and customs. Fortunately, the Japanese authorities did not check whose and what luggage went on board, or they would hardly have considered various trunks, suitcases and three massive wooden crates essential for a two week visit to Hong Kong. Had they spotted it, I

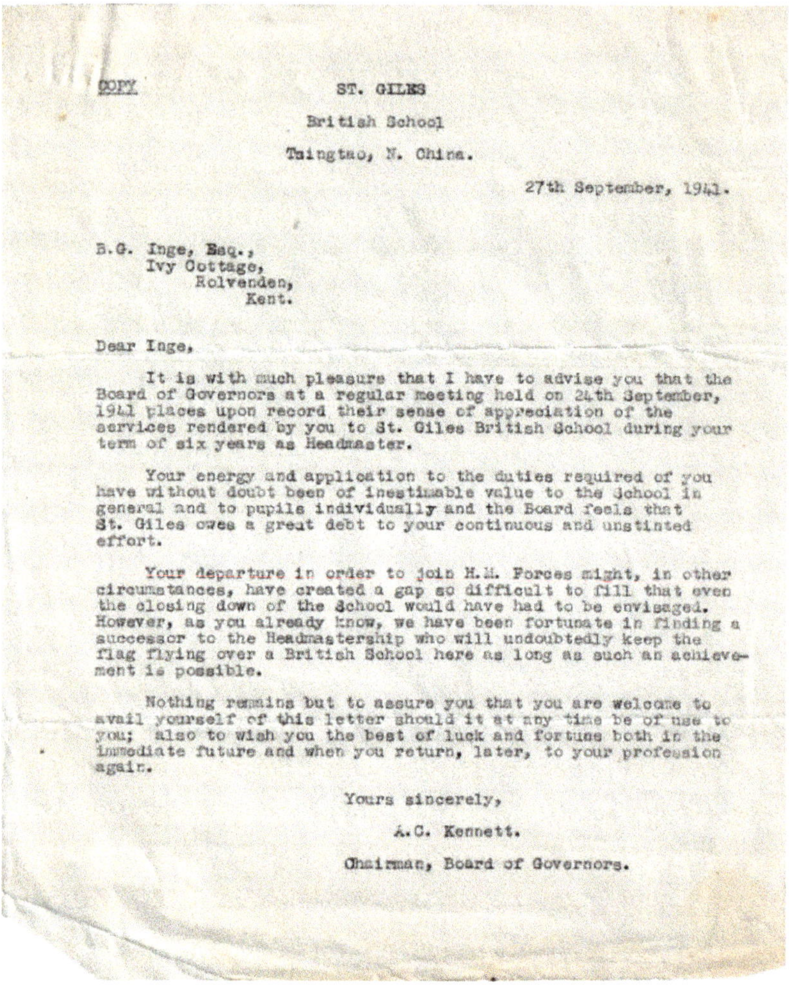

COPY

ST. GILES

British School

Tsingtao, N. China.

27th September, 1941.

B.G. Inge, Esq.,
Ivy Cottage,
Rolvenden,
Kent.

Dear Inge,

It is with much pleasure that I have to advise you that the Board of Governors at a regular meeting held on 24th September, 1941 places upon record their sense of appreciation of the services rendered by you to St. Giles British School during your term of six years as Headmaster.

Your energy and application to the duties required of you have without doubt been of inestimable value to the School in general and to pupils individually and the Board feels that St. Giles owes a great debt to your continuous and unstinted effort.

Your departure in order to join H.M. Forces might, in other circumstances, have created a gap so difficult to fill that even the closing down of the School would have had to be envisaged. However, as you already know, we have been fortunate in finding a successor to the Headmastership who will undoubtedly keep the flag flying over a British School here as long as such an achievement is possible.

Nothing remains but to assure you that you are welcome to avail yourself of this letter should it at any time be of use to you; also to wish you the best of luck and fortune both in the immediate future and when you return, later, to your profession again.

Yours sincerely,

A.C. Kennett.

Chairman, Board of Governors.

Figure 37 - Testimonial from St. Giles School

should most certainly never have got out of Tsingtao, nor should I probably be writing this.

First stop: Shanghai, where I had to wait for a few days for a ship for Hong Kong and said farewell to many friends. Local Old Blues (ex-Christ's Hospital boys) gave me a farewell evening - and what an evening! It went on till 2:00 am, and I was very happy to lie in my bunk on route to Hong Kong the next day. I took with me on my trip home the Old Blue register of Club members, home and overseas, and whenever we looked in at a port and an Old Blue was there, I looked him up. I was invariably looked after, entertained and welcomed most warmly; they were a splendid lot.

From Shanghai to Hong Kong, where at last I could breathe. Shanghai too was under the Japanese and anything could have happened, but Hong Kong was under the Union Jack. It may be difficult for those who have not experienced this sort of thing to realize what a tremendous relief it was to see and be under the British flag again.

I had to wait several weeks in Hong Kong for a boat to England and was lucky to get a passage on the SS *Mentor*, a Blue Funnel cargo boat of 11,000 tons. It only took six passengers anyway, and there were about five of us in the end.

Figure 38 - SS Mentor

"Lucky" is the right word because so many people were wanting out of Hong Kong to safer climes, and the latest crack Blue Funnel liner carrying 600 passengers and fully booked was blown ashore by a typhoon just before the passengers embarked. How they got away - if they did - I do not know, but I was thankful for my uninspiring ship and bunk, and was relieved to hear that my luggage and all three crates were on board.

In Hong Kong I stayed, as usual, with some parents, but my ship was constantly having its departure delayed owing to technical difficulties, such as the refrigeration not working and so on. Meantime I looked up friends, played cricket with the Navy once on the famous ground (now regrettably lost to cricket), played ten-pin bowls at the Club, golf at Fanling on the mainland and so on.

Incidentally, then or earlier I met two men famous in the recent annals of China; soldiers of fortune, they might be called, One-

Arm Sutton[23] and Two-Gun Cohen[24]. Very mild and pleasant they were over a beer!

Eventually, the ship was ready to sail, so down the Peak I went on the famous tram, dropped in at a jeweler's I had been casing the day before and bought a jade engagement ring. Each night on the long trip home I put the ring (together with other jewelry) in the pocket of the coat I would put on at once if we got torpedoed en route. Fortunately that didn't happen, but there is a sequel to all this. The *Mentor* and its sister ship *Stentor* were due to leave Singapore at the same time, one to be routed home by the Panama Canal and the other via the Cape in South Africa. We, *Mentor*, happily got the Cape route; the *Stentor* was torpedoed just before reaching the Panama Canal. I was in fact even luckier than I knew, for the *Mentor* herself was torpedoed in the Caribbean on her very next voyage![25] Lucky indeed.

Next stop Singapore, where my sister Norah was head of a Girls' Missionary School. She invited me to stay, to the astonishment of all and sundry; apparently no man had ever stayed in the house

23   Major General Francis "Frank" Arthur Sutton M.C. (1884-1944) was an English adventurer known as "One Arm Sutton" after losing part of an arm to a hand grenade at the Battle of Gallipoli. A product of Eton College, Sutton studied Engineering at University of London before working in civil engineering in Argentina, Mexico, and the US after 1906. He held a commission in the Royal Engineers during World War I, then built railways in Mexico and Argentina and mined for gold in Siberia and Korea. Sutton travelled to China where he had purchased manufacturing rights for the Stokes Mortar that he provided to various warlords. He became a major general for the Chinese warlord Zhang Zuolin. During World War II he was interned in Hong Kong, where he died of dysentery.

24   Morris (Moishe) Abraham Cohen (1887–1970), better known as "Two-Gun Cohen" and also by his Chinese name Ma Kun, was a Polish-born British and Canadian adventurer of Jewish origin who became aide-de-camp to Sun Yat-sen and a major-general in the Chinese National Revolutionary Army. After being nicked by a bullet in battle, Cohen wondered what he would do if one of his arms were injured, started carrying a second revolver and found he was ambidextrous. A long-time defender of Chinese rights in Canada and elsewhere, when Japan invaded China he procured weapons for the Chinese and worked for the British SOE. He was interned in Hong Kong when it fell, but released in a rare prisoner swap in 1943, and post-war became a liaison trusted by both Communist and Nationalist Chinese leaders.

25   See page 179.

before! I had about five days there, time enough to look up some friends, see "*The Reluctant Dragon*" with Norah, and watch some Indians play hockey (the first time I'd seen Indians as a team; their stick work was fabulous).

The *Mentor* then went up Malaysia to Penang, where I looked up another friend. People move around so much in their jobs from port to port out East that you get to know someone everywhere. Walking through a coconut grove, littered with the huge entire coconuts - not just the small insides that we see - scared me a little in case one dropped on me, but all was well. Then back down to Port Swettenham[26] and by car to Kuala Lumpur, where I astonished CT's brother, who was a big noise in the Police there; we had last met at Downsend! I think it was in Penang or Port Swettenham that we took on board large quantities of rubber in flat sheets. We had driven through rubber plantations and somehow I found out that ammonia dissolved rubber. This piece of information came in very handy later when removing anti-splintering rubber solution from windows in Oxford, put on against possible damage by air raids.

So off to Ceylon, where we "parked" in Colombo harbor. HMS *Norfolk* was there, and we watched and listened to the Royal Marines band playing on deck. It was a Sunday, and that night there was a most awful thunderstorm, too. The next morning a large shape

Figure 39 - RMS Aquitania

was seen approaching us over the horizon; we thought it was the *Queen Elizabeth* or *Queen Mary*, but it turned out to be the vast ship RMS *Aquitania*. She was not as big, I think, as the two *Queens*, but I believe she was much higher out of the water with all her decks. She

26   Now Port Klang.

absolutely towered over us.

There were two odd things later on connected with the *Aquitania*. When at RBCS I wanted some more double bunks, I found on buying them that they had come from the *Aquitania*, when she was broken up. Odder still, when I was talking about this coincidence to Morris and Bob Nicol in Pewsey they said, "Do you know the shop fittings, drawers, etc. we have in our shop? They came from the *Aquitania* too!" It's an odd world.

When we left there, as usual at every port, the ship went up and down outside the harbor degaussing. Ships had a cable all around them, which was a device to avoid trouble from magnetic mines, and I gather (though I cannot understand it properly) that this cruising up and down was to do with the removal of some probability of the ship setting off such mines.

And so to South Africa, amidst flying fish, dolphins and the rest, with albatrosses keeping us company as we went further South. Astonishing birds, for they swooped around the ship and kept up with us while I can't remember seeing a single wing being flapped. Big chaps, too; not as big as I had been led to expect, but no wonder the Ancient Mariner didn't like having one round his neck! Durban was our first stop, on a lovely summer day; the course that we were following meant that we kept up with summer and the sun right up until we left the West Indies and got near Virginia.

I looked up an Old Blue there who took me home to dinner. There was an unusual feature of the house, a fairly large entry hall with a mass of paintings, I believe by his wife. In the middle was a smallish photo of one house. The explanation? My friend had won £75,000 on the old Henley Sweep. I always felt the house should have been given a distinctly larger photo as a "thank you" for its success.

We stocked up with various supplies then scarce in England, such as butter and sausages, all tinned. We were allowed to take only small amounts home, and I gave one of the tins of butter to Joyce's Head Mistress to her surprise and delight. I'm not sure whether it was as a thankfulness for getting home or as an apology for taking Joyce away, but it went down well!

One day in Durban, then off to Cape Town for two days, where I bought some ascorbic tablets from a chemist (who was also an Old Blue!). The food on the board was pretty grim and we had almost no fruit or green stuff whatever, so I had to get something to make up. I am convinced, as we all were, that the Purser/Steward was making a very good thing out of his contract to supply the passengers' food, so anything to help or relieve the monotony of very average meals - and small ones, at that - was most welcome.

You may wonder what on earth we did on a small, non-passenger boat to pass the time over all these months. Mostly we played Bridge, and came near to manslaughter at times over one particular ex-Chief Petty Officer who "knew it all". We read books; the ships "library" of some 40 books was thoroughly explored, and I was even reduced to reading Dickens. We played quoits with rope rings on the iron deck, and for some time we kept a <u>very</u> close eye on one very pleasant but unfortunate passenger who suffered such agonies from sinus trouble that he appeared likely to throw himself off the ship. Fortunately he recovered, but we had some anxious moments when he stood gazing out over the ship's rail.

Desperate for exercise and longing to get rid of some surplus energy, I also went coal shoveling with the Chinese stokers, who after their invariably cheerful manner roared with laughter every time I turned up and clearly thought I was mad. (So did the Captain, Officers and other passengers.) A few days of that filtered off sufficient energy and I returned to Bridge. Every evening without fail the Captain joined us, and four of us had two games - just two, no more or less - of Chinese Checkers, a splendid game which is really two Halma games going on at once.

After we left Cape Town with its most striking Table Mountain (and where I met another posse of Old Blues!), we found to our surprise that we were not going up to Freetown - that route was far too vulnerable to submarine attack - but over to the West Indies. The old ship fairly belted along, with the result that we had to put into Norfolk, VA, with a twisted propeller shaft later on. The reason for our hurry - she was an old ship, and "belting along" is comparative – was not merely the desire to get home; a radio message conveyed that there were submarines around, and that there were even a few boatloads of armed enemy men drifting around too.

Anyway, it didn't seem too healthy to linger, so off we went and fetched up in Saint Lucia, a delightful little island in the West Indies, in lovely summer weather. We went on shore in summer clothes, white shirt, white shorts, topee, and stopped to look at the latest Reuters bulletin posted up. We wished we hadn't, for there it was: "U-boats are now hunting in packs in the Atlantic" and so forth. Normally we didn't worry during daytime, we just enjoyed the sun and sea breezes, though we were desperately short of exercise; there wasn't far you could walk on this boat.

But at night, with the ship darkened all over, it was another thing. The majesty of the stars, which it seemed you could almost touch, and the phosphorescence of the ships wake were beautiful, but when you got onto your bunk every evening you always wondered… after making sure your lifebelt was handy, with its little red light which you would switch on if you wound up in the water in the _very_ vague hope that someone might (improbably) see you and if so might (even more improbably) risk being torpedoed themselves by stopping to pick you up. Gloomy but unavoidable thoughts, which did not disappear the longer the trip went on.

St. Lucia, however, provided us with grapefruit, our first fresh food for about two months. This day I remember as being December 14th, and nearly the end of our lovely summer "cruise". We only stayed there a day and then left for the North Atlantic and for Norfolk, VA. And then, too, it really got cold.

Here we got a tremendous shock. We had heard vague news about a Japanese attack on Pearl Harbor but it didn't seem to rate very highly. Obviously full details had been banned for security reasons, and after all we'd been used to some terrible attacks by the Japanese on Shanghai, Nanking and elsewhere already. This sounded like just another such affair. Then I saw a copy of _Time_ magazine with the most horrific pictures of the holocaust at Pearl Harbor, with capital ships sinking, battered beyond recognition or on fire; it was terrible. Presumably these photos were deliberately released in the States for reasons of their own, but not a hint of such devastation was put on the air where it could have been picked up internationally, especially by the Allies, and might presumably have been extremely bad for morale.

Certainly when I got back to England no one had either seen or heard anything but the very bare bones of the facts, to the extent that the Japanese had attacked the American fleet at Pearl Harbor and that the Americans had sustained some damage. _Some_ damage would have been more accurate, for the copies of _Time_ (a very popular American magazine in England also at that time) which were sold in England had all the photographs (and probably news) about the attack removed before being sent over here. At least they had better luck than the School Certificate (the old GCE) exam papers for our children in China, which were sunk on route for the East. We managed fortunately to have duplicates sent out.

We arrived at Norfolk on December 24th. I strolled downtown and looked in at a local YMCA, where a Christmas party was going on; one of the officials invited me up to his house to lunch on Boxing Day. Christmas Day was terrible, with nothing to do on the ship. I went to a service in an old church in Norfolk, with large box pews, all very English in origin of course, in Virginia. It had as a souvenir of the War of Independence a cannonball stuck in its square tower, still stuck there after all these years; it had, it was believed, been fired by the British. I have seldom felt so appallingly lonely, so I staggered over the snow and ice to a cinema.

I was put in touch with the Rotary Club, who invited me to lunch. I forgot to mention earlier that I had been Vice President at the Tsingtao Rotary Club, but resigned to avoid any possibility of being President, which I didn't want. It was a splendidly international affair; when I joined there were British and Germans, Americans of course, Chinese and Japanese and any other nationality you like. As the various wars broke out, of course, some representatives dropped out but "it was fun while it lasted." It eventually became extremely tiring partly because of all Tsingtao Special Police night duties, and we were actually relieved when the Japanese eventually took over the town.

Also on Boxing Day, I had been invited by an American businessman to listen to Churchill addressing the House of Representatives. It was magnificent speech, and won tremendous acclaim from the Americans, while - I must admit - I was so choked with pride that I could hardly speak. It was the most moving occasion.

I got in touch with some great American naval friends of mine, the Magruders. John Magruder had been Captain of the USS *Augusta*, flagship of the American China fleet, at Tsingtao; we became great buddies and had seen a great deal of each other. They were now in Philadelphia, about three hundred miles north, and as I found that we were due for a fortnight's stay in Norfolk I had several days in which to look them up. After an all-night journey (part of which was on a ferry whereon was a party of RAF Officers going to the States for

Figure 40 - USS Augusta
Photo signed by John Magruder "To Bernard Inge...and that indomitable spirit that will never die." Given to BGI "in recognition of his stout defence of his homeland against the American assumption that the UK was finished following Dunkirk," according to Joyce.

further training), at last I arrived at the Magruders' house about 8:00 AM. This was on December 31st, 1941.

In Philadelphia we went to see that splendid film, "*How Green Was My Valley*", just released, and then watched the annual parade on New Year's Day. This was quite a "do". All the various Guilds, Societies and Associations spent the previous 12 months preparing for it and the costumes, bands, inevitable majorettes and floats make a tremendous and long procession. But what a day to have it on, bang in the middle of the American winter. The very wide streets of course provide a wonderful opportunity and background to show off the elaborate displays, but what happens when it's snowing madly? Fortunately, this day it was fine, if cold, and anyway Esther Magruder and I watched most of it from the comfortable lounge of a big hotel. Afterwards we consumed, for the first time for me, vast quantities of Lobster Newburg - splendid.

In the evening John took his wife Esther, his daughter (15, also Esther) and me out to dinner at the Merion Cricket Club - yes, MCC[27]. It was the second-oldest Cricket Club in the United States,

---

27   Marylebone Cricket Club, the original "MCC", was founded

and the walls, as we went down the thickly carpeted staircase, were covered with pictures of cricket being played in earlier times. It was a pleasant evening and I thoroughly enjoyed such a wonderful meal (off yet another vast menu of every conceivable variety of food) after the sparse fare on board. But it was the wonderfully relaxed atmosphere which perhaps contributed most to the evening. America had only just entered the war and there was certainly at this time no lack of any food of whatever kind, and always peace.

For months we had traveled under daily strain through fear of being torpedoed, for months we had to listen helplessly to the radio which recorded disaster after disaster for the Allies, not long after we had left a particular port or country - and now a marvelous, brief break. Hong Kong had fallen; what had happened to all the children and parents we knew so well? We knew quite enough about the Japanese military to fear the worst, and only too often our fears turned out to be justified. Singapore went, that "impregnable" island, whose massive guns were discovered to be all facing seaward so that when the hopelessly under-estimated Japanese came down over land, the guns were useless. Singapore, where as far as I knew Norah still was. (Happily, she'd been sent to India in charge of a multitude of Japanese women and children internees.)

In one blow the great HMS *Repulse* and HMS *Prince of Wales*, battleships both, were bombed into helplessness and sank. And all the time the Japanese were getting nearer Burma - and then India? Meanwhile Allied shipping losses grew at a frantic rate, and we might be the next victims. No wonder we enjoyed the fortnight's break.

The weather was by now very cold, and off we went to Halifax, Nova Scotia, joining a convoy. We left Halifax as a convoy of 40 ships; a few shot ahead out of the convoy on their own, quite unofficially and to the wrath of the officials. These ships were usually faster than some and preferred to risk being on their own, believing that their greater speed would give them a better chance to avoid being hit by a torpedo. They thought that risk preferable to being forced to keep to the inevitably slow rate of the convoy (whose speed is necessarily that of its slowest member) despite having a naval escort of destroyers, frigates and, near land, of airplanes. Never have I seen anything roll at sea like those frigates, and John Roberts would doubtless bear out that destroyers rolled almost as badly. It must have

in London in 1787 as the governing body of cricket. The Merion Cricket Club was founded in Pennsylvania in 1865.

been fantastic trying merely to keep one's feet.

After two days we were about 8 ships short at least, those having shot ahead. Numbers grew less, then down came the fog at night. Next morning, we could only see one other ship and there hadn't been any enemy attack. In that we were particularly lucky, for some lunatic ship bang in the middle of the convoy had set off a gigantic flare by accident, and there we all were nicely silhouetted against the sky for any U-boat to pick off. Happily none were about, but it made us feel absolutely naked, especially as the ship had been darkened overall ever since we left Hong Kong and we were not even allowed to smoke, let alone light a cigarette on deck in the blackout. This, by the way, was one of the things which was so wonderful about Norfolk and Philadelphia; no lighting restrictions, and the towns and shops all blazed with light.

But back to the convoy. Only one other ship in sight. Our Captain flashed the other Captain, "Where is the convoy?" Back came the helpful answer, "Don't know; we've been following you all night." So we plodded on. We found that one or two ships had gone adrift on the Irish coast, but the others were scattered far and wide. So it was with a feeling of both triumph and amusement that the *Mentor*, one of the slowest ships in the convoy, steamed up the Mersey, first home to Liverpool. There we were faced with skeleton building after skeleton building, smashed buildings, complete devastation it seemed, after enemy bombing, the whole scene covered with a thick fall of snow. And the date: 20th January 1942, the day before my 39th birthday.

We stayed on board that evening and the Customs men came on to clear us. They were extraordinarily, and rightly, good with the crew. If a chap produced a bottle of Scotch, for example, they would say, "Go and have a drink out of it and then come back"- no duty. One chap produced a lovely roll of silk; the Customs Officer looked at it carefully and said, "Looks like cotton to me, off you go!" I doubt if either crew or passengers paid duty on anything. As far as we were concerned, I think they felt (and how right they were) that we were lucky to be alive and so had earned a little laxity with the rules.

It was sympathetic treatment of people who were having a pretty grim time. The crew's year consisted of about five months outward and back, six weeks or less leave, then another five months at sea, always, always in imminent danger not only of torpedoing but from air attack. To counter the latter, as soon as the *Mentor* came within the range of land-based planes we took it in turns (not by choice!) to be up on deck with a heavy machine gun (a Browning, I think), a tin hat and a good deal of optimism. If we saw an enemy plane coming at us, we were supposed to fire at it. Not a shot was fired by any of us, for three very good reasons. First, it was extremely difficult to judge what direction the plane was coming from. Secondly, there was no way of telling until it was overhead whether it was enemy or a friend, and finally, owing to the speed of the plane, by the time you had it in your sights (having solved the previous two problems) the plane had gone. I did see one, but it escaped unharmed, and so did we.

The next morning, 21st January, my birthday, I phoned home (and Joyce) who were all considerably relieved I had got home safely. So was I! But there was more to it than just that. After we were engaged Joyce had tried hard to get out to China and I had tried hard to get her out there. The order, unfortunately, was that no one between 16 and 60 was allowed to leave the country. Between us we wrote to Prime Ministers, Foreign Secretaries, Ambassadors, all to no avail. So when I left Hong Kong I had sent a wire to Joyce saying that I was leaving that day.

Consequently, for the next few months on the trip I wondered daily – for we had not given up hope – whether Joyce might somehow have eventually got permission to go out to China, and was on her way there while I merrily passed her going in the other direction! It was always a possibility, and a very worrying one. But Joyce was on the end of the phone when I rang, and all was well. Once again, things had turned out right. If Joyce <u>had</u> got out to China and Tsingtao, I should not have left the school and we should both have been put "in the bag" by the Japanese. Whether we should ever have got out again is another matter.

Teaching – England

So next day off the ship and up to London, where I met Joyce at Waterloo Station. Finding somewhere to stay was an appalling problem. I got a taxi and we went all around the place, but eventually I did find a small room somewhere.

We went down by coach to my Mother's home at Rolvenden in Kent together, and on the way, as that part of Kent was a "restricted" area, police came on board and asked for our "Identity Cards". I had never heard of these and said (unintentionally rather loudly), "I haven't got one; I only came back from China yesterday." There was a deathly hush over the coach, and heads were turned in my direction while people craned to see what this mysterious person looked like. I think they expected a two-headed Chinaman with a couple of pigtails. Anyway, the police let me through, and we were warmly greeted at home, especially by Ron, who said, "Glad to see you, old boy, because I'm off to Ceylon on Monday."

We Inges do travel about. At that time Marnie was at the bottom of South America, Ron shortly off to Ceylon, Norah in Singapore or India, Daphne in Nigeria and I had just got back from China. Only Betty was at home, with Mama. We'd always been brought up to write home once a week, or as near as we could; in Canada I once had to apologize for writing in pencil as the ink had frozen solid in my bedroom.

The result was that Mama had a wonderful correspondence and, acting as an information center par excellence, when she wrote to us (as she did every week) she included news about the rest of the family, so we were able to keep pretty well in touch.

When I was at school, she used to write on Saturday, pay one penny (in old coinage) for a stamp and the letter arrived at school at Horsham in Sussex on Sunday morning. *Quantum mutantum*[28]

A few days at Rolvenden and it was time to go job hunting. What I could <u>not</u> do was get warm. I had had six very cold winters (and six very hot summers) in China but the cold was always dry, and the damp English cold really got into my bones. It was literally months before I could get warm.

---

28   Things have changed.

We were married on April 7th, 1942, at the Parish Church, Hove[29], a vast church which could hold about 1,200 people, but on this occasion, with the war being on and Hove being in a restricted area, there were exactly 12 of us all told. And so began a new era in our lives, and really what is Volume III of this story.

Figure 41 - April 7th, 1942

---

29   The town where Joyce's Father, Norcliffe Roberts, had retired.

Dragon School

The next thing was to find a job, so I went up to stay at Bookham.[30] On Ron's advice to "Try the family profession," Joyce was teaching (PE) all day, but we managed to have most evenings together. Eventually, I applied for the salaried Headmastership of a Prep School. I had to write to a Mr. A. Retey, who replied that he regretted that the job had gone but that had taken the liberty of showing my letter to Joc Lynam, the Headmaster of the Dragon School at Oxford. To cut a long story short, I was offered a job at the Dragon to start in a few weeks, to be resident for a term and a half, and then non-resident until the end of the summer term. I joined them in February; Joyce went on teaching at Bookham until the summer.

Figure 42 - Joc Lyman

Figure 43 - Dragon School lodge, today

So much depends on luck and/or grasping your opportunities. If Tony Retey had not contacted Joc Lynam, I quite likely would not have obtained an Oxford - or possibly any - degree. In my last years at Downsend I had made a determined effort to get a degree by correspondence course, but had failed my finals.

---

30   Near Leatherhead and not far from Epsom, Joyce's home.

Because of Tony's action, I got a job at the Dragon. I joined the local Home Guard, and found in my section an Oxford Don of 60 (which I thought then was very old!); he helped me to get into Exeter College, merely on the strength of my London Matric 20 years earlier. Because I was living within two miles, I could take a degree in my spare time without attending any lectures; it was all done by tutorials in the evening.

Figure 44 - Dragon School, Oxford, today

So I finally got my degree, which was absolutely essential to my career. Without it I would never have got a Headship - and what a Headship, which lasted until my retirement and which enabled us to have a lovely family and to bring them up in some sort of comfort, even if not affluent. And all this dates from Tony showing that letter to Joc. It is, in my mind, a quite incredible chain of circumstances.

I find it extraordinarily difficult to continue with the story from this point onwards, because you - the family – know most of it[31], so I should probably confine my further writing to things which you may not know much about.

Joyce and I had our first home in Charlbury Road, Oxford, in the home of Sir Adrian and Lady Holt. After a year we moved to Banbury Road, to a house owned by three elderly "Dickensian" sisters, of whom the eldest was the "dragon" and boss of the other two. The middle one I remember nothing about, and the youngest was quite pleasant when allowed to be. However, when a baby seemed to be in prospect we were politely asked to move on.

After walking miles and miles and miles, Joyce eventually

---

31   See Appendix 1 for an attempt to fill in some of the gaps.

found a flat at 86c Banbury Rd. She had given up teaching now, but Jill was on the way and it must have been heartbreaking and exhausting in the extreme for her to have to go on looking and looking. However, triumph at last, and on August 25th, 1944, Jill turned up, on a beautifully sunny Wednesday afternoon. And I'd finished my degree exams. Our cup of happiness - if not our quiver - was full.

Figure 45 - 86 Banbury Road today

All this time I was fully occupied with (1) teaching, (2) Home Guard, (3) working for a degree. Joyce was marvelous; every evening if I wasn't "soldiering" or attending tutorials - and sometimes after I had been - we had three solid hours of silence while I struggled with my work. The only break we had in term time was on Friday nights, when I always had a bridge four, almost invariably with Dragon Staff. Thanks to our joint determination I passed all necessary exams a year early, but the authorities wouldn't let me have my degree until the three years compulsory residence was fulfilled. (That was a BA; I eventually took my MA Oxon in 1949.)

The four years I had at Dragon brought both Joyce and myself the greatest happiness. Joyce helped at the Dragon and taught PE, at one time at three Girls' Schools at the same time, tearing from one to the other, while I endeavored to get Common Entrance candidates through Latin, French and Maths. It was and is a magnificent school, completely "sui generis" - very strange to start with but once you are acclimatized, delightful, utterly sensible and extremely happy.

Home Guard

Meantime, I joined the Home Guard. When I got back to England I approached the authorities because I wanted to join up. "What do you do?" they asked. "Teach," I said. Then with one of those flashes of inspiration for which officialdom is famous, they said, "Then go on teaching, and join one of the Home Defense units." As several Masters at the school were in the Home Guard, I joined them, a unit attached to the Ox and Bucks Light Infantry. As a matter of fact Tony Retey (he and his wife, Dolly, became two of our best friends) was in the Auxiliary Fire Service, and had I discussed it with him before joining the Home Guard I should probably have joined the AFS. I wonder if I then would have met anybody who could have got me into Exeter, and if not what line would my life have taken then? The world is indeed a small place, and opportunities must be seized.

Now, the Home Guard has been mocked endlessly. There was indeed much to make us laugh, but we did work - and work hard - to make ourselves efficient. Several of the more amusing moments occur to me. One was when our gallant Major (a genuine one brought back out of retirement) was tossing onto the counter light-heartedly some Mills Bomb primers. Why nothing went off I shall never know; this was in the Armory, with ammunition, etc., all around. On another occasion I ran in a hurry to hang up my greatcoat, which I had discovered was too warm. Along the stone passage two <u>primed</u> Mills Bombs shot out of the pouches in my webbing and crashed onto the floor. Fortunately, neither pin came out, nor did the primers break, but I knew ever afterwards the meaning of "breaking out into a cold sweat".

On yet another day (or evening, rather) we were carrying out field training in the University Parks, crawling on our tummies and so on. We all reported back to HQ at about 9:30 PM, which was a normal time for "dismiss" so that we could collect a pint or so at one of the locals with which Oxford is so happily supplied before going home. We then found at HQ that we were one man short. He was eventually discovered in the pitch dark, still crawling towards the unseen enemy half an hour after both they and his fighting comrades had gone home. A hard life...

Then there was the occasion when the country was so short

of rifles that ours were taken away for the Regular Army. So on our night duties we had to stand guard with a <u>pike</u>, so help us, a length of heavy-duty piping about 6 feet long with a bayonet fastened on the end. Well, we did it, and in weather which reminded us that a rifle butt is made of wood while this piping nearly froze to our fingers.

But for me the most hysterical moment of the war came when I was studying military history for my degree, and at that moment in particular the Battle of the Marne. Before posting the sentries one night at Mansfield College (I was by then a Sergeant) I looked around at my section and saw a myriad of metal ribbons, for we had old soldiers and all nationalities in the Home Guard. So I said, "Look, you chaps, I can't make out exactly what happened at the Marne. Can any of you help me? By the look of your ribbons someone must have been there." And a quiet voice said cheerfully, "Ja, I vos dere." I had never been so stunned in my life and very hurriedly changed the subject. (Very few people believe this story, but as I live and breathe it is absolutely true!)

We had Sunday morning parades, plus two evening parades, and also some courses away from Oxford if one wanted to go. As a Schoolmaster I had more holidays than most, and so I was able to go on two courses. One, a fieldcraft course in Sussex, was, to quote the circular, "meant to be tough". On arrival we were "asked" to volunteer for essential jobs - getting bedding, food supplies, etc., things mostly which needed doing several times a day. So I chose the latrines, mainly because all I had to do was (1) dig them at the beginning of camp, and (2) fill them in at the end – and I knew no one else would volunteer. After all, I had once spent time mucking out the most noisome pigsties and cowpens, and I could let others do all the other jobs.

It worked beautifully, but on the second day at midday we were absolutely exhausted, which is where I first learned the value of relaxation. We were all told to lie down on our backs, legs apart, rifles within reach, and relax, just for 10 minutes, when on the blast of a whistle we were to <u>leap</u> to our feet and would feel fine. We dropped like logs, dead beat, then, as ordered, when the whistle went, shot to our feet, got in line and felt wonderfully fit again. It was quite extraordinary. We only had about five more hours work but we simply couldn't have done it without that 10 minutes relaxation. Very odd - to me, anyway.

There was a pleasant sequel to this course. By previous arrangement I was met at the station at Tunbridge Wells by Jean Eckford, then about 16 or 17, one of my ex-pupils from China, the Eckfords being my greatest friends out there. Jean took me to her Uncle's house for the night - nothing unusual about that - and I was restored with some good Scotch. It was the next morning which produced the shock. A knock at the bedroom door; "Come in." Enters a soldier in uniform. "May I have your boots to clean, please, Sir, and is there any of your equipment which needs cleaning?" It appeared that Jean's Uncle, who was an officer in the Army, had his own resident batman! I was, as they say, completely taken aback, but accepted the offer and my boots came back most beautifully polished. But I think it must be the first time ever that a modest Corporal (as I was then), and in the Home Guard at that, had his shoes cleaned by a batman.

The other course was a totally different kettle of fish. It was a sub-artillery course and took place at Woolacombe, North Devon. We had lectures on fuses, explosives, various machine guns, a Blacker Bombard (of which more later) and the abominable Smith Gun. We had heard rumors about the Smith Gun, and our fears were <u>not</u> allayed when our Instructor started off by saying, "Now this gun is not dangerous to handle" - which immediately put the wind up us. Justifiably so, for a few weeks after we left Woolacombe two Guards Instructors were killed by one at the course.

It was an extraordinary gun and I don't know that it was ever fired in anger - unless you include the anger of the men who practiced on it. It was a small gun firing a shell about 10 inches long, three to four inches in diameter. The great thing about this gun (they said) was that you could tow it anywhere behind a baby Austin, and I believe that was true. The two wheels were solid discs about four feet across, and when you got your firing point you heaved the gun over, with one wheel acting as a base and the other as cover for the men firing it. Ingenious. But the shell had a long tape wound around the blunt end, with a piece of lead on the end; when the shell was in flight, this gradually unwound, and when fully unwound made the shell instantly live. The only snag was that unless you were very careful the tape would unwind in the barrel and then of course the whole thing blew up, which was, one imagines, how the two instructors lost their lives.

Figure 46 - The Smith Gun

Our only casualty was a Private (actually a practicing doctor) who reacted so violently when the gun went off in trials that he bashed his head against the upper wheel, and cut his nose unpleasantly as his tin hat was forced down on him with some violence. Only a few of us, happily, had to fire this wretched thing, but the *piece de resistance* was the Blacker Bombard. This was a "portable" gun, which meant that three men tottered along each with one of the three tripod legs, another carried the barrel and others the "bombs". When you set it up it sat down only about a foot off the ground on its spread-out tripod. To fire it you lay flat on your tummy, there being a metal shield between the firer and the "shell", a slit in the shield enabling you to take aim and also to preserve you from most of the flash. It went off with a rather frightening roar, and then you watched the extraordinary missile solemnly wobbling its way towards the objective.

Our target was one of the anti-invasion posts sunk into the famous Woolacombe Sands. Can you imagine it? Three miles of 8-foot-high posts at 12-foot intervals over the whole area - and still we managed not to hit one on one occasion. Let me describe the missile. It had an oval-shaped bomb placed on the end of a steel tube about 3 feet long, with fins at the back. I've seen some odd objects in my time but this one beat the lot, and I should hate to have had one coming at me. No wonder one poor little rabbit died; nothing hit it, he just died of shock, happily the only casualty on our course, which lasted a week.

Figure 47 - The Blacker Bombard

But we were thereafter always one up on many of our fellows and even on some "Regulars", to whom we would say casually, and with an air of insouciance, "Of course, the Blacker Bombard (what a lovely sounding name) is a pretty useful weapon; have you used it?" Most people hadn't a clue what we were talking about, so we chalked one up with happy regularity. I don't believe the animal ever went into action, like the Smith Gun. If it had, the enemy would probably have died laughing.

There were other "toys" we played about with - Mills Bombs, for example. The first time I held a live one in my hand I was - as most people were - terrified to think that if I did anything wrong it would kill me. But, and this was common experience too, once you had (1) removed the pin, (2) hurled the thing in the right direction with a bowling action, (3) instantly ducked down behind the trench and (4) heard the considerable explosion, you suddenly felt full of confidence and wanted to go on hurling Mills Bombs all night. All very odd. We had "plastic" Mills Bombs, too, also unpleasant. We did plenty of firing practice, had the odd route march, and played with a most unpleasant "sticky" bomb, while there were Molotov cocktails available. These latter were bottles filled with petrol, which when hurled upon incoming tanks, etc., burst into most unpleasant flames all over the attackers.

But the "sticky bomb" was fairly unique. It was a round shape with a protruding stem, all enclosed in a metal casing which you removed before use. You were then left with this large bomb, about 6 to 7 inches in diameter, which was covered in some very sticky substance. Its use? Well, this was the idea; as a tank came along you leapt out of your cover, jammed the bomb onto the tank where its sticky substance made it stay on, and retreated madly before it blew up. As far as I was concerned - and I had friends! - I prayed devoutly that I would never have to use the things, or if I did that the enemy, in other tanks or vehicles or elsewhere, would kindly refrain from shooting me until I was safely back under cover. No, the prospects were a bit daunting.

On other occasions we would spend Sunday morning parades blocking main roads with vast angle irons, which we dropped into slots in the road. And I remember one Sunday morning when we careered madly but enthusiastically through the gardens and over the fences of houses in north Oxford, not at all the sort of thing the residents particularly appreciated. Probably our moment of greatest actual danger came when our beloved Major (a nice chap but a bit of a menace) was examining a loaded Sten gun in front of his loyal troops - actually about 15 yards in front of <u>me</u>! He hadn't seen one before, and as his fingers wandered idly around the trigger more prayers went up in 30 seconds than had ever been known before. Happily a coolheaded Officer gently disengaged his hand, and we breathed again. As far as I remember there was no safety catch on the Sten; I may be wrong. But two dozen of us at that range could easily have been wiped out. The perils of war are not always, or only, the more obvious ones of being in action.

As it happened, Oxford never saw any action on the part of the Home Guard, except for one historic occasion when one of <u>our</u> planes, having forgotten the correct landing signal for the day, flew madly backwards and forwards across Oxford while the demented pilot tried to land, avoiding the happily harmless stream of shells aimed at him by the Home Guard ack-ack battery. Certainly life is not dull, taking one thing with another.

I was one of the few who never got the Home Guard medal. That's because it was awarded for a minimum of three year service, and although I joined up in February 1942 the Home Guard was disbanded before the three years were up. Come to think of it, why, before the end of the war? Anyway, there it is.

So there you are. It was pretty strenuous at times, being on top of one's normal work, and it was especially tough after an all-night guard. Being by then a Sergeant, I had to remain awake all night in charge of the guard, and then go off, have a bath, change and do a full days teaching. But I shall never forget the lovely peace of an early spring or summer morning as I cycled home along the Banbury Rd, each garden with its flowering shrubs and trees. Sheer delight, and a considerable change from one of our "sleeping and guard" HQs in a dilapidated building where rats ran over you. I never did like rats anyway.

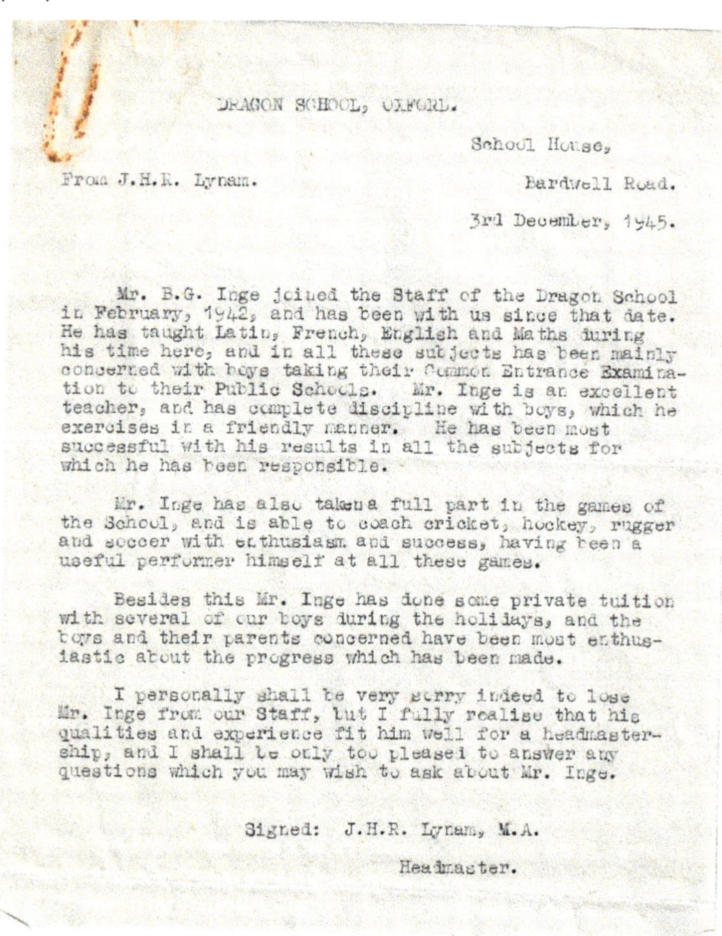

DRAGON SCHOOL, OXFORD.

School House,

From J.H.R. Lynam.
Bardwell Road.

3rd December, 1945.

Mr. B.G. Inge joined the Staff of the Dragon School in February, 1942, and has been with us since that date. He has taught Latin, French, English and Maths during his time here, and in all these subjects has been mainly concerned with boys taking their Common Entrance Examination to their Public Schools. Mr. Inge is an excellent teacher, and has complete discipline with boys, which he exercises in a friendly manner. He has been most successful with his results in all the subjects for which he has been responsible.

Mr. Inge has also taken a full part in the games of the School, and is able to coach cricket, hockey, rugger and soccer with enthusiasm and success, having been a useful performer himself at all these games.

Besides this Mr. Inge has done some private tuition with several of our boys during the holidays, and the boys and their parents concerned have been most enthusiastic about the progress which has been made.

I personally shall be very sorry indeed to lose Mr. Inge from our Staff, but I fully realise that his qualities and experience fit him well for a headmastership, and I shall be only too pleased to answer any questions which you may wish to ask about Mr. Inge.

Signed: J.H.R. Lynam, M.A.

Headmaster.

Figure 48 - Dragon School formal testimonial

DRAGON SCHOOL, OXFORD.

From J. H. R. Lynam.

Telegrams: 'Dragons, Oxford.'
Telephone: Oxford, 5560.

SCHOOL HOUSE,
BARDWELL ROAD.

22nd February, 1946.

My dear Bernard,

First of all I am afraid you must have thought
me very careless in the matter of the last note which
you sent to me, as I realise now that it contains other
items of interest besides the matter of the Changing
Room! I am extremely sorry, but I must confess that
I have only just read the rest of the note, and
realise that I did nothing about your maths set, and
that I have not sent you the Latin papers for which you
asked. Do you still want these, because if so send a
boy over for them now and you shall have them?

With regard to your earlier letter, it is good of
you to write as you did, and I think you know how very
sorry both Hum and I are to be losing you. It will undoubtedly leave a very real gap here which, I may say,
it will not be easy to fill; but I am sure that you are
right in seeking for something more ambitious, and I
hope that your new appointment may lead eventually ~~lead~~
to something even of wider scope. In the meantime I
feel that the job at Reading is a very worth while one,
and if at any time I can be of help to you, either
directly or indirectly, please don't hesitate to ask me.

If I may be allowed to give you one especial pat on the back,
from my own point of view, I should like to say how
extremely pleasant it has been to be able to work in such
friendly co-operation with a person who has himself been
at the head of things, as you have, but who has never
on any occasion let that appear as any sort of obstacle
to working in complete harmony here.

Unless you wish it, I do not propose to make any
public announcement about your leaving us after to-morrow.
I never think that much is to be gained from such announce-
ments, but I will certainly tell the boys if you would
like me to do so. I hope that, although you actually
cease to take classes after to-morrow we shall see you
round about here often until you go to Reading, and
even then I think you will have to make a note in your

diary to be here for the sing-song at the end of
term.

With every good wish,

Yours ever,

B.G. Inge Esq.

Joe.

Figure 49 - Personal note to BGI from Joc Lyman, Headmaster at the Dragon School

Reading Blue Coat School

Eventually I returned to Headmastership, at the Reading Blue Coat School. After the first shortlist interview I went home and said that "I wouldn't have the job if it was offered to me!" However, I was put on a short list and invited back for a further interview. When called before the Trustees for the second time on that day, the Chairman, the delightful Bishop Parham, smiled amiably and said, "By the way, Mr. Inge, there is one thing we haven't asked you. Would you accept the post if it was offered to you?" Frankly, I had not made up my mind, but on the old principle of grabbing your chances, after a few seconds of furious thinking I said "Yes, Sir," and that was that.

There were about 176 applicants for the post, so you had to have some luck. I think two things helped; I had been at Christ's Hospital - <u>the</u> Blue Coat School of them all (though there was no formal link between CH and Aldworth's Hospital, as RBCS was originally called) - and I had had six years already as a Headmaster. I don't know if one other matter had any effect. The Bishop said, "I see you were at Exeter College. That," he went on, turning to Ted Blandy, Secretary to the Trustees, "makes three of us, including myself." You never know!

I took over officially on the 1st March, 1946, (at the Bath Road site), and the last and longest part of my teaching career started. The school had fallen on difficult days, and a few months earlier there had actually been a proposal to close it down altogether. However, thanks to the determination of Harry and George Dunster (two Old Blues) and Bishop Parham, this move was blocked, and it was decided to advertise for a new Headmaster and see what he could do.

The first thing which struck me was that the school could neither be made viable nor expand where it was, so, to put it briefly, before I had been there a month we were looking for a new site. We examined three; one at Purley was not suitable, with insufficient grounds and/or buildings and playing fields. I believe it is now a home for handicapped children. The second, at Spencer's Wood (and since demolished) had over 1,000 German prisoners still in residence and was therefore not available as soon as we wanted.

The third, Holme Park at Sonning, struck me as the ideal site, with an imposing main building and plenty of room for more

BLANDY & BLANDY,
W. & H. BLANDY.
J. R. B. SMITH.
C. J. B. H. TOSER.
SOLICITORS.
COMMISSIONERS FOR OATHS.

Telephone
READING Nº 3066 (3 Lines)

Please return   *1. Friar Street.*

Reading

5th February, 1946.

B. G. Inge, Esq.,
   86c, Banbury Road,
        Oxford.

Dear Sir,

<u>Reading Municipal (Church) Charities.</u>

<u>Reading Blue Coat School.</u>

On behalf of the Trustees of the Reading Municipal (Church)
Charities, I am writing to confirm the decision of the Trustees at
their Meeting held yesterday for the appointment of yourself as
Headmaster of the Reading Blue Coat School on the following terms
and conditions:-

(1)   Your duties to commence on the 1st March, 1946.

(2)   Your salary to be at the rate of Six hundred and fifty
pounds (£650) per annum, and in addition, you are to be entitled to
residence at the School, full board, lighting and heating for yourself
and your wife and children, free of expense.

(3)   Your wife is to act as Matron at the School at an additional
salary of £120 per annum, or you are to be responsible for securing
the services of an independent Matron at the same salary with board-
residence, free of expense.

(4)   You are to be in full control of and responsible for the
general administration of the School, including the teaching and
domestic staff and the engagement and dismissal of such staff, but
you are to keep the Trustees, or the School Committee on their behalf,
fully informed from time to time on all these matters.

(5)   Your duties also to include the collection of school fees,
the passing of accounts for payment by the Assistant Treasurers, and
the payment of small accounts out of a fixed float.

(6)   The selection of Foundation boys will be dealt with by the
Trustees in conjunction with yourself, but you will be responsible
for the selection of all fee-paying boys - boarders and day-boys.

(7)   Your appointment is to be for the period of one year
on probation, and if your appointment is confirmed and accepted
by you at the termination of that period, a formal contract shall
be entered into by the Trustees and yourself embodying the terms
of your appointment.

As the School is a Church of England Foundation, it is
essential, as was pointed out at the Trustees' meeting, that due
regard shall be given to the training of the boys in the doctrines
of the Church of England.

Will you please let me have an acknowledgment of this letter,
confirming your acceptance of the appointment on the above terms
and conditions.

I need scarcely add that the Trustees will be willing at all
times to co-operate with you in the carrying out of your duties,
and to give you every assistance that they possibly can.

Yours faithfully,

Arthur. Reading

Chairman of the Trustees.

Figure 50 - Letter of Appointment to RBCS

Figure 51 - The Bath Road site

buildings and for games.[32] Indeed, the Trustees purchased it for the ridiculous price (nowadays) of £16,750. Thanks to Harry Dunster, they got £11,000 pounds for the old Bath Road site, after the Reading Council's preliminary offer of £5,500 - double the price!

There was so much to do at the school, so many things needed improving or altering. Actually, the school standards in education had been going up gradually, but the whole setup at the Bath Road site was hopelessly handicapped by lack of money, insufficient room to take more pupils (who would have provided more money through additional fees), and thereby insufficient qualified staff, and only a cinder playground. It was "up to Prospect Park" for games. The staff consisted of one senior unqualified master, three "trained teachers" and two pupil teachers - not a degree in sight. Salaries were pretty abysmal but under my predecessor they had begun to crawl out of the depths of the £70/year stage.

All in all it was "move or bust", so we moved, in January 1947 and in what weather - snow and ice on the roads. It took a week, and what a week. The large Pickfords vans ploughed their way through snow and ice simultaneously with our stripping the school of everything movable – a task which in the end I gave to two boys who were persistently in trouble. They really satisfied their lust for destruction, having it last a free hand to smash (certain) things up.

32   The estate covered 46 acres, with extensive frontage to the River Thames at the foot of a steep, wooded hill.

We had one hair-raising episode; at the top of the hill leading down across Southampton Street the vast van responded neither to brakes nor anything else, because of the icy road. So, desperately, we slid down the hill right through the red lights across the cross traffic and, like Saint Paul, "arrived safely at the other side." How on earth we didn't collide with anything on that very busy crossroads I shall never know; Providence must have been working overtime. It was quite a week.

Figure 52 – The front of Holme Park shortly after the move, before the railings were torn out.

I had allocated everything as far as possible to different rooms in the school and all spare stuff (and there was masses of it) which was not needed at once was moved to W, X, Y, Z, these being horse stables, cattle and pig stables, and so on. The Pickfords men at the beginning of the week were full of laughter and bonhomie, but by Saturday the air was getting blue.

Imagine the picture, then, at the beginning of term. An entirely new building, only about four masters and four boys who had been in it, no one except me knowing for sure which rooms had been allocated for what; we hadn't had time to familiarize ourselves properly with the building. Where were the dormitories, where the classrooms, where Sick Bay? - and so forth. We opened on January 1st, 1947, and I'm happy to say that the Trustees all had lunch at the White Hart, Sonning, and took me with them. Not Joyce, unhappily, but (a) it was a stag party and (b) Joyce was much cumbered with family, at that time Jill and David (who was just a year old).

It is useless and impossible to describe the School's gradual development over the next 21 years, so I will try to give a brief picture of it as it was on that day. We lived in the main house to start with. There was no one on the staff who had had any experience of Boarding Schools, so I had perforce to oversee that side of things with a Housemaster.

You went into the School through what was actually the original back gate of the "mansion" - an old chestnut paling gate. On either side were fields, the one on the left being the only playing field in existence then; no pavilion but fenced around as all the fields were. Cattle in the fields on the right, all the way up to the house, opposite which was another field, inevitably fenced all around. No classrooms outside, no tuck shop, no gymnasium, no Sixth Form Block, no Library, no anything in fact! We used rooms in the house as Staff rooms, dormitories and classrooms, and put other classrooms in outbuildings such as ex-stables and other such buildings. Some still bore the legends inscribed by our predecessors, the Royal Veterinary College, who had rented the place from 1939-46 from one Captain Stephenson, who had earlier used it as a Prep School. So you might go to a room which bore the title "Bone Room", "Dissecting Room" or "Path Lab".

Further, the garden had been rented out to a man who was a market gardener. I had a job getting it back for the school and had to appear before an Agricultural Tribunal. Stressing our need of the garden to help feed about 100 souls, I was staggered to be asked by one aging member, "But why, Mr. Inge, do you need the garden at Holme Park when the school is on the Bath Road?" This was at least a year after we had left Bath Road and did not enhance my opinion of official tribunals. I replied gently, as one having pity on a half-wit - and we got the garden back.

I should have mentioned earlier the fact that when I took the school over there were 108 boys, 57 Boarders and 51 Day Boys. We had already started to grow before we left Reading, and were at about 119 when we went to Sonning.

It was a terrible winter for snow, ice and, inevitably, floods. The land between Sonning and Reading was completely flooded on each side of the Thames. As if that wasn't enough, the two 2,000 gallon water tanks on the roof of the house overflowed as their "mechanics" froze up. Joyce and I, amongst others, had water pouring through our bedroom ceiling one night - not,

happily, through the nursery ceiling next door. So we moved up
to the Drawing Room (much later on this became the Office), and
housemaster Tony Davies spent some very noble but extremely
frozen hours trying to save us from even worse deluges, in which he
was fairly but not completely successful - not through lack of effort
though!

*Figure 53 - The rear of Holme Park. BGI's study is the ground floor room to the left
of the arched doorway, and looked out over the rose garden, a goldfish pond and the
extensive Big Lawn.*

Gradually things took shape. The "huts" were moved from
Bath Road to the site they occupied at Holme Park until September
1977, and provided two bitterly cold classrooms. We got sorted
out generally and then the cattle had to go. So I made a pact with
Mr. Laughton, the farmer whose cattle were on the rented fields.
These were very rough and pretty useless for games in their present
condition, but even so football and cricket, through sheer lack of
space elsewhere, had to be played merrily amongst the cowpats for
some time. "If," I said to Mr. Laughton, "you care to plant these two
fields in two successive years, one at a time, with corn, you can have
the entire crop, providing you leave the field level and sown with
grass." He played ball, got a tremendous crop of wheat off each field,
and left the fields in splendid condition. I also took the opportunity
to do some sheaf pitching again, and thoroughly enjoyed myself.

So, the cattle gone, I climbed on a newly-acquired Ferguson
tractor which the Trustees didn't know I had purchased (I don't quite
know how I got away with that one) and hauled hundreds of yards of

136

iron railings out of the ground.[33] I knew it would make things look better, but I was astonished at how much difference it made. The whole school was opened up and became most attractive to see as soon as one got inside the gates.

Figure 54 - RBCS in 1947, on the grass "island" in the gravel drive in front of the main entrance.
BGI and Joyce are seated in the center of the front row; to Joyce's left is Chris Way, Housemaster and BGI's right-hand man for many, many years.

Shortly after this we were told that the Maidenhead bus shelter was for sale, as a new one was being put up. We bought it for £250 and converted it into a cricket pavilion, the big room being where the conductors had rested and the small room being reserved for passengers. Pickfords brought it over in one piece, only the tiles having been removed to save weight. It was an astonishing sight as it moved up the slope at the entrance, like a tile-less ark, and it was then lowered gradually - with the lorry sinking up to two feet in the grass – onto a prepared concrete site. The kitchen and loos were added later by the Parents Association and Old Blues.

Something not many people know about took place somewhere around the 1950s; I was informed just before tea time that the Prefects had all gone on strike. This was apparently due to their taking objection to the work they and the other boys were expected

33   Dad also acquired a set of gang mowers to tow behind the tractor, and could very often be found at weekends mowing the playing fields and big lawn. Tim took over these duties as soon as he could (age 12 or so), driving the tractor and mowing very competently.

Figure 55 - RBCS staff, summer 1949
L-R, back row: Miss Blenkinsop, H. A. Nuttall, H. Price, R. F. Goodings, P. B.
Clarke, B. T. Moraes, Maurice Edelston, Betty Inge
Front row: A. C. Davis, Miss Pougher, BGI, Joyce, F. S. ("Chris") Way, Miss
Falder

to do around the place and which was part of the school tradition, whether it was making paths, sawing up wood, shifting coke (in earlier days), and so on. Anyway, this called for instant action - but what? I had never had a strike on my hands before, and here were all these Prefects without their badges of office, which they had removed, pretending to be ordinary members of the hoi polloi.

Over to the school I went and inspiration came - but would it work? The Prefects always had their tea at high table, but now were sitting at the other tables with their fellows. This of course wrecked the food arrangements, so much being provided at each table for the normal number of boys there. So I simply pitched into them with all guns firing, asking them what on Earth they meant by messing up all the carefully made arrangements for every single table, interfering with the housekeepers' and cooks' work, and more, ad lib - and then walked out. No reference was made to anything else; on went the badges again, and back went the Prefects to their duties.

I don't think I ever knew or worried who was behind it, I was merely thankful at being inspired to take the right line at the right time, but it was a sticky moment. Would they return to duty or not? I was, I think, very lucky, looking back. Had I delivered a tirade on responsibility and maintenance of discipline, I feel I might have come up against a completely blank wall - and then what? Anyway, with common sense on both sides the incident passed off peacefully, with no further reactions (outward, anyway).

This last item was something of a diversion, but I am glad to have recorded it as I think it has evaded the school record, unlike the occasion long, long ago when there were 15 Boarders at the old School, long before my predecessor's time. They all ran away, all except one, poor fellow, who got stuck in the window through which they were emerging.

One of our educational difficulties was getting qualified staff. We were not then "recognized" by the Ministry of Education. Normally no good man would want to come to an unrecognized school, and we couldn't be recognized until we had properly qualified staff. It seemed an insoluble problem, but gradually good men did come, together with some not so good. Eventually, with the loyal help of people like Chris Way and Mick Bertram, we gradually developed a hard core of good staff, around which other good men gathered in time. It was a long process but we battled on, getting fairly frequent visits from HM's inspectors who would usually (and not always fairly) make their criticisms regarding equipment, dormitories, staff, no gymnasium and so on, sometimes very much ad nausea.

Eventually, 12 years later in 1959, we attained recognition, just one year too late for me personally to have the quite considerable benefits available on retirement. For that you have to be on the Burnham scale and recognized for 10 years as a minimum. Due to retire in 1965, that left nearly nine years, and when I tried there was nothing I could do about it. The Trustees were generous when I left, within the limits of their funds, but were quite unable to match Burnham's standards, which would have (both lump sum and pension) come from State funds. This made a considerable difference to my pension and was all the more galling in that my efforts to obtain recognition had benefited everyone on the staff except me! There must be a moral somewhere. That I received as much as I did I feel certain must have been due to the efforts of my very great friend and Trustee, George Dunster, whose advice and help over more than 20 years had proved invariably kind and invariably sound and helpful.

So, as the years went by classrooms sprung up, Science labs developed, as did a tuck shop and Library, cricket pavilion and nets, swimming pool, gymnasium, boathouse, extensions to dormitories,

Figure 56 - Opening of the Dunster Block of classrooms, 26 September, 1955

the creation of Big School (two large rooms thrown together to make an assembly hall) and other items such as epidiascopes[34].

Many of these improvements were provided by funds from the annual fête, the first of which raised £150 in 1947 or 1948, the last one (in 1977) £1,000 pounds. These fêtes were run by Parents and Old Blues together, who gave wonderful support both to the school and to me personally all the time I was there.

But everything which was done to improve the school owed a tremendous amount to individual members of the Staff, whether it was complete reorganization of the Library, or the introduction and development of rowing, or the CCF (Combined Cadet Force). In fact, nothing new could have thrived as it did had it not been for the enthusiastic hard work of the Staff. My annual thanks to them at the Prizegiving always seemed inadequate to me, genuine though they were, but effusiveness might have been worse. Some I could repay when they left by writing a warm testimonial. I remember one Master coming to me with the testimonial I had written in his hand, saying "Thank you very much, Sir." "Is it alright?" I inquired. "All right, Sir?" he said. "I didn't even recognize myself. It was marvelous!" One wins sometimes.

So went on the building up of numbers, standards, introduction of the Sixth Form, the sending of our first boys direct to university, and the widening of sports activities to include rugger,

---

34   Early overhead projectors

Figure 57 - Opening of the swimming pool, 11 July, 1958

county athletics, squash and more cricket and soccer fixtures.

At the same time our own family was growing. Jon joined the family in 1948 on February 17th, and Tim turned up on May 9th, 1950, both young men deciding that the middle of the night was the right time to make their debut. This point of view was not altogether shared by their parents, particularly their Mother who only just got to the nursing home in time before Jon turned up. And that completed a marvelous family, who have given and still continue to give me so much wonderful happiness - a great tribute to the way they were brought up by their Mother. As a matter of rather intriguing interest, when we joined school Jill was 18 months old; when we left, Michael, Jill's son, was 15 months old. So our time at RBCS just covered one generation!

We had a most tremendous "splurge" in 1960, this being the Tercentenary of the opening of the school in 1660. The school was thought to have been <u>founded</u> in 1646, when Richard Aldworth[35] died and his will starting up the school came into legal effect. But thanks to legal wrangles it wasn't <u>opened</u> until 1660. My predecessor had

---

35   Richard Aldworth was a merchant of The Skinners' Company and a Governor of Christ's Hospital; the School was established near St Mary's Minster Church in Reading. Its original name was Aldworth's Hospital, providing "Education and bringing upp of twenty poore male children" and for a "Godly and learned man to be Schoolmaster". The original uniform was a 'Blue Coate and Cappe', based closely on that used by Christ's Hospital.

already issued Tercentenary medals dated 1646-1946, but my Trustees (who didn't seem to know anything about them until I told them) blithely ignored that. They had a new set stamped and printed 1660-1960 – no doubt a puzzle for some future historian if he gets hold of both medals and doesn't know the story behind them.

Figure 58 - A view of RBCS showing the rose garden and goldfish pond. The modern extension to the left is York Dormitory, added in the 1950s on top of the Chapel and Library. The Cottage (Headmaster's house) is just out of the picture to the right.

At the Tercentenary we had a great Thanksgiving service in St. Lawrence's Church, Reading, where the school had worshipped for 275 years before moving to Sonning. This was followed by sherry at the School and then by a splendid lunch, attended by dignitaries, Trustees, the Mayor of Reading and other prominent men, the whole meal being tape-recorded and well lubricated by ample drafts of wine. Then followed the opening of the boathouse (after a walk down a Gaderene slope through the woods), a few more speeches and then, exhausted by it all, we made our way slowly back to school; the boys had been especially well regaled on this day. The lunch took place in a vast marquee on the lawn, in the same place as a quite fantastic farewell party was given by the Parents to Joyce in myself in 1968 - of which a little more later.

Incidentally a photo in the local Reading paper of the top table party at the Tercentenary Dance had underneath it, "Mr. and Mrs. van Straubenzee." Firstly, Bill van Straubenzee (our local MP) was not married, and secondly "Mrs. van Straubenzee" was Joyce!

A more personal major event at the School was Jill's wedding to Tony Stock – my Chemistry Master! – on 6th August, 1966. They were married at St. Andrew's Church in Sonning, and we held the reception at RBCS, with the happy couple descending the grand staircase into the Marble Hall before leaving in Tony's 1946 MG TC. Tim had kept the car safe from pranksters and drove it round to the gravel drive in front of the school for them to climb into.

One day the next year, the School Governors unexpectedly turned up to celebrate my 21 years at RBCS, and gave me a golden key as a symbol of "a perpetual welcome for you at the School". It was a complete surprise, and very delightful one, organized in complete secrecy by Joyce as "a get-together for drinks" occasion!

I wanted to stay on at the School for a few years more after 1968, but the Trustees wouldn't play, and in view of the strain under which I found myself at times (involving disappearances for a break of a week or two), I now think they were right. It wasn't until after I had been retired for some months that I suddenly realized what a tremendous strain I had been working under, and what a huge burden had dropped off my shoulders, like Christian. It probably was time that someone younger and fresh took over, but it was not easy to see it that way at the time.

However, our departure was made at least a little easier by the incredible generosity and kindness of everyone connected with the School towards Joyce in myself during our last term. The CCF presented us with an engraved silver tray, after several abortive attempts to get us on our own after morning prayers! The Staff as usual were most generous with their check, having already marked my 50th and 60th birthdays as well as our Silver Wedding, and they threw a sherry party for us, while the Prefects dined us one night at the George Hotel. The domestic and garden staff combined to present us with a splendid clock, the Trustees gave us a complete set of china in a design of our choice - this was their <u>personal</u> gift - while the Old Blues made a special "do" of their Annual Dinner, inviting ladies as well, and saw us off nobly with a delightful check and a gold watch each.

The climax came with the Parents' "Leaving Party" in a vast marquee on the lawn. The tent was splendidly decorated, the food was magnificent, ditto the wines, and in between various speeches of farewell and of an undeserved generosity, Joyce and I first of all had to withstand the shock of seeing my portrait in oils. (I don't feel quite like the Churchills did about Graham Newland's portrait, but I found

Figure 59 - BGI portrait

and find it difficult to recognize myself.) The portrait had been commissioned by some American parents, the Kents, who had tried to express their appreciation of what the School had done for their youngster, Frank. Following that came the presentation of a superb and large cut glass vase with the School Crest engraved on it, together with my initials and 1946-1968, a very considerable check, and two tickets and all financial arrangements for a fortnight's holiday in Majorca. The final touch came when one Parent also arranged for a car to take us all the way from Pewsey to Gatwick, a most touching gesture.

We were, of course, quite overwhelmed by all this and did our best to express our thanks. What was perhaps the happiest and most moving feature was that the Parents present at this dinner represented those boys we had known all the way from our first days in 1946 right up to the present. Even then the evening wasn't quite over, for two large parents seized me, lifted me on their shoulders, and carried me in state right around the vast marquee[36]. All my family, together with Priscilla, had been invited to the dinner by the Parents, and I was naturally very proud to have them there, though somewhat embarrassed at times. But I believe they all enjoyed the evening thoroughly, and if ever "a good time was had by all" it was on that night - except for one person, for poor old David was sitting there the whole time with a collapsed lung. No one knew it until the next day - nor did he; he just knew he wasn't feeling too good, poor chap.

So, down to earth again the next day, and school proceeded apace. There were the usual "alarms and excursions", and some unusual ones too, but in general life went on much as expected.

So we came to the end of the summer term, and the end of our life at the School. Even that had it slightly humorous side. My term of engagement ended on August 31st, but the Trustees were anxious to get hold of the Cottage where we lived, in order to convert it into offices and a flat for the housekeeper before the next term.

36   Brandy in hand!

144

So, in short: "Could we please manage to leave a month early?" A
month! This only gave us about 10 days after the end of term, which
is no way to hand a School over. Fortunately, I had been (and kept)
in close touch with my successor (Patrick Richardson) so we made
it in time, and as we left the School in a downpour we passed the
delightful new Headmaster's house which the Trustees had decided to
build for the new man.

Actually, the Cottage did need a tremendous lot doing to it[37]
and in many ways it was not by any means the ideal Headmaster's
house, but it did, I think we would agree, make a very delightful
home in which we all found great happiness. So I'm not bitter about
the new Headmaster's house, as I don't think I should like to have left
the Cottage, but the timing of its construction strikes me as slightly
comic, or unfortunate. The School Committee, obviously thinking I
might get pretty upset about it, never discussed any details with me,
and seemed anxious never to mention it in front of me. However, the
School Architect one day very shyly produced the plans (in his office)
and said, "I didn't dare show you these before!" By this time I had got
used to it anyway, and the committee didn't know I'd seen the plans.

I'm not sure I didn't have the last laugh, however. The site
they proposed was barred by the planning authorities, because being
at the bottom of the field it meant another opening into Sonning
Lane, which they - the Planning Authorities - would not allow, and
which I thought was a bad site anyway. So once again, we looked for
another site. I picked what I thought to be the best site, and it was
approved, and there the house sits to this day - unless another tree has
blown down and this time has demolished the house. In spite of my
having had all possibly dangerous trees felled near the site, not long
after my successor moved into the new house a vast elm descended
with very considerable force alongside the house, fortunately without
damage to life or limb (except to those of the tree).

By way of a postscript, most people have been fed up with
their jobs at different times and wanted a change. I was no exception,
and three times during my career was offered posts outside teaching.
One was selling advertising space in an engineering magazine,
another selling refrigerators (Electrolux), and finally as a radio

37   For example, it had no central heating (just two open
fireplaces and an electric water heater) and the single pane, metal framed
windows in the upstairs bedrooms quite often had ice on their inside
surfaces in winter.

announcer for the old Radio Normandy, full of advertisements and very like Radio Luxembourg - the salary for which was £5 a week.

Either the need to give the school a term's notice stopped me from accepting, or some hesitancy as to my capabilities in these other directions - or I just lost my nerve. I don't know which. It's amusing to wonder how I should have ended up in any of these other careers, but I have no regrets at all - once I got my degree - at having stuck to teaching, if only from the vast number of friends I've been able to make. Not to mention a wife whom I collected en route through my career, as it were!

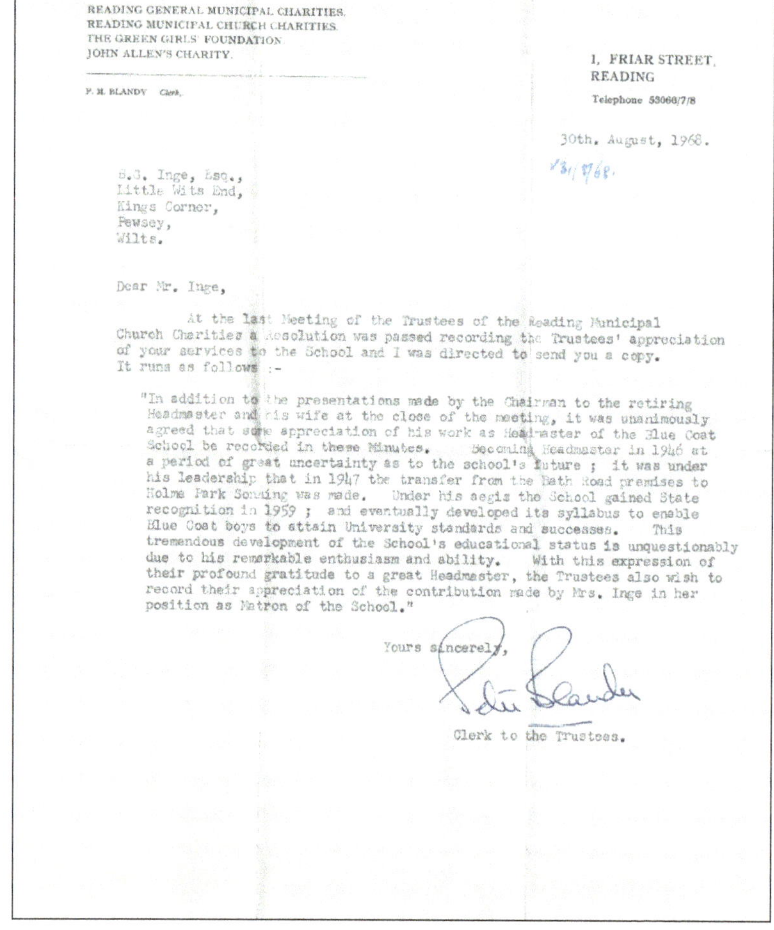

READING GENERAL MUNICIPAL CHARITIES.
READING MUNICIPAL CHURCH CHARITIES.
THE GREEN GIRLS' FOUNDATION
JOHN ALLEN'S CHARITY.

P. M. BLANDY   Clerk.

1, FRIAR STREET,
READING

Telephone 53066/7/8

30th. August, 1968.

B.S. Inge, Esq.,
Little Wits End,
Kings Corner,
Pewsey,
Wilts.

Dear Mr. Inge,

At the last Meeting of the Trustees of the Reading Municipal Church Charities a Resolution was passed recording the Trustees' appreciation of your services to the School and I was directed to send you a copy. It runs as follows :-

"In addition to the presentations made by the Chairman to the retiring Headmaster and his wife at the close of the meeting, it was unanimously agreed that some appreciation of his work as Headmaster of the Blue Coat School be recorded in these Minutes. Becoming Headmaster in 1946 at a period of great uncertainty as to the school's future ; it was under his leadership that in 1947 the transfer from the Bath Road premises to Holme Park Sonning was made. Under his aegis the School gained State recognition in 1959 ; and eventually developed its syllabus to enable Blue Coat boys to attain University standards and successes. This tremendous development of the School's educational status is unquestionably due to his remarkable enthusiasm and ability. With this expression of their profound gratitude to a great Headmaster, the Trustees also wish to record their appreciation of the contribution made by Mrs. Inge in her position as Matron of the School."

Yours sincerely,

Clerk to the Trustees.

Figure 60 - RBCS testimonial

Retirement

So ended that "chapter" in my life, and off we went to Pewsey. We left the school on July 31st, 1968; the removal vans took everything down to Pewsey into store for the night. Joyce and I spent the night "camping out" at *Little Wits End*, and the next day we entered upon our new life. The furniture arrived, various members of the family arrived to help, and we set to to make the place habitable and to turn it into our new home. Everybody worked themselves to the limit, and by the end of August we had our home looking and feeling pretty good. At which point Joyce and I left it all behind and went off to Majorca on the holiday the Parents had so kindly provided, and which they had with touching thoughtfulness arranged to start on the very day after I officially left the school. Some very kindly thinking had gone into the whole thing.

We arrived back a fortnight later in appalling weather. A sort of cloudburst had hit southern England, but, with grateful thanks to Tim who got thoroughly soaked bringing the car to meet us, we did get home after hours of traveling on incredibly flooded roads, and we settled down at last in our new home.

I see that I have not mentioned the splendid holiday Joyce and I had in Canada in 1977, thanks to the generosity and kindness of Tim and Trudy. I doubt if the family have avoided hearing full details of it, but it should be duly recorded, especially as it enabled me to fulfill a 50-year-old wish to visit Canada again. True, not where I wanted to revisit, but Canada is Canada, and Canadians are Canadians, and so I was very happy to renew acquaintance with the country and its people. So there we are.

You know the rest.

However, to round off this record I'm going to write something about games and music, as they have concerned me. Nothing sensational but they had and have a very large place in my life.

And so this "saga" ends, and ends with my most humble and grateful thanks to the one person above all who has made my life such a happy one - Joyce - and with her, to my family, for none of them will ever know fully how much happiness they've given me.

I hope this lengthy account will not seem in anyway boasting or immodest. I have merely tried to give an honest record of what I remember of my life, with some of my views which I hope may be of interest. If in any way I have bored or offended, I beg your forgiveness. Remember, you asked for it -literally!

Should I have failed to explain anything properly, or omitted anything either in full or in detail, which any of you would wish me to have written more about, I shall do my best to comply with your wishes, given due notice. I must have left out a good deal but I can't remember everything at the drop of a hat, and anyway I've had a very full life and a very happy one. Can one ask for more?

Finis coronat opus.[38]

B. G. Inge, January 29th, 1978

---

38   The end crowns the work.

Postscript 1: Games

Games have played such a large part in my enjoyment of life and as this is supposed to be a record of that life, I feel I should put in a little bit about them. They have not only given me great pleasure but have provided me with a very necessary outlet from my abundant (some say super-abundant) energy! Further, they have enabled me to have a very wide circle of friends everywhere I've played in the world, and I like to think that they have helped me to acquire at least to some degree a sense of tolerance and understanding, or appreciation of the other man's point of view. In case this sounds a bit pompous, may I add that games and sports have been the source not only of a tremendous amount of laughter - a sense of humor being essential to the enjoyment of games - but of moments of real hilarity, common to all sportsmen.

Games provide such varied enjoyment, whether going round a golf course on one's own or playing in a team. Some games are far more "sociable" than others, especially cricket, for example. You spend all day in the company of people you like (most of them, anyway), at a game you like, and go down to the local with them all in the evening. There is always much laughter amongst cricketers who do not necessarily regard the game as a sacred ritual. Play it hard, play as well as you can, but having said that, keep a sense of proportion and of humor.

In all games I've always believed in attack. I found that I was very fast and thoroughly enjoyed trying to score goals at hockey or soccer, playing on the wing or at center forward, or hitting out hard - especially sixes - at cricket. Squash satisfied me completely in all respects. In cricket I developed a desire to hit at least one six on every ground I played. This accounted not only for some sensational shots but also for my getting out for 0 on far too many occasions! For the record, when playing a Navy game at Wei-hai-wei in China, I remember hitting the ball out of the ground, over the pavilion and into the sea, where it got very wet.

I was not a good cricketer, but I loved the game and taught myself some of the art of leg-break bowling, which proved a great help to me. Once in China the Americans and British challenged each other to hand ball and cricket. We were hammered at hand ball but, boy oh boy, when I bowled leg breaks I got my own back. The Americans simply could not cope with balls which came so slowly and which changed course <u>after</u> hitting the ground. Had I sent down full tosses they would have hit them to Kingdom come.

And China (of all places) certainly provided us with some odd cricket. The pitch (of matting) and ground were inside the racecourse (as at Ascot, by the way), and as a lucky hit to square leg could easily have landed amongst the ponies and jockeys we had to stop play every time they came into the finishing straight. When that happened, too, the band at the racecourse broke into "galloping" music, so all in all it was quite a show.

But we had another kind of show when the Japanese were with us. During a game we noticed Japanese soldiers exercising over the inside of the racecourse. At the beginning of one over we suddenly noticed that they were advancing straight through us, flinging themselves on the ground and then getting up and charging. The Japanese, as I have mentioned before, being bayonet- and trigger-happy, we stopped playing and remained motionless until the wave of soldiers had passed right through the game and emerged out the other side of us. I frequently had the feeling that this was all very deliberate but we weren't buying that one.

I had a splendid game at Hong Kong (Navy again), and once at Wei-hai-wei had to employ "coarse cricket" tactics to get rid of an excellent batsman, still there at lunch. The usual gins preceded lunch then some of us decided to persuade the batsman to have a glass of port, and, after tremendous difficulty, a second glass. It was hard work, but in the blazing sun the port did its work and it was fascinating to watch this man get gradually a little slower and still a little slower in his strokes, eventually missing the ball altogether. Whereupon, with dignity and with a good score, he retired slowly to the pavilion to sleep it off, while we breathed again.

For some reason this brings to mind a totally different experience. This was at Shirley House, the first school I taught at, where on the occasion of the Parents XI versus the School match, one Father was late. I persuaded the Headmaster (called The Colonel, that being his correct title) if I could substitute in the field for him - all keen I was. He agreed, but regretted it fairly quickly, for in two overs (it being one of my lucky days) I had made two catches, one easy, one difficult, and run out a third victim with one stump to aim at from square leg - thus accounting, unfortunately, for three of the schools best bats. This was too much for The Colonel who shot out of the pavilion and in a parade ground voice warned, "Mr. Inge, you are supposed to be a decrepit old Father!" and removed me pronto from the field. *Vive le sport!*

As I have hinted before, my progress in skill at games was hindered by my inability to play for clubs during term time, owing to School games commitments, but I had some good times in the holidays, especially one summer when I played for Aylsham, near Norwich. There was a cunning 60-year-old slow bowler who welcomed me with open arms as I held lots of catches for him in the slips, where I fielded most of my life. It was at Aylsham also that I was confronted by a harmless looking bowler in brown shirt and brown trousers, and braces[39]. Here we go for six, I said to myself. Wrong again; the ball was fast and straight, and while I carved an immense slice out of the air my stumps were demolished. Never underestimate the enemy.

I once bowled a couple of overs or so for the Parents against Maidenhead Grammar School, for whom Tim was captain and keeping wicket. By that time of life my bowling had deteriorated from being Slow into Dead Slow and almost Stop. I think I got wickets by mesmerism, for the batsman watched the ball in a sort of hypnotic trance as it soared up into the air and made its way slowly up to the other end. The Headmaster, seeing the boys rather puzzled by this, said amiably to me, "I don't think they've seen this sort of bowling before," and who was I to argue with that ambiguous remark. Anyway, they very soon got the hang of it!

One of the best times I had in cricket was when I got up a side called the Yokels (it consisted of friends); a certain cricketing skill was helpful, but not essential. We played on Sundays, I bowled endlessly because I was determined to get all the exercise I could - Len Siney bowled most of the afternoon with me - and we all had a good time, but few if any of us could have told you the result the next day. That wasn't the point of it; what mattered was that we should all enjoy ourselves, the whole object of cricket. I believe you are given a bat to hit the ball with, and hit it as hard as you can, one characteristic I certainly passed on to Tim who nearly decapitated me with a terrific straight drive past my head off my own bowling! No sense of filial

39   Suspenders, for our American readers.

duty, that lad… One Yokel match was played in part in a snowstorm and pouring rain, but we still enjoyed it, at least when we were in the pavilion. *L'audace, toujours l'audace!* I would always rather win (or even lose) a match by five to four or four to five then scrape around defending a one goal lead.

Being a rugger man I had scorned soccer, but at Lowestoft there <u>was</u> no rugger club in 1926, so I took up soccer. Then at Downsend in the holidays I joined a hockey club, and started to play squash with one of the Staff. Tennis was a great favorite of mine, and in those days many people had their own tennis courts and would hold tennis parties on Saturday and even Sunday afternoons. So by the time I got out to China I was more or less capable of playing any game which was available.

Out there I also played softball once, but the oddest experiences were concerned with field hockey. All our teams in Tsingtao were very international, though the cricket team was nearly all Englishmen, for obvious reasons. But sometimes for exercise and pleasure we had "pick-up" games, and for hockey we used to invite some of the women and girls.

Mixed hockey, of course, has long been known as the most dangerous of all games! For some extraordinary reason, charming ladies and attractive girls, who are normally so delightful a part of our lives, become fiends incarnate in the game of mixed hockey. There is no reason for this; it just happens. Given the merciless manner in which women attack the men with their sticks when tackling them, I was prepared for a good deal - but the unexpected always happens.

Once when I was bolting down the pitch at a rate of knots after the ball, the left back, a lady(?), picked up the ball and threw it at me! Fortunately she missed, but she was apparently new to the game and thought that was all part of the fun. Even more extraordinary was another occasion, when again belting down the pitch with the ball, absolutely flat out, I saw looming up a very large German woman, who as before was playing left back. I swerved nimbly to avoid her when she stepped straight into my path, with the inevitable awful collision resulting! There really was a monumental crash. After picking myself up and then her, I apologized profusely for knocking her over, when she smiled amiably and said, "Why do you apologize? Isn't that what I'm supposed to do, get in your way?" She wasn't interested in the ball, just in blocking the body, and seemed well

qualified to join American football. I'm happy to say that while we
stayed on friendly terms socially we never again met on the field of
battle.

I was not always on the receiving end. One Petty Officer
in goal had his peaked hat removed by a shot from me which, on a
rather loose patch of gravel, I had undercut. It was a hard shot but
a brilliant if unintentional save, for the ball instead of going high up
in the net hit him violently on the forehead, knocked off his cap and
went sailing over the bar. But his day was not yet done; in the second
half I sent in a pile-driver, which caught him bang in the middle with
a horrid-sounding crack. His knees buckled (a thing I had never
actually seen before) and he sank almost in slow motion to his knees.
Quite incredibly, he not only recovered quickly but went on playing
in goal - stern stuff, our sailors.

On the other hand it wasn't St. Giles' day either when we
played HMS *Delight's* team, for they had two burly players at back.
Tearing down the field to be met by the ball coming head high at
screaming speed took all our prayers and faith to continue.[40] It really
was frightening, for if one of those clearing shots had hit any of us
we should have been appallingly injured. They dropped these two
players once after we protested, but they turned up again later. It was
the only grumble we had against the Navy, ever!

On another occasion, the school was playing HMS *Suffolk*
on a bitterly cold day, so cold that our opponents played in grey
trousers while we were as usual, bravely but foolishly, in shorts and
the girls on the team in tunics with no stockings. This, by the way,
was the first time I'd ever seen legs <u>really</u> blue with cold! The cold
was so intense that stick after stick snapped, and the joint reserve of
five sticks was soon exhausted. Another stick went; what to do? The
opposing goalkeeper knew the answer. He was the *Suffolk's* Chaplain,
a large and most likeable chap; he offered up his stick, saying that he
preferred to keep his hands in his pockets, "today, anyway." He would
defend his goal with his legs, padded of course, and for anything
higher, with his stomach - which he actually did. It was interesting to
see the amount of rebound there was off his stomach from a hefty hit.

I was once playing soccer for Tsingtao against the crew of
a French cruiser, when trying to push the ball between the legs of a
<u>large French back I trod on the d</u>arn thing, and there was a horrid

40   In field hockey, the ball is supposed to be kept below knee
height.

noise as various bones cracked, etc. It was painful, of course, but members of the French team ran to pick me up. I was about to ask them to go gently, but of all moments it was then that I, who always prided myself on being able to speak French reasonably well, could not remember <u>a single French word</u> of any sort! Pride has its falls. Suddenly one of the French body-bearers, seeing that I wasn't enjoying it much, called out to the others, "*Doucement, doucement*" (gently, gently for, for the uninitiated.). Saved, I ended up taking the trip to my car with a cloud of "Doucements" coming from my mouth like balloons in a cartoon. But fate hadn't finished with me. On the way to the match I had taken some of the staff and pupils down to watch, and they said how comfortable the car was. Airily I replied, "I'm glad of that, but I wouldn't know because I've never sat in the back." Guess where I sat on the way home while someone else drove the car?

Still looking for exercise I took up riding. Now all the ponies we rode out there were Mongolian ponies with mouths like iron, and if they got the bit between their teeth you would only hang on and pray that you could keep on. My particular beast ran away with me once on the stony and very hard rough metal road. There was nothing I could do except sit tight and hope, and eventually the animal ran out of steam, but I didn't enjoy it much! If I thought the pony was feeling a bit too frisky, I used to head him for the hills and point his nose up a long, long slope. By the time he got to the top he was almost ready to eat out of my hand. I wish now I had ridden more, but you can't do everything.

The Club had a ten-pin bowling alley and we all had teams using it regularly, once or twice a week. It really is a most strenuous game, and our limbs were lubricated by beer at the rate of a pint a game - four games being the sum for a match. After that we had Prairie Oysters and hoped that we would feel alright in the morning, which we did.

The other sporting activity which has given me so much fun is golf. I never was good at it, but as with other games I was good enough to give other people a fair game, which is really what matters. Golf has these enormous advantages; you can play it by yourself (though not for preference), you get away from all worries for three to four hours, no telephones, and no official visitors or business. It's a very friendly and sociable game (especially at the 19th hole!), you can find a golf course almost anywhere in the world, you are made welcome at any Golf Club, and you can play with a complete stranger who, within a few holes, might have been a lifelong friend. I played a good deal at Tsingtao with Ian McGillchrist; we even used to go out sometimes when the course was frozen and the pins had been taken out of the holes. We nearly froze, too, but a few hot rums in the bar put that straight.

As usual one has the odd special memories of golf. The Japanese, whose favorite form of play was the three ball, were dead keen on golf and I believe actually owned the Tsingtao course. They had (some of them) some unusual ideas on the correct dress for the game, and I especially cherished the sight of one Japanese who was perfectly attired - except that with his plus fours (a fashion regrettably extinct) he wore short white socks with suspenders. And on one occasion I sliced my drive most horribly, and knocked the club out of the hand of a Japanese golfer who was minding his own business inoffensively on a tee at about 45 degrees from me. I expected wrath and recrimination as he came towards me. A little way off, however, he removed his hat, bowed to me and said, "Verree sorree, verree sorree." There was no answer to that. I tried to apologize but he stuck to his "Verree sorree" and so we both ambled off to our own games.

During the Sino-Japanese war, in order to save petrol the Japanese authorities in Tsingtao banned the use of petrol for cars to take Japanese golfers to the golf course, which was a few miles from the center of the town. It had never occurred to me that the Japanese golfers would disobey such an order, being what they are, but it was surprising and delightful to find that human nature is the same whole world over, for there seem to be very little diminution in the number of Japanese golfers. They merely hired cars or a small bus, drove to the bottom of the hill which led to the golf course and walked up to the clubhouse.

On one occasion I was about to drive off the third tee when Ian quietly said to me, "I should wait a bit if I were you." "Why on earth?" I asked. He pointed to the bunkers about 100 yards ahead, bang in the middle of the course. There was a familiar sight, but in an unfamiliar place; Japanese marines lying undercover behind the bunkers, their rifles and machine guns pointing straight at us! As with the cricket episode mentioned earlier, they were practicing advancing over fairly open ground, but it still makes me feel slightly sick when I think what might have happened had we driven at them and (all too probably) hit one of them. Life had its little excitements.

In winter, apart from bowling we had played quite a bit of billiards, with the occasional game of snooker, and of course amused ourselves with various dice games, especially Liar Dice and Cameroons, at the Club. This was a pleasant place with most of the more usual English magazines and papers available, though of course a little behind the times owing to the distance. Reuters kept us up to date with news bulletins.

I think that about concludes the "sporting" side of this report. I always have wished that I was better at most games, if not all, but I've had tremendous pleasure out of my average ability. And after all, I have played golf at Gleneagles, cricket in China, golf in Hong Kong, Singapore and Royal Blackheath, both sorts of football, hockey, squash, tennis, ten-pin bowls, and have also enjoyed swimming and riding. It would be greedy and ungrateful to ask for more.

And now I have taken in a big way to bowls, now that owing to years and heart trouble I can no longer run and rush about the place. And, as ever, once again I have found a new skill to learn, great companionship, not a little humor and great enjoyment.

Curiously enough it was not for a long time that I found something that I feel sure I could have been good at and which was not affected by my lack of inches - cross country running. I was quite good at school. However, as I grew and developed, if I could have had the training and coaching (which also applies to other sports) I really believe I could have done something. I <u>knew</u> I could do it even at school, just as I knew that my lack of size not only gave me an inferiority complex at <u>other</u> games and sports but definitely hindered me doing well at them. But overall, I have no regrets, just thankfulness for all the fun I've had, and thankfulness too that my body <u>and</u> mind, which insist so relentlessly still on exercise, can now have their needs so readily and conveniently filled by walking.

I suppose my greatest thanks ought to go, oddly enough, to the Turnbulls in Canada for the relentless way in which I was made to stick to jobs, often beyond my strength, thus developing simultaneously an intense dislike of the Turnbulls and a really strong and tough constitution, the process furthered more pleasantly by the Prossers. Considering what a weakling I was at the beginning of my life it must have been a near miracle that I survived as I did, and so again I have much to thank Providence for. Just as I am grateful for the opportunities I had to practice various other sports or watch them being played, which gave me an understanding of them and made one *au fait* with them, even if not deeply.

Amongst these must be mentioned (on the principle I always followed off "trying anything once") Real Tennis played at, of all places, Lords (where there is a court for this variation - actually the original form - of tennis, played with "lopsided" rackets); fly fishing in Scotland (my host's brother caught and displayed a 30-pound salmon! I got nothing); badminton, played once in Hong Kong, basketball in China, and shooting with a 12-bore shotgun lent to me by one of the Trustees. Incidentally, I was wandering around the woods at Holme Park at 6:30 AM one morning when I was nearly shot by the gardener, who in the semi-light mistook me for something else! I went sailing a few times in China and on holiday at Shaldon, and I watched in Shanghai the fantastic game of jai alai, better known in the West as pelota. And I don't know whether going up in a helicopter from the school lawn counts as a sport!

Now, I think, one final story. I was playing cricket on the Merton College grounds at Oxford and banging away merrily as usual, with some success. I had just hoisted a ball satisfactorily to the boundary and was about to play the next ball when the wicketkeeper said, "I should look at your bat if I were you." I did - my bat was split vertically completely in two right up to where the handle was fitted into the blade, and there was at least an inch or two between the two parts. I've wondered ever since just what would have happened had I connected violently with the next ball, for I had noticed nothing at all. Odd, very, but true.

BGI

Postscript 2: Music

This is difficult. There are so many forms of music, but my chief regrets are two. First, that Mother allowed me to stop having music lessons when I was seven because I didn't like them - a most unusual concession on the part of my Victorian parents! Second, that through circumstances my introduction to classical music was so late.

Music of a sort there always was, but this was hymns in church, and hymns on Sunday morning. There were class singing lessons in school, to learn popular old English traditional songs and so on, and then I had to practice singing scales in an effort to get into St. Paul's Cathedral Choir School - and how my family suffered!

Then at St. Paul's we were confronted daily by some chants, anthems, oratorios and so forth, which had the virtue, apart from being splendid choral music, of teaching one to read music at sight easily. I was in the choir at Christ's Hospital and have since sung in choirs in many, many churches. More secular music, such as Gilbert and Sullivan operettas and songs sung as solos at concerts (school and village), gave me tremendous pleasure.

I had a baritone voice which while not sensational apparently pleased many people, but the greatest thrill of my singing life was when we at Ashtead produced a small choir for the villages competitions in the Leith Hill annual festival. By ourselves we were nothing much, but in the evening some 40 choirs combined to sing together the songs we'd been practicing all winter for the competition.

The concert was conducted by the great Vaughan Williams, and I can still feel the indescribable emotional thrill I felt as the massed voices soared in "Blessed Pair of Sirens" and other songs. It was so overwhelming that it was almost impossible to sing at all, but to be one of that triumphant chorus was beyond description. Singing can give one immense pleasure en masse, whether possessed of a good voice or not.

But it is instrumental music which we missed out on so much. It must be remembered that in our youth there were hardly any gramophones (and _no_ radios), and we couldn't afford one anyway. Then when I eventually acquired one, tastes seemed to have depended largely on popular dance records and other music which one "ran across".

In 1925 some Parents gave me a gramophone and some money for records. What to buy? I cannot for the life of me imagine how I made my choices, but I remember very clearly that I bought such diverse records as *"The Parade of the Wooden Soldiers,"* Liszt's Second Hungarian Rhapsody, and the Ballet Egyptian Suite.

So I discovered that I liked most ballet music, and by trial and error my taste gradually developed, but not much until I was in my early 40s. Bach, Beethoven, Brahms - they meant little or nothing to me. They were "classical music," and I had no one to introduce me to them. I think I shied off them because "classical music" was too close to the "classics" such as Dickens (whom I couldn't stand, after one little effort), and as "classics" were "good for one" I instinctively shied away from them.

And now that I have been able, largely through radio and records and TV, to become acquainted with so much lovely music, my regret is greater than ever that I did not merely not know it before, but I was unable to introduce the family to it. Only now, i.e. in recent years, are we all beginning to become even acquainted with much of the wonderful enjoyment of the great classical composers. One can never catch up with it all, of course, but I wish so much that we had all met it earlier. It would be interesting to see how the family's interests develop individually.

I think this may sound as though I am only interested in Beethoven and company. Far from it; my tastes are very Catholic, and include even some modern "pop" and other music. Dance music is always a favorite, choral and solo singing, solo instruments especially the piano - in fact, from The Beatles to Wagner. So be it. One may never become particularly knowledgeable about any composer and remain very ignorant in music in general, but variety is the spice of life.

There is so much to enjoy in life that one simply cannot embrace it all. Neither should one really grieve that one cannot have a complete knowledge of music or anything else unless one is a supreme authority on that subject - and then how much fun would you miss by knowing nothing about so many other things? The world is an exciting place - let's enjoy it.

BGI

160

Postscript 3: Coaching

There is one part of my life and career which I have not
mentioned and which is of no great importance perhaps, but it
may fill in a few gaps and in any case gave me some very pleasant
moments. I refer to coaching, not of games (which I did for so much
of my career) but of academic subjects, in the holidays.

I somehow acquired the information at my first teaching
job that, if you felt like it and could get one, a job coaching boys
in the holidays would be a useful financial help! And as, like all
young schoolmasters in those days, I was more or less permanently
"broke" I thought I would try it. I was told that you got the best jobs
by advertising in *The Times*, a paper I never read and which was
well beyond me both in content and price at that stage of my life.
However, in 1925, in went the advertisement, and I got a job coaching
a boy for five weeks in the summer holidays, four weeks with the
family at Hardelot, near Boulogne, in France, and a further week with
them at Bexhill. For this I got free travel, free staying at the only and
rather posh hotel in Hardelot, and £10 - in those days, untold wealth.

The only snag, which I didn't discover until the first morning
of coaching, was that while I had been engaged to teach the boy
"Science", he and I meant different things. His "Science" meant
the engineering studies and mechanics done at his school (which I
believe from a distance of 50 years was Pangbourne Nautical College),
of which I knew absolutely nothing. "Science" to me meant what we
call Science at school, i.e. chemistry and physics. So there was I, in
France, on the job, with five weeks ahead of me, absolutely stumped.

Eventually we found a little common ground, mostly
trigonometry, and somehow or other I held the fort for five weeks -
and some very uncomfortable moments I had, feeling that I was there
under false pretenses due entirely to neither the boy's Mother (who
interviewed me) nor myself having discussed the word "Science"
or the subject to be taught. It was rather terrible at times, but both
parties survived. I am still astonished that the boy's Father, a *puisne*
(minor) judge (English) from India, never discussed the boy's
progress with me. Had he done so "all would have been lost!"

Apart from that horrible shadow in the background I had

a marvelous time. I was invited one evening at the hotel to join
what seemed to be a family party, one of the ladies coming over to
me as I sat in my lonely chair in black tie (every night of course)
in the lounge and asking me if I would like to join them. So I did,
and we played almost nightly some fairly foolish card games such as
Hearts. The party consisted of two families, one the wife of the top
"policeman" in London (the Chief Commissioner) and her daughter
Pat (the sister, I discovered, of that great English Test cricketer G. O.
Allen) and with them was the daughter of an American Admiral, a
girl called Loveday (I can't recall her last name).

The other family was a Mother also on her own, plus two
sons of 18 and 16 who were at Charterhouse. So we had a handy
four, the 16 year old being naturally excluded from the rest of us. I
suppose our ages were 22 (me), 18, and the girls… about 18, I believe.
We played tennis, swam, went for walks and danced, for there was
dancing every night after dinner - on a stone floor! After I had done
my two hours coaching each morning I was free to do what I liked, go
with my friends or join the family - judge, wife and two boys - with
whom I came out; I only coached one of the boys. His family stayed
in a pension while I was put up at the hotel - a splendid arrangement!

I was given my hotel bill each week, which I then handed to
the judge, who gave me the money plus a small drinks allowance. As
I was TT then, I consumed vast quantities of citronade, an incredibly
sweet sort of lemon squash, and I often think what I could have had
out there in France! I played golf with the judge periodically (and
very badly) at a course which had an old ruined castle inside it, so
that at one hole you drove off the highest tower onto the fairway. It
- the castle - also had the only "oubliette" I have seen; along a dark
passage where undesirable prisoners could be shunted along with
spears behind them, in the dark, unable to see the gap in the floor
through which they disappeared into the depths below.

We danced nightly, as I've said, having split up into two
couples merely by mutual arrangement – Pat and I, and Loveday and
the Charterhouse fellow, Richard. The weather was superb nearly
all the time, with beautiful evenings which led to Richard and me
deciding to walk into Boulogne one night, and back, just for the
fun of it. It was some six or seven miles away and we set off in high
spirits, which, however, flagged a little. So we took off our shoes to
ease our aching feet and paddled along the tarmac until we decided

we weren't going to get there anyway. So we turned around, somehow
got back and crawled through a side window into the hotel about
four in the morning (the hotel being completely shut up at that time),
sinking into exhausted sleep. Richard was alright, he could sleep in,
but I had to go round and coach in a few hours, and kept nodding off
during the lesson. No comment was made, fortunately.

Richard and I once took the girls out to dinner and the
theater, and I only mention it because that was one of the very few
occasions when I wore white tie, tails, white gloves - the lot - <u>which
you were supposed to do if you sat in the stalls of a theater</u>. Then,
later, it became black ties and dinner jackets, and now? I'm probably
being old fashioned when I regret the passing of "tails and white tie,"
but I had never met anything else which made you feel absolutely
looking "the tops". I have worn them occasionally since, twice at
RBCS functions such as the Tercentenary Dance; they make you feel
just great!

One evening while dancing, two of us men with two girls
decided to have a competition (with the girls' assent) to see who
could spin round longest on the dance floor without stopping. I
thought I was going to win this, but suddenly my partner explained
rather hurriedly "a few more turns and I shall be sick". So brakes
were hurriedly applied and we had to acknowledge defeat. What
I've not explained is that the other man in the contest was not
18 year old Richard, but what I then considered to be an elderly
gentleman of perhaps 55(!). He had proved a delightful person and
a good companion, and to my amazement as a "still wet behind the
ears" young Assistant Master in a Prep School turned out to be the
Headmaster of one of the best Public Schools in England - Sedbergh!
You just never know.

He it was who on learning that I had no degree urged me
to get one; "Teaching in a prep school at 30 is hell," he said. I found
later in life that I didn't agree with him, but the advice was welcome.
Further, when I got back to England he sent me a vast box of special
"non-throat" cigarettes, a kindly thought to lead me off the worst
perils of smoking. But his kindness and his even noticing me meant a
tremendous lot to a callow youth.

There was one terrible tragedy while we were out there. A
party of some two dozen French Boy Scouts had been along the beach
paddling, not swimming. Now the beach, a very splendid sandy one,

had lots of "lagoons" along it, which of course were quite invisible with only a few inches of water over the sand, completely hiding the "dips" and "drops" of one or two feet at the most. It was not a rough sea at all, but apparently a long, gentle, rolling wave came in and somehow caught the boys unawares. This must have made them panic because, I repeat, in the deepest shallows there were not more than two feet of water, but thirteen of them were drowned. It was horrible.

Little white coffins were laid in the local Chapel until funerals could be arranged, but what followed was incredible. The hotel band, which played nightly for dancing, continued to do so that night, unbelievably. A crowd gathered in fury outside the hotel where the dance music could clearly be heard, demanding that it be stopped, which, thank heaven, it was.

I would like to end on a happier note about this holiday, so here goes. We had a fancy-dress ball one evening and I went into Boulogne where, for the vast sum of £2 I hired a Red Indian outfit, thus fulfilling another youthful ambition. (The other thing I've always wanted to do is to turn out dressed like a Roman Centurion, but I've had no luck that way.) Anyway, to make the illusion complete, and being in complete ignorance of the principles of makeup, I smeared a sort of red-brown greasepaint all over my face, most of my hands and the front of my neck. I smelled like a walking greasepaint factory and found that partners were rather scarce, much as I fancied myself with headdress and an immense trail of feathers hanging down my back to my feet. Worse was to come; I had the most frightful job getting the greasepaint off, and nearly decided to keep it on until it wore off. Never again.

And so ended that particular coaching job, which I nearly didn't get to anyway because the Passport Office (then as now?) ignored my instructions to send the passport to my school and sent it home. 24 hours to go, and no passport. I roared up to the Passport Office and explained what had happened; I produced the only spare photo I had, and they issued me with the new one on the spot. A narrow escape indeed.

One other sporting activity I indulged in was sand yachting at Hardelot. A few local chaps had these, and they were great fun, both tearing along and sometimes with two wheels only on the sand (out of three), tilting well over in the breeze, and then spinning the

craft right around on its own axis in order to stop. Just another thing
for the record, that's all. They were most generous with their loan of
the yachts, along three miles of sand.

Another post I had was coaching an 11-year-old who lived
at Richard's Castle near Ludlow, with his widowed Mother. This was
just a pleasant ordinary job, resident of course, because I neither
applied for nor wanted anything else, in lovely country. However,
after a week we went off on holiday by car to Borth, in North Wales.
Borth is known locally as the "despair of would-be suicides by
drowning", for the bathing is so safe and the beach so even, gentle and
level, that it is claimed to be impossible to drown, however hard you
try. Later on the boy's Mother invited me out to dinner and a theater.

This coaching business so often involved staying in pleasant
hotels, free of course, which saved the expense of "digs" etc. in
holidays. I seldom used to go home, as I knew no one outside the
family and preferred to be amongst the parents and friends I knew
around the school.

Another year I got a job (again through *The Times*), coaching
a boy of 11 or 12 in London. I was to stay in the hotel and, apart
from two hours coaching in the morning, my time was absolutely
my own. Staying free in a hotel in London? Heaven! Otherwise that
was just an ordinary job. I had another two weeks once staying in
Hampstead with a doctor whose son I was teaching at Downsend. A
very pleasant time, and the doctor and I played golf regularly every
Thursday - his day off - at Stanmore.

Often in the holidays when I was teaching at Downsend I
would have local boys to coach. On one holiday I had three boys
to coach, one hour each daily. Fortunately, I had my OK Supreme
motorbike then, so by haring around from house to house I managed
to fit them all in before lunch. Rates of pay then were ten shillings
an hour (50p) if visiting, resident £4 a week, which with free board
wasn't too bad and helped enormously during the holidays.

This was especially so as Prep Schools then only paid their
staff at half term, or sometimes only at the end of term. The result
was that, for instance, you felt as rich as Croesus at, say, the end of
July, having a full terms salary in hand, but you were inevitably broke
before the end of the holidays. Worse, you had nothing coming
in until the next half term or even in some cases until just before
Christmas. An iniquitous business, especially as the Headmasters of

all these privately-owned schools insisted naturally that all school fees
must be paid before the beginning of term, so they had the interest on
the fees for a couple of months increased merely by not paying their
staff monthly.

I might add that many of us found it impossible to live
this way, especially when married, and we eventually persuaded
Headmasters to pay us monthly like anybody else. We had grumbles
of "complications", etc., but ignored them and got our pay properly
each month. We started this at the Dragon school, a few of us, and
I believe it is now common practice there, as it certainly is at most if
not all other schools. Certainly it is so with all State schools.

BGI

Postcript 4: Royal Navy Ships Visited

<u>List of HM Ships we met in Tsingtao</u>
(we also played hockey against most of them)
<u>Cruisers</u>:
HMS *Suffolk*
HMS *Dorsetshire* (I traveled from Tsingtao to Hong Kong in her)
HMS *Birmingham* (Tony Blackley[41] served on this ship!)
HMS *Kent*
HMS *Cardiff*
<u>Destroyers</u>:
HMS *Duncan*
HMS *Delight*
HMS *Daring*
HMS *Defender*
HMS *Duchess*
HMS *Decoy*
HMS *Dainty*
HMS *Diamond*
HMS *Diana*
<u>Sloops</u>:
HMS *Grimsby*
HMS *Berwick*
HMS *Folkestone*
HMS *Lowestoft*

<u>Additional ships I travelled on, lived on or visited</u>:
- HMS *Medway* – submarine depot ship, stayed on board twice for 1-2 weeks
- Several HMS submarines, including HMS *Perseus*
- HMS *Adventure* – minelayer, acting as a target-tower for gunnery practice.

NB: In the harbor at Hong Kong there was – and perhaps still is – an aged sloop named HMS *Cornflower*. It happened that she started to leak, so she was towed to dry dock where her hull was filled with a concrete lining to keep out the water. This done, the dock was

41   Brother-in-law; after the war he married Joyce's sister, Bunty.

flooded in order to let the ship pass out into the harbor.

The water rose - but the *Cornflower* didn't. They had rather overdone the cement!

BGI

Appendix 1: Filling in a Few Gaps

Jon Inge

Dad left out quite a lot about his life after he started at RBCS, on the assumption that those (the immediate family) who'd pressured him to write this "Saga", as we always called it, would already be familiar with the details. Not entirely true and in any event for those outside the immediate family I thought it worthwhile to add a few comments to round out the story.

Dad didn't mention much about his own parents, other than that his father Walter wasn't around much after the war. The school he started having gone broke in 1912, Walter signed up for the Army and doesn't seem to have re-joined family life, then or after the war, in any meaningful way. Family lore has it that he had joined Military Intelligence - there's a shipping manifest showing him crossing the Atlantic on his way to Guatemala in 1912 – and he was listed as a Captain in the South Staffordshire Regiment in 1916. At point he gave the family house on Dunsany Road, London (where they'd moved from Kent in 1915) as his residence.

Figure 61 - Walter Inge

If so, he wasn't there very often. Another manifest has him returning to England in December 1925 from an unknown location, and census records for 1933 show him living in Hammersmith with one of his relatives. Dad's brother Ron, after he graduated from college, had bought a house in Kent in 1924 and moved the rest of the family there. Walter's financial support of his wife Edith (née Ely) and six children (Margaret ("Marnie"), Ron, Norah, Dad, Yvonne ("Betty") and Daphne) was minimal at best, and it was only thanks to the support of various Ely relatives that they could afford the house on Dunsany Road at all.

Knowing Ron's generous nature and sense of responsibility, I suspect that he sent most of his Navy and Air Force pay home to his mother Edith to help support the family. The children's higher education was entirely dependent on their getting full scholarships to whichever establishment they wanted to attend, but fortunately they were all up to the task. These financial straits also explain Edith's mandate that Norah not go into missionary service right after school; she already had two missionary daughters and knew how little the profession paid.

Figure 62 - BGI's mother Edith Ely and her family
l-r: Edith, Alan, Milton, Anna Selina Ely, Arnold, Joseph Bird Ely, Bernard, Ethel

Mum told me that Walter continued to work in Military Intelligence in Central America and the Caribbean, and contracted a tropical disease there in the late 1930s that he declined to have treated. He returned to the UK but the disease had progressed too far, and he died in London in February 1940. Edith outlived him by another ten years.

One of the most striking things about my parents to me was the bond they had from the very start. When they met Mum was just 14 and he was twice her age! When he left for China in July 1935 he was 32 and she was still only 17. He certainly wrote to her from there; I don't know how often but she kept the stamps from his letters in an envelope. I haven't found any of the letters themselves.

When he asked her to marry him in September 1940 (by telegram), when he was 37 and she'd just turned 22, she didn't hesitate despite their age difference and her not having seen him for five

170

Figure 63 - letter to Joyce (at her father's retirement address) from Tsingtao

Figure 64 - From Tsingtao through Hong Kong on 21st May, 1940

Figure 65 - Amongst the stamps Joyce kept from his letters are these, including from his vacation in Peking just before he left China, and from Hong Kong and the US on his way home. I wonder if she received these letters before he arrived himself!

years. She borrowed a bicycle, rode to the Post Office and sent a one-word telegram ("Yes") to China, in wartime! He returned to England in January 1942; on April 7, aged 23, she married a man she hadn't seen since she was 17.

Their bond never wavered; her support for him was total and loving their whole life. Whatever would help him and school was exactly what she would do, with grace, love and a wonderful smile, and he appreciated and loved her totally in return.

Originally housed in a few rooms in the main school building (where the ceiling leaks Dad referred to occurred that first 1947 winter), the family soon moved into The Cottage. Just across the yard from the school kitchen, this had originally been a coach house (converted to a workshop) facing on to the yard, with various rooms at the rear where we lived, overlooking a garden.

After a year or so the upper levels of the building were remodeled (I remember it happening, so it must have been around 1951 or so), with a floor installed across the upper part of the coach house/workshop to create two new bedrooms (for Jill and

David) and a bathroom. There were two other upstairs bedrooms, one for Mum and Dad, and one for Tim and me. Our old bedrooms downstairs were then usable as guest bedrooms, though not

Figure 66 - The Cottage (the family home at RBCS) in 1994 after it had been made into offices. The upper window of the main school building on the right is the apartment where we lived while The Cottage was converted into a home. The circular flower bed was originally a huge water tower.

Figure 67 - The garden behind The Cottage
Painted by Dad's sister Yvonne ("Betty"), who taught art at RBCS. She took a little artistic licence with it - there were actually four silver birch trees in a row in front of the artist, not one, and a second tall acacia tree in the flower bed at centre – but it captures well the beautiful results of Mum and Dad's efforts.

conveniently; one had to go through the first bedroom to get to the second, and the only downstairs toilet was at the other end of the house, by the back door!

The amount of energy and enthusiasm Dad put into the School was truly amazing. As others have noted, he would head over to his study around 7:00 am to go through the morning post, then into breakfast with the boarders and staff. In the evenings he would return to The Cottage for dinner, but then often go back to the school to talk with staff members, check on a project or help some pupils with one-on-one coaching. After Tim started at school and Mum was free to start full-time work as the school Matron, Dad would often stay to have dinner with the boarders and staff; dinners for us children would be sent over from the school kitchen as Mum no longer had time to cook for us.

At weekends he would lead work parties of boys into the woods to collect firewood for the school's many fireplaces, or drive the tractor and gang-mowers to keep the playing fields usable. On walks around the school grounds with us at weekends he always had a walking stick with him, not for support but to wreak havoc among the stinging nettles and blackberry canes encroaching on the paths. When we went on family excursions, whether on holiday or at weekends, he would lead us on extensive walks for exercise, and encouraged our understanding of and love for nature. At the beach he'd lead us on scrambles over the rocks, turning over clumps of seaweed to show us the crabs hiding underneath.

But he didn't always enjoy the best of health. He mentions his stress-caused issues in China; he was also a long-time smoker, first with cigarettes (Olivier), and then, on his doctor's recommendation, pipe tobacco (Three Nuns Empire, which kept Tim and I well supplied with useful tins to put things in; I still have a couple!). We often tried surreptitiously to take the burning pipe from his mouth when he dozed off watching TV, but always woke him. After retirement he had a cataract operation and was ordered to give up smoking to avoid irritating his eyes. During a six-month check-up he mentioned his frustration with this and was told it was supposed to have been only for a week, so he went back to tobacco only to find that it had become far too expensive and made him cough! So that was that.

In his 50s he had at least one episode of a slipped disc, which laid him up for a few weeks in traction. He was confined to bed at home, with a heavy weight strapped to his leg on a cord that went over a pulley at the foot of the bed. He could pick it up and carry it to walk to the bathroom, but otherwise was not allowed out of bed for at least two weeks. Nonetheless, as soon as he was better he returned to his usual vigour and relentless pace.

As he noted the RBCS buildings were a great foundation for a school, but needed very considerable development to bring the facilities up to government standards. I remember the construction of the swimming pool, the Dunster block of classrooms, the addition of York Dormitory over the Chapel/Library, installation of oil-fired central heating with two massive boilers under the kitchen (in what had once been the coal cellar), the Boat House on the river and the construction of the woodworking shop. All of these, and everything else that was added later such as a gymnasium and Sixth Form Centre, were major projects for which he had to raise funds and constantly monitor progress.

A big fund-raiser every year was the School Fête, held on the Big Lawn. Two huge marquee tents were erected for covered stalls and the performance of a play, and many other stalls were set up on

Figure 68 - Big Lawn

the lawn. Mum and some of the female staff would spend hours creating beautiful small posies, which they would lay out on woven baskets and sell to pupils' mothers as they strolled around the lawn. Dad would escort the Mayor of Reading, our local MP and other dignitaries throughout the afternoon.

Dad was responsible for hiring all staff (teaching and domestic) and for maintaining good relations with all the parents, on whose willingness to keep paying school fees the entire operation rested. As in China, many of the boarders came from families based overseas. Their travel schedules at term end meant that a few pupils sometimes had to stay on for a day or two after term had officially ended, and Mum and Dad acted as surrogate parents for that time. As Mum was responsible for organising the boarders' laundry as well as for the Sick

Figure 69 - The RBCS Fête, 1948
L-R Mum, David, Dad, General Sir Andrew and Lady Thorne

Bay and everyone's general health, there was a pretty strong family feeling in the school anyway.

Mum and Dad took a group of pupils to Switzerland every Easter for a 7-10 day walking holiday, usually to somewhere different every year – Interlaken, Grindelwald, etc.– making all the travel and accommodation arrangements themselves. They arranged for a sitter - one Miss Egar, from Harrogate - to stay with us while they were gone. We always looked forward to the gifts they'd bring back: model chalets, cuckoo clocks, toys and wonderful Swiss chocolate!

Christmas was a major event, of course. Christmas Dinner in the school dining rooms was the full, traditional feast, to which we children were invited. Mum made centrepieces for each of the dozen or so tables, using logs stood on end, covered with plaster of Paris at their upper ends to resemble snow. Little figures, fir trees and cottages were embedded in the plaster to create small mountain scenes, along with a couple of candles. In the evening our village doctor, Dr. Hammond, would arrive dressed as Father Christmas, and would distribute gifts to each and every child (including us) from the pile under the huge Christmas tree in the marble entry hall. Mum and other staff members did all the gift buying and wrapping, with knowledge of what each child's interests were, an amazing annual task for a school of around 150 boarders. And Dad knew every one by name, as well as their parents, with whom he stayed in touch throughout his time at RBCS and well into retirement.

Speaking of names, as happens to all teachers he acquired a nickname, in his case "Chad". In the early 1950s, when strict rationing was still in effect, a little cartoon character called Chad regularly appeared in the newspapers, hanging over a wall and complaining about the latest shortage: "Wot, no eggs?", "Wot, no bacon?" etc. One frosty morning at RBCS Dad was late arriving for breakfast, keeping everyone waiting; one of the boys quickly drew Chad in the condensation on one of the windows, with the caption, "Wot, no Headmaster?" It met with instant approval, and stuck for the rest of his life there.

Figure 70 - Chad

He mentioned his abiding love of singing, especially Gilbert & Sullivan operettas, and he often took us to local G&S performances in Reading and Windsor. He also sang in the St. Andrew's Church choir every Sunday, and often just when walking around the house and school. I recall one RBCS concert where he led the boys and parents in four successive choruses of "Land of Hope and Glory", just because he found it so thrilling to sing! A love of the stage and especially comedy made trips to London to see Brian Rix farces a regular occurrence, and he delighted in driving around the City beforehand introducing us to its various landmarks.

Speaking of comedy he had a keen ear for a good pun, in Latin or Greek as well as English, and enjoyed swapping jokes in Greek or Latin with his brother Ron and the more erudite cousins such as Philip and Priscilla Oakeshott. A favourite was this well-known Latin "verse":

> Civile si ergo,
> fortibus es in ero.
> O nobile deus trux.
> Votis inem Causan dux.

which looks like Latin but doesn't make any sense. However, if you read it phonetically comes out as:

See Willie, see 'er go!
Forty buses in a row!
Oh no Billie, dey is trucks.
What is in 'em? Cows and ducks!

He was very fond of nonsense rhymes (Lewis Carroll was
a favourite), and often amused himself (and others) by writing
impromptu doggerel poetry, such as:

<u>My Father's a Poet!</u> (so said David)
My Father's a poet
And my word does he know it.
He just churns out verse
Getting steadily worse.
You can't get him to stop
Till he's ready to drop.
Now my rhyming has fled
And I MUST go to bed.

Retirement to Pewsey was very hard for him, initially. The
Trustees refusal to extend his service at RBCS for the short time
needed to qualify him for the higher Burnham-scale retirement felt
especially personal, as did their decision to build his successor a
new house at a considerable distance from the school. The Cottage
may have needed a lot of work, but the new house was much larger
and more modern, and its location meant that the new Headmaster
wouldn't be able to stay in such close contact with the boys and staff,
something Dad believed was essential at a boarding school. He had
always had to fight the Board of Trustees hard for funds for the school
projects, and despite active and solid support from the Dunster
brothers and a couple of others, he must have made a few enemies
along the way.

The reduced pension available to him limited his and Mum's
search for a retirement home, and they looked at several options
before deciding on Pewsey. They'd already selected the *"Little Wits
End"* name for it, knowing that "Little" was all they'd be able to afford
and that they'd be at their wits' end by the time they found it! After
finding the house he quickly reported back to us that he'd walked
from the house to the Post Office in the village, and passed thirteen

Figure 71 - Little Wits End, Pewsey

pubs on the way! (We're not sure he actually *passed* all of them…)

The state of the house at least gave him a number of significant projects to keep him occupied. Originally three small dwellings in a row, walls were demolished to make it into one, staircases and central heating installed, carpets laid and the whole place rewired, replumbed and redecorated. As it had been at Sonning, their new home was full of mementoes from Dad's travels.

Then there was a garage to put up, a brick terrace to lay and the whole garden to be dug over and planted, all of which were excellent outlets for his still-abundant energy. Mum joined him in all of these projects, including laying the brick terrace and planting the garden, which became just as beautiful as the one they'd made at The Cottage.

He joined the local lawn bowls club, developing his knack for spin bowling at cricket into the subtleties of curving a ball towards a target at ground level, and was active enough to be named Member of the Year in his second year. Still looking to occupy his time and feel productive, he was delighted to be asked to help a local school with a building expansion project, his years of experience of such things at RBCS proving invaluable. He took a teaching job in Devizes as he really missed the contact with eager pupils. However, the driving became an increasingly tiring factor, especially in winter over snowy roads, and he had to give that up after a few years.

The past popped up for him unexpectedly one evening in

1983 while watching an episode of the BBC TV program "*This is Your Life*", featuring Bob Arnott, Captain of the Cunard liner *Queen Elizabeth II*.

One featured episode was in May 1942 when Mr. Arnott, then a midshipman on the SS *Antilochus*, rescued one Peter Jackson from a lifeboat in the Caribbean after his ship had been torpedoed. They became friends, both joining Cunard Lines after the war. Mr. Jackson rose to command the QE2 and eventually became Senior Master at Cunard; Mr. Arnott took over the QE2 from him.

The ship Mr. Jackson had been on? The SS *Mentor*; she'd been sunk by a u-boat one day out from New Orleans on her way to Bombay. Dad wrote to Captain Jackson to see if they'd met on the *Mentor* on Dad's voyage home from China, and on 19th April, 1983, received a courteous note back regretting that they hadn't, but only by chance. He should have been on the *Mentor* during that trip but had been hospitalized in Glasgow with appendicitis and missed it, rejoining the *Mentor* in Liverpool in January 1942, a couple of days after she'd brought Dad home!

The *Mentor* then left Liverpool on Friday 13th February, 1942, for the Panama Canal and Singapore, but suffered heavy weather damage crossing the Atlantic and put into Bermuda for repairs. By the time she left Bermuda on Friday 13th March (was fate being tempted?) Singapore had fallen to the Japanese and she was diverted to New Orleans, where she stayed for ten weeks. Re-routed to Bombay, she left on 26th May, 1942, and was torpedoed in the Caribbean the next day. Mr. Jackson the the rest of the survivors had been in their lifeboat for a day when they were rescued by the *Antilochus*. His memory confirmed Dad's that the *Mentor* was "very austere and spartan" with "awful food."

Exercise in some form was essential to Dad, and his regular walks throughout the local countryside were immensely rewarding, not just for the exercise itself but also to keep in touch with the natural world he had always loved so much. An allotment in the village allowed him to grow many vegetables for the house; he always loved growing things, whether they be plants or young people.

Eventually his joints, muscles and heart began to fail him, to his intense frustration. He acquired a small electric scooter, which he used not only for getting into the village but also for driving around the garden with a hosepipe, watering the flowerbeds. A chairlift was installed to help him get upstairs to the bedroom and bathroom, and he delighted in giving rides on it to the grandchildren, whose parents found it invaluable for transferring their suitcases up the narrow stairs during visits!

In failing health for several years, at 86 he finally succumbed very suddenly, on 29 October, 1989, just after sitting down on the chairlift, from either a stroke or an aneurysm of some kind.

Mum stayed on at Little Wits End for the next 15 years, on her own but visited often by family and friends, not only from Pewsey but also from their many contacts among the parents and old boys from RBCS around the world. She stayed active in the local Women's Institute branch and helped out in the local tea shop, printing the church parish newsletter on a duplicator and contributing to village life in any way she could. Her own health gave out gradually over the years, and she died from cancer on 27th August, 2004 in hospital in Salisbury, just before her 86th birthday.

They were a truly remarkable couple.

- Jon Inge, April 2024

Figure 72 - Mum and Dad, 1974

Appendix 2: Admirable Siblings

Dad certainly had an adventurous life, but the rest of his siblings were equally remarkable in their willingness to travel and to "do the right thing." Details on their lives will be covered in a separate volume, but the following brief summaries will give an idea of the strength of their characters. The rest of us have a lot to live up to.

Marnie

Margaret "Marnie" Kingsford Inge (10 June 1896 – 5 Jan 1958). Marnie married the Rev. Geoffrey Morris Oakeshott on 4 July 1925. Sadly their first child, Margaret, died within her first month (1928), but they had four other children: Nigel (b. 1929), Phil (1931), Priscilla (1933) and Beth (1938).

As a minister Geoff had the livings at Pertenhall and Swineshead in Bedfordshire, but in 1938 was sent to Punta Arenas, Chile, on a three-year missionary assignment to run the Anglican Society there. They took the two young girls with them; Nigel and Phil followed in 1939, going down unaccompanied (aged 10 and 8!) on a freighter.

The family lived in Punta Arenas until December 1944; the contract was up in 1942 but no-one wanted six non-combatants back in the UK. Geoff continued teaching, at a small school he'd started there and also when they moved to Argentina, to the Buenos Aires suburb of Quilmes where he worked at St. George's College. After the war they returned to the UK, arriving in January 1947; Geoff became Rector of Barton le Clay, in Bedfordshire. His health was not good, and he died on 30th October 1955.

Nigel bought a house in Spalding in the spring of 1956, and Marnie and Beth moved there. Her health deteriorated, however, and she died on January 5th 1958, age 61.

Ron

<u>Ronald Morice Paul Inge</u> (22 Jan 1898 – 23 July 1974). Ron
lied about his age to join the Royal Navy
at the outbreak of war (he was 16 and told
them he was 18). Two years later he joined
the new-formed Royal Naval Air Service
(the forerunner to the RAF) as an observer.
Shot down in the English Channel twice,
the Germans rescued him the second time
and put him in a POW camp. He escaped
three times but was recaptured each time.

After being repatriated after the
war he took two months leave to recover his badly-affected health.
However, feeling that he hadn't sufficiently done his duty, in 1919
he volunteered for the Archangel Force, an Allied effort fighting on
the side of the White Russians in North Russia to prevent military
equipment falling into the hands of the Bolsheviks. His plane crashed
again and injured his back, arm and leg, and he was sent back to
England. (I have his photo album from this campaign.)

He entered Jesus College, Cambridge, had to take a year out
for back surgery (he wore a back brace for the rest of his life) and
graduated in 1924 in Mediaeval and Modern Languages. Father
Walter having left the family without support, Ron took responsibility
for mother Edith and his two younger sisters, Betty and Daphne,
rented a considerable mansion in Hawkhurst, Kent, and started a
tutoring establishment for boys.

Three years later (1927) as his sisters became self-supporting,
he gave up the Hawkhurst house, took a 16th Century cottage
in Rolvenden as a family base for Edith and became a resident
schoolmaster, starting at Stowe. The next year he moved to Campbell
College, Belfast, where he taught for the next 32 years.

In 1941 he took a leave of absence to rejoin the RAF (still
feeling that he hadn't done his duty), serving at home and in air traffic
control in Ceylon. Post-war he returned to Campbell, teaching with
distinction and retiring in 1960.

He then taught at Wymondham School, Norfolk, and bought
a bungalow in Sproughton, Suffolk. Norah joined him there after

retiring from teaching in Leicester, and Betty moved in in April 1964. He became a strong supporter of the local church as a Diocesan Reader, often taking two services on a Sunday. He also did much work for the Samaritans, and was a part-time guide/lecturer for the National Trust. Ron passed away on 23 July, 1974, at Sproughton.

Norah

<u>Norah Newbury Inge</u> (14 August, 1900 – 15 Sep, 1995).

Norah had always leaned towards missionary work, joining the missionary volunteers at college. However, her mother Edith insisted on a different profession because of its low pay; she feared debt very strongly.

Norah became a maths teacher instead, but kept in touch with the missionary society. In 1933/4 she was asked to go to Kandy, Ceylon, where the missionaries were desperate for a maths teacher. Returning to England in 1936 she was given proper missionary training, and was then assigned to a post in Singapore. When war broke out in Europe in 1939 she carried on teaching and working to establish Girl Guide troops there. Dad dropped in to see her in late 1941 (Sep/Oct) on his way home from Tsingtao.

The Japanese invaded Malaya on December 8, 1941, the day after Pearl Harbor. As the Japanese forces drove south through Malaya the British police rounded up all Japanese citizens living there (it was a British protectorate) and sent them to Singapore for internment.

Per the Geneva Convention, responsibility for internees fell to the civilian police, not the armed forces. Norah had become good friends with the Police Commissioner and his wife, a fellow Girl Guide Commissioner. When the Police Commissioner needed someone who could organize a group of 200-300 people his wife recommended Norah, who'd very competently organized Guide camps of that size. She was given a locked dispatch bag with a key to wear around her neck, and was told "When you get to wherever you're going, give that to whoever you find. Whatever you do, we'll say it's right."

The male internees were housed in Changi Gaol on Singapore

island, but 978 women and children were sent to St. John's Island, just south of Singapore island, under Norah's supervision. After six weeks, at the end of January 1942 and with the Japanese closing in (they invaded Singapore on February 8), the women and children (and Norah) were put on a British India ship heading south, with no declared destination.

Five days later they landed in Calcutta, India. They were sent to New Delhi to be reunited with 2,000 male Japanese internees, and all were housed in 8-person tents inside an old walled fort in the desert. After about 18 months in the fort, in late summer 1943, everyone was moved to barracks buildings in Deoli, Rajasthan, about 270 miles SW of Delhi and far out in the desert. They lived in rooms in several wings, so families no longer had to share tents.

In other wings (not under Norah's control) there were some 400 Germans, several hundred Italians and about 60 Javanese. The camp also had three anti-Nazi German doctors "who were magnificent, truly excellent professionals," according to Norah.

The police guards were often rotated out of duty every three months because the harsh climate was tough on everyone, but Norah wasn't allowed to leave; she'd been told she had to stay with the Japanese until the end of the war, as she was their only link back to Singapore. Her health suffered badly as a result, and she caught beri-beri, malaria, dengue fever, dysentery, pneumonia and whatever else was going around. She was never really free of anything, but survived thanks to the German doctors.

After VJ Day the internees became increasingly restive at the delay in their being repatriated, and eventually rioted for several days. The riot was only stopped by the police shooting; about 40 were killed. Arrangements were finally made for the internees to leave on a ship in June 1946. Norah was allowed to leave for home in May and took a train to Bombay; she still had to wait five weeks for a ship, but finally got a berth on the "*Andes*", arriving in Southampton on 4th June, 1946.

Word of her experiences eventually reached the Imperial War Museum, and she agreed to be interviewed by them for their archives. Recordings of these six interviews are now in the family archives.

Norah had been promised that she wouldn't have to go back to Singapore, but the staff and pupils at her old school wrote to the bishop and implored him to send her back – so she went. She returned in 1947, and a year later became Principal of St. Margaret's Primary School, the oldest school in Singapore, retiring in 1958.

Her bishop then posted her to the school board, and subsequently to a school for the blind. She remained heavily involved in the Girl Guide movement, being awarded the Medal of Merit in 1950 and the Beaver Award for services to Guiding in 1959, and serving as Colony Commissioner until Singapore's independence in 1965.

Norah finally returned to England for good shortly thereafter and retired to her brother Ron's house in Sproughton, Ipswich, along with her sister Betty. When Ron died in 1974 she and Betty moved to a nursing home in Wantage, Berks, where (of course) she became involved in its administration. Norah died there in 1995, a born administrator and remarkable woman.

Betty

<u>Yvonne Florence Inge</u> (27 October, 1904 – 16 July, 1985). Despite her given names, she was somehow linked to the name "Betsy Jane", possibly after a popular doll of the time, and was thereafter known to parts of the family as Betty and to others as Jane.

She moved around with the family from Kent to London and back to Kent, attending St. Paul's Girls School en route and then joining her mother Edith and brother Ron in Rolvenden, Kent. Not much is recorded about Betty's life from here until after the war, but she did work for a while as a tutor to a family in Stuttgart, Germany. It's not noted when Betty's artistic talents first became apparent, but she was certainly an accomplished artist.

At some point in her late teens Betty came down with diabetes. Complications set in during her late 30s/early 40s; she had first one toe amputated, then the remaining toes, and eventually she had to have her left leg amputated. She was fitted with a metal artificial leg (which she called Reggie, after the surgeon/consultant who treated her and with whom she became good friends), a handicap which she never let slow her down.

In 1947 Dad hired her as Art Teacher at RBCS. She moved

into a one-room corner apartment in the main school building, with views over the grounds in two directions but at the top of three flights of stone stairs. Despite having to climb those stairs several times a day with an artificial leg, she never complained.

She acquired and learned to drive "Ladybird", a three-wheeled invalid carriage which she painted to resemble the insect, and became a well-known local sight in it. Later she exchanged this for a more robust but still three-wheeled Reliant car, converted with hand controls (an accelerator lever on the right side of the steering wheel and a stiff pull-lever for the clutch mounted to the gear lever), which she called just "The Bug".

Her health was never good, and she spent much time in Battle Hospital, Reading for problems with her spine. She spent the rest of her life wearing a plastic neck collar to support her head. Her left wrist also gave her trouble, no doubt triggered by the hand clutch lever on The Bug, and she often wore a plastic wrist splint. As always, she just accepted all this and never complained.

Betty retired from RBCS in 1964 and joined Ron and Norah at Ron's house in Sproughton. When Ron died in 1974 she moved with Norah to a nursing home in Wantage, where she continued to paint and hold exhibitions. As her eyesight began to fade she switched from landscapes to abstract painting, and maintained that her composition improved as a result. When she could no longer see she moved on to clay modeling and sculpture, sensing what she was creating with her hands. She died there on 16th July, 1985, an excellent artist and teacher, and a determined, much-loved woman.

Daphne

Daphne Mary Brunhilde Inge (2 March, 1908 – 2 November, 1998). Long attracted to missionary work, Daphne was assigned to the Niger Delta in 1936. She was met off the ship by John Mabey Carr, who'd been on missionary assignment there since 1933 and who introduced her to the local staff, dignitaries and the area.

They took a liking to each other but not smoothly; although they became engaged in 1939, when John reached England on four weeks leave he was welcomed by a letter from Daphne calling off the engagement! Nevertheless, they married in early 1940 and their son Peter was born that December. Believing that the climate in Nigeria was unhealthy for babies, however, they took Peter to South Africa on a vacation to see friends (it being impossible to get to the UK at that time) and left him with them for the next three years.

Shortly after fraternal twins Robin and Jenny were born in 1943 it became possible to return to the UK, so they collected Peter from South Africa (though he hardly knew them), and boarded a boat home. The captain decided to head straight for England instead of first crossing to the USA to join a convoy, a risky manoevre made far worse when the ship broke down in the Bay of Biscay, prime u-boat territory! Fortunately they were not attacked and eventually made it home safely.

John took a living in the Portsmouth suburb of Cosham, then moved to Matlock in the Midlands in early 1945, where Sue was born in 1946. In 1953 a bishop who John had appointed in the Niger Delta asked him to go to neighboring Cameroon to establish some churches there, on his own.

Daphne agreed as long as she could take the children there on vacation at least once, which she did in 1955. They flew out on a Vickers Viking via Biarritz, Tangier and Lagos to Tiko, Cameroon. Returning by sea via a banana boat from Tiko, they landed in Garston, Liverpool, on 19th October, 1955.

John returned to the UK in 1956 to take up a living in Leicester, and in 1966-7 took over as Vicar at St. Peter's and St. Paul's church in Shiplake, Berks. He retired from there in 1975 and moved the family to Caversham, near Reading.

Sadly, Daphne developed dementia late in life. She and John moved to Lancaster; he died in October 1994, and she followed him in November 1998.

Appendix 3: Eulogies

The first was given by John "Gubby" Allen at Dad's funeral. John was a House Master and long-time friend of Dad's at RBCS; he acquired the nickname from sharing a name with cricketer John "Gubby" Allen.

<u>IN MEMORIAM - 2nd November, 1989</u>

<u>The Lesson</u> - read by Alan Sanders, Headmaster, Reading Blue Coat School

Death is nothing at all...I have only slipped away into the next room; I am I and you are you... whatever we were to each other we are still. Call me by my old familiar name; speak to me in the easy way you always used. Put no difference into your tone; wear no forced air of solemnity or sorrow. Laugh as we always laughed at the little jokes we enjoyed together. Play, smile, think of me, pray for me. Let my name be ever the household word that it always was. Let it be spoken without effect, without the ghost of a shadow in it. Life means all that it ever meant. It is the same as it ever was, there is absolutely unbroken continuity. What is death but a negligible accident? Why should I be out of mind just because I am out of sight? I am but waiting for you, for an interval, somewhere very near just around the corner... all is well.

Part of a letter by Canon Henry Scott Holland.

<u>Address</u> - John ("Gubby") Allen

We are here to bid goodbye to Bernard Inge, and reflect on his outstanding and influential life of eighty-six years. Eighty-six years for which, if life is just, he will have been repaid in some measure, however inadequate, for the enrichment he brought to the lives if so many.

Our first thoughts are surely of love, support and heartfelt sympathy for the current emptiness being felt by Joyce, whose self-sacrifice and devoted care throughout Bunny's life (but notably in his last, frail years) brought him so much comfort and freedom from anxiety. And our thoughts extend to his family, to Jill, David, Jon and Tim and their families, for having to undergo the pain and readjustment and feeling of deprivation at the death of the head of the family, which was bonded together by the love he demonstrably manifested to them all.

I am certain that none here feels adequate to pass, on succinctly speaking to Bunny's family and close friends at the end of a life of a man of so great a calibre and stature - certainly I'm not. I can but recall with all humility my experiences of working with Bunny Inge at the Reading Blue Coat School for eleven years.

Bunny went from St. Paul's Cathedral Choir School to Christ's Hospital, before taking off at the age of seventeen for a farm in Canada.

189

Although this gave him experiences to draw on and anecdotes to recount later, the life wasn't sufficiently rewarding to hold him, and when he returned to England after three years, he acquiesced to the suggestion of his schoolmaster father that he "join the family business", as he said. And so he, like his sister Betty and brother Ronald, became a teacher.

When war came, he was Headmaster of an English school in China, but he returned by the legendary "slow boat" to marry Joyce (who had accepted his telegram of proposal) and in due time he took up an appointment at the renowned Dragon School at Oxford. There in Oxford, a fellow member of the Home Guard found a way for Bunny to read for a degree at Exeter College while he was teaching, while he was adjusting to his new married status, and at the same time manning the home front. He passed the necessary examinations in two years, but still had to dine in hall and fill the requirements of another year in residence before being allowed to take his degree and seek a more fulfilling appointment.

Reading Blue Coat School at that time was not an impressive establishment. It survived the war only due to the shrewd financial management of Headmaster Freddie King. When he left to take up a new career in commerce the trustees appointed Bernard Inge to succeed him, although all concerned realised that the three-hundred-year-old school had no future as it stood at that time. Historians have recorded, and all will acknowledge, the dominant part that Bunny Inge played in shaping the strong, sound and thriving Blue Coat School of today from the establishment he took over in 1946, but it was from the next period, when the character of the school and the personality and human qualities of the Headmaster became inseparably interwoven, that I gained the experiences that are my only authority for speaking now.

The Blue Coat School I joined some ten years later had a pervasive warmth and personal friendliness that extended to all its boundaries. It originated in Bunny's heart. There was scarcely a dividing line between Bunny's family and the members of the school, nor was there any division between his family home, the study and the staff room, and the boarding house. Bunny's love for the young, the generosity of his spirit and the spontaneity of his affection for all members of the community at Holme Park knew no limits.

Those who were members of the school in this period have a wealth of rich memories to treasure. I could talk about Bunny's love of sport in general and cricket in particular, his love of choral singing, his humour and the way he would relish a witticism or bon mot. I should perhaps mention his enthusiasm for novel office gadgets, but his impatience with their instructions; it will surprise no-one that he never espoused the personal computer! But I will confine myself to just two aspects of Bunny's character with effects that reached us all.

The first was his boundless energy. Each day at 6:45 the study boys took his polished shoes to The Cottage. Then the sound of his voice singing "Oft in Danger, Oft in Woe" - which was ostensibly to himself but really to act as an early warning system for any boys misbehaving - would signal his arrival in the study. At his desk, he'd been through his own post by 7:30 - and everybody else's by 8 o'clock. And after breakfast with the boarding house, then assembly, lessons and lunch, then games or more lessons, he allowed himself a brief visit back to The

2

190

Cottage for tea, then back to the study for special lessons for boys
slipping behind with their Maths, or Latin, or French. He played golf
with his friends, squash with the boys, and cricket and hockey for
selected teams. Bunny coached the Colts XI, took a leading part in the
annual play, led boarders on pioneering parties with bow saws on Saturday and Sunday afternoons to keep the Holme Park fires supplied with
logs.

In the Christmas holidays, Bunny fed the school pigs and chickens to let
the gardeners enjoy their break. In the Easter holidays, he took the
school's annual Swiss trip on energetic walks up the Alps, and in the
summer holidays he drove the tractors to gang-mow the school playing
fields. And for the boarders' annual Christmas party, he personally
selected the "Tom and Jerry" cartoons. And though his body weakened,
his mental energy never faded; it's now only a week since Alan Sanders
received a bubbling, impulsive 8-page letter brimming with enthusiasm
for the school's activities.

Of his powers of leadership, I should point out that Industry & Education now organise courses and qualifications in Management. This is so
that a leader may know what strategies to employ to get the best out of
his team. Bunny would have had no tolerance or patience with such
irrelevancies. His own supreme powers in this direction came instinctively. His intuitive gift of understanding went straight to a person's
heart, and a sign of encouragement or approval from the Head could
make a boy or master feel ten feet tall. If he noticed particular efforts
from a master he would say, "I'll take your lessons, you spend the day
at Lords (or Henley, or Wimbledon)." The notoriously straitened circumstances of schoolmasters' finances restrained him from suggesting
that they take a day at the races...

His birthday every year coincided with the anniversary of the school's
movement to Holme Park, and it thus provided the excuse for an annual
party at The Cottage. Spanish Chablis had just found its way to England, and Bunny used to come round, fill your glass and confide, "It's
just the thing for parties, it's very cheap." Knowing the uncertainty
that spread through the school as his retirement approached, the Head
called a special staff meeting to say, "I should like you to know that
Patrick Richardson, who is succeeding me, is the nicest man I've ever
met." One strategy never failed to defuse a colleague expressing impatience or anger with an aspect of school routine. Before he would hear
the grievance, Bunny would sit the plaintiff down, tell him to take a
deep breath, and not to speak until he had enjoyed a substantial tot of
whiskey. I commend this to all present.

Doctor Embling, who knew the school as Director of Music for fifty
years, summed up what I have to say with the words, "Bernard Inge
has the gift of spreading happiness." I cannot speak for the family or
former pupils of Bunny, but I can certainly vouch that countless
friends, colleagues and acquaintances have found Bunny Inge's warmth
and generosity of spirit an enduring inspiration. We thank God for the
privilege to have had his example.

3

The second was given by Nick Siney (son of Len Siney, another House Master and long-time friend of Dad's) at Dad's Memorial Service:

On November 2nd last year, many of us here today joined Joyce and the family at Bunny Inge's funeral at Pewsey and I know that hundred of others, who couldn't be present, were there most certainly in spirit, as with sad hearts we bid farewell to a truly remarkable and charismatic man. A man who truly lived up to the School Motto - VERITAS OMNIA VINCIT (Truth Conquers All).

Today we have joined Joyce and the family again, at this Memorial Service to celebrate and honour BERNARD INGE who, along with Joyce had such an influence on both the staff and boys who were more than fortunate to have been at the Reading Blue Coat School during Bunny and Joyce's time there.
I am quite certain we are joined today by many of Bunny and Joyce's friends from the village of Sonning, a village which Bunny loved and made quite certain became an integral part of the school when it moved to Sonning from Bath Road. These ties remain today.

Anybody who answered to not only BERNARD INGE but also BUNNY, THE OLD MAN, CHAD OR PLAIN SIR, had to have a great sense of humour, which can be borne out by some of the things he said in my school reports, which, I might add, I have kept under lock and key ever since, so my children would never see them.
Needless to say, Bunny subsequently told both my boys at cricket one day, the stormy of how I threw the Malthus Service into total confusion when I was reading the First Lesson, but concluded by saying 'Here endeth the Second Lesson'. When I apologised to the Bishop afterwards, he told me Bunny had told him I was, no doubt, thinking about the next day's cricket match and whether to bat or field first - and in any event, maths was not my strongest point - as a certain Antipodean gentleman who doesn't live very far away from this Church will testify.

I am certain that if you asked any Old Blue about their years at the School when Bunny was Headmaster, their memories would be happy ones, and that is why I feel he would want us to chuckle and smile and celebrate his life today, rather than be sad.

In normal circumstances, I am quite certain the present staff and pupils cringe when they hear yet another geriatric Old Blue reminiscing about his time at the School - which is precisely what this geriatric Old Blue is about to do - but trust they will put up with it on this very special occasion.

Unfortunately for many of the pupils here today, they will only know of BERNARD INGE from the stories that have been handed down and from the oil painting hanging in

Big School.

Big School, or Chapel as it was called in my day, doubled up as Classroom/ Chapel and had various functions including Dining Room, where Bunny and Joyce entertained the cricketers amongst us to lunch during the school cricket week. This was a week when Bunny would play for the Staff Xl on Monday, Aldworthian Xl Tuesday, Jack Stratton's Xl Wednesday, Farmer Bob Smith's Xl Thursday, his own Headmaster's Xl on Friday and the Old Blues on Saturday, and somehow managed to open the bowling at every match with slow, high trejectory leg spins, to devastating effect - particularly after lunch when he had made certain the batsman 'not out' had been well fed and watered with one of his favourite malts.

The Chapel, or Big School also served as Joyce's Dancing Studio, where she would gather the fifth formers prior to the Leavers Dance, and endeavour to teach the basic rudiments of ballroom dancing, so that on the allotted day of the dance, we would appear, hopefully like 'Debs Delights' ready and able to quick-step and waltz without crushing the toes of the young ladies present. For those of the congregation who don't know the Chapel/Big School, it is very long in length, but narrow in width, consequently if you ask any Old Blue's wife what their husbands dancing capabilities are, they will no doubt say 'very good going in a straight line, but definitely suspect when trying to negotiate turns and corners.

When Bunny Inge took the School to Holme Park in 1947, you have to remember this was before the advent of central heating as we know it today, and long before Marks and Spencer started selling duvet covers and quite definitely was before young ladies started sitting at the desks that we did - and in those spartan days had you asked a boy what a computer was, he would no doubt, have answered 'someone who travels to London each day to work'.

Bunny Inge almost single handed drummed up support, and with the then Bishop of Reading Trustees and Governors, Old Blues and Friends of the School, mounted an Appeal to raise the necessary funds to purchase Holme Park.

Bunny was, as far as I am concered, very rare for an Academic, because he had the ability to take off his mortar board and act like a Chairman or Sales Director of a major company. It was this business accumen and commercial awareness for banging the gong which galvanised the new School and its move to Sonning in 1947 - but one of his greatest qualities was the ability to charm the sparrows out of the trees.

There is no doubt that without his enthusiasm and strength, and Joyce as the power behind the throne, and if he hadn't been in the right place at the right time, it is unlikely that the School would have survived as we know it today, and his contribution ranks alongside that of The Founder, Richard Aldworth and Benefactors Messrs West, Hall, Malthus and Rich.

In 1947/8 after the school moved to Holme Park, ragwort and thistles grew in abundance on the playing fields, due to cattle and horses being the previous incumbents. At the start of each summer term, Chad would line up the staff and pupils down one end of the grounds. On his command, all would move slowly forward, like a swarm of locusts, devouring ragwort and thistles as they went. A potato crop was planted in various parts of the grounds, and when the time came for lifting, Bunny again operated the ragwort pulling system - the potatoes subsequently being consumed by the Boarding House.

In those far off days, every boarder started the day by being rudely awakened by the Duty Master at 7 am followed by a lukewarm shower, if you were lucky, and then trade work. This consisted of a variety of jobs, from polishing, scrubbing or peeling potatoes down in the cellars under the supervision of the stoker, a man called 'Fritzie Frost', but the most sought after job was that of the Old Mans study monitor. The most important job he had was to make sure that when Bunny came over -rom the cottage first thing in the morning to read The Times before breakfast, he had a cup of his favourite china tea. I well remember one April Fool's Day. One, Mike Foster, decided to disguise Bunny's cup of tea which he always drank minus milk and sugar, by making it with Worcester sause, which as you can imagine must have reached parts that even a well known Lager doesn't reach today.   Bunny did see the funny side of this - and I think Mike Foster did too after hopping around Stone Hall after his swift and sharp punishment.
I remember playing football in Big School with a pair of rolled up socks with Steve Dunster. We were having a whale of a time, until we realised that Bunny had been watching us for some minutes through the window. He came in and gave us a dressing-down - then proceeded to show us just how you should take a penalty by sending the goalie the wrong way, and then - regardless of the fact Steve's dad and uncle were Trustees and Governors of the school and he played cricket nearly every weekend with my father, gave us both 3 whacks on the backside for good measure. A drop of corporal punishment did us no harm, the same as it didn't for numerous other boys who subsequently went on to leave school and do National Service, knowing exactly what discipline and helping those less fortunate than yourselves was all about - thanks to Bunny Inge and the staff.

Even on school holidays abroad, Bunny would use every day things as examples to teach us something. On one holiday in Kandersteg in Switzerland, we all had packed lunches in pristine white paper bags, which Bunny said had to be kept off the snow for obvious reasons. However, not thinking I put my bag on the snow whilst we had a snowball fight, which was interrupted by a giant snow plough, which not only cleared the road where we were playing, but also my packed lunch - As an apple flew at great speed in one direction and my sandwiches in the other, Bunny turned to me and said "bad luck Siney, but at least you will always remember Isaac Newton's theory on gravity - although your lunch travelled quicker going up than it did coming down" - and that story is perfectly true.

Bunny Inge was warmhearted, generous, kind and tremendous fun to be with. Not only did he and Joyce remember every Old Blue's name, but that of girlfriends, wives and also children. As I have said he was a truly remarkable man, and will now close by using the very words Bunny used at a Memorial Service held 19 years ago on the 11th March, when he stood where I am today, and gave the address at my late father's Service -

"When he entered the gates of heaven the trumpets sounded"

These have been just a few of the many personal memories I have shared with you today at the Memorial Service to celebrate this remarkable and loveable man's life but the most important memories are your own, which I hope, like mine, you will cherish for ever.

Appendix 4: Cars Owned

In his youth Dad had a brief motorcycle ownership, a 350cc OK Supreme, but after falling off several times in the rain gave motorcycling up in disgust. Although not blessed with mechanical aptitude he always had a liking for interesting cars, something a little different from the masses. He mentions various cars he drove pre-war, including an Austin 12, a baby Austin, a Citroën and the big open Fiat he ran in China; to the best of my memory, the following are the cars he had during his RBCS years. I don't have photos of <u>any</u> of his cars, much to my regret, so the following images are of similar models, not his actual vehicles.

<u>Daimler</u> (1940s?), dark green – its sunroof leaked in the rain, dripping onto whichever child was sitting in the middle of the front bench seat. It's engine eventually ran a big end while we were on holiday in Somerset (David thinks it was in Dorchester, either on the way there or back), and Dad replaced it on the spot with the most appropriate car the garage had, which was a:

<u>Ford Pilot</u> (late 1940s), black, with a quite powerful side-valve V8 engine; it would cruise nicely at 80 mph, and Mum enjoyed driving it! Eventually it was traded in at Vincent's, in Reading (where Dad acquired all his cars until he retired) for:

<u>Standard Vanguard Phase II</u> (1954), black, a very solid car. It

had good performance from a 2.2 litre four-cylinder engine (with overdrive) that was also used in the TR2 sports car. We had a lot of affection for this one! It was eventually traded in for:

<u>Ford Zephyr Mk.2</u>, turquoise. This had a 2.6-liter six-

cylinder engine with a Raymond Hays-modified cylinder head for more power, which made it quite fast and enjoyable to drive. These cars were quite successful in rallies, including the Monte Carlo. After a while Dad traded it in for something he'd always dreamed of:

<u>1937 Rolls-Royce 25/30</u>, black, Park Ward body with a wind-up glass division between the driver and the rear-seat passengers. This really did make the rear seats almost completely isolated from outside sounds, and as kids in the back seat we often took advantage of it to feel quite "lordly"! I'm sure Mum and Dad often appreciated our being in a soundproof part of the car, too.

Dad had Vincent's take it out to the RBCS for Mum to test drive, as it was a heavy car. She gamely pronounced it "not as heavy to drive as I expected," (I suspect that she didn't want to disappoint Dad, who clearly had his heart set on it) so Dad bought it. The gear lever and handbrake were on the right side of the driver's floor, just inside the (rear-hinged) door, and care was needed to avoid one or both going up one's trouser leg on entry.

It was an amazingly solid car; all four doors shut like a bank vault. Tim once swung the wheel over a little too soon when backing it out of the garage, and took out two bricks in the wall with the end of the car's front bumper. There wasn't a mark on the chrome. It lasted for several years but eventually (1963-4) developed a ticking sound from the engine. Vincent's diagnosed a broken piston ring, but quoted £200 to lift the cylinder head and another £200 to replace the ring(s). As Dad had only paid £525 for the car in the first place (it was just an old car back then!), he traded it in on, of all things:

<u>1957 Borgward Isabella</u>, maroon. A highly unusual choice

after the Rolls, but a remarkably good car; 1,500cc, four-seat, two-door, 4-speed column gear change. I learned to drive on this, but after a couple of years (in 1966?) Dad traded it in on:

<u>1955 Daimler Conquest Century II</u>, dark green. A very nice, classy car, with a 2.4 litre straight six engine producing 100 bhp (hence "Century").

Mum and Dad then retired to Pewsey, where the Daimler proved a tad expensive to run on a retirement budget, especially after Dad took a part-time teaching position in Devizes with significant mileage (and fuel costs) each day. He replaced it with a Mini, much to our surprise! That was certainly economical, but increasingly hard for him to get in and out of. Eventually Mum and Dad went through a variety of other small cars, including a nice Triumph 1300.

200

Appendix 5: Traveling to Tsingtao on the Trans-Siberian Railway, 1935

During his trip Dad borrowed a typewriter from a French traveling companion and used it to record his notes and impressions. He later compiled these into the following story, which was published in the school magazine of either Christ's Hospital or the RBCS; it's unclear which. (The closing paragraphs of the preceding article by one A. H. C. Hill on life for a new boy in whichever boarding school it was are a little worrisome…)

After a man has been beaten by a College prefect, of which
there are 18, one receives a piece of toast from him. The
Junior Prefect of all is called "College Nurse", and it is his
duty to spank anyone of the new roll out of bed after 8-45 p.m.
(Note the difference between "beat" and "spank".)

I found things a bit easier to get into perhaps through
knowing both the Andrews (the younger was Staunton's pater)
and Morgan and Ounsted, who were friendly and helpful in
information.

Believe it or not, it is quite easy to get settled down in three
weeks at the most, which would appear incredible to some."

A. H. C. HILL.

THE ROCKET.

The sky is dark,
The wind's soft breath
Stirs the dead leaves
As if from Death . . .
A sudden flash,
The rocket flies
Out into the murky skies,
Rushing with a tail of light,
Like a comet in the night.

Upwards, upwards, farther, farther,
Where will it find its silent end?
And all its path is filled with golden light
With which the planets blend.

C. R. BENZECRY.

THE TRANS-SIBERIAN RAILWAY.

We got on the Trans-Siberian train at Negoreloze and were
greeted, as we stepped on the train, with a blare of music
coming from loud-speakers fitted flush with the ceilings and in
the dining cars. Very pleasant at times, but some of the stuff
relayed is pretty trying, especially the Russian songs and
speeches which come over the air at times. We have both
wireless, and records transmitted from a compartment on the
train itself. When they play dance music it's not too bad and
seems to come through not too badly, but the other stuff is too

169

loud and rasping as a rule. Still, it provides variety, although it probably amuses me more than most people on the train. The first-class compartments are really rather nice, with only two in each one. Very comfortable seats and beds, with a private washing place shared with the next compartment. I think they are a bit bigger than the usual ones on European trains. My companion is a queer bird. He is a Russian officer of very high rank; in fact I am told that there is only one rank higher, but that does not prevent him from going to bed clad only in the brightest pair of blue pants I have ever seen. He sleeps the clock pretty well round and has breakfast later than most of us, which is saying a good deal. He cannot speak a word of English or French, and as they are the only two languages I know our conversation is negligible. However, we get on very well and wave amiable courtesies to one another. He is full of smiles, and between us we wreathe the compartment with airy grins. All very jolly if a bit dull at times. Fortunately I am not dependent on him for company. There are some seven of us who speak English and we stick together as a rule. Two of us are English—if you count a Scotchman— and the others vary. I got up a bridge four which is composed of a Frenchman, a Dutchman, a Scotchman and myself.

The food is quite good at times although rather exotic. The mid-day meal laid us all out on the first day through the number of its courses, but we have got wiser now and leave some of them out. Caviare abounds, but none of us except a Swiss has much use for it, especially when it is followed by the rest of the fish, a sturgeon, as you doubtless know. There is a gigantic menu which is presented to you with a great flourish, but, as about three-quarters of the items are permanently " off ", the choice becomes not only dull but very limited. The chef on this train happens to be rather a bad one ; he is lazy and anything you ask him to do is greeted with a giant umbrage. Rather a pity, because some of the chefs on these trains are rather good and helpful, as are most of the officials. We have a " guide " on the train with us who speaks Russian and English, and he is both cheerful and helpful. Occasionally he tries to put a bit of propaganda down our throats, but as we refuse to take him seriously he is finding it heavy going.

We passed a homeward bound Trans-Siberian Express this morning, and at least one person would rather have liked to have got on it! The train stops several times a day for about ten or twenty minutes and we then get out and stretch our legs, or walk briskly up and down the platform in true British style, but how long we shall have the energy to do so remains to be seen. The appearance of the average person in the waiting rooms at the stations is terribly poor and dirty, while the smell is usually decidedly strong and revolting. It is a very common sight to see people lying flat on the stone floor, dead to the wide. And before I forget it I must tell you of our trip round Moscow.

As time was short we were taken on a little conducted tour, in the course of which propaganda was shot at us a good deal of the time. Our guide was a Russian girl and she was pretty efficient. All the decent new buildings were pointed out to us, and each one seemed to be either an Institute for culture, physical or otherwise, or else a building for Medical research, students, etc. There were exceptions, of course, but not many.

One's first impression of Moscow is not encouraging; the roads are awful, the buildings drab in the extreme, and the people all so poor looking and none too clean. Most of them seemed cheerful enough, but I do wish they'd try to look cleaner; it's so depressing. Then we were taken round the better parts. Here the roads were very much better and very smooth, but there seemed to be no shops worthy of the name. Women again seemed to be doing the same work as the men, and a policewoman on point-duty was greeted by us with cheers, but she didn't seem to appreciate it. Then to the Kremlin. This—we only saw the outside—was magnificent. Now, of course, it is all turned into political headquarters, but when the Tsars lived in it it must have been a really superb sight. It overlooks both the Volga and the huge Red Square, where Lenin's tomb is now placed. We were unable to have a look at the embalmed Lenin as it appears that it is the close season for him, but the tomb itself, of polished red and black granite, is a fine effort, though utterly out of place in its present surroundings. After paying for our guide at the official office—the guides get paid a regular salary by the state —we were taken on the Metro.

This has only been open three months and the Russians are justifiably proud of it. As you go in it seems an exact replica of Piccadilly Circus Station. But there the resemblance ceases, although the moving staircases and the lights are the same. For the platforms are long, wide, beautifully lit, and all of what seems like marble, although I don't know if it is. Each station on the line is constructed on its own different architectural lines, as regards the style, although the main features are the same. Each station also has its own colour; nothing violent, of course, but in soft tones. We only saw three, and they were in grey, a very gentle brown, a soft blue, and—we must have seen four after all—all white, though again a soft white. There are no advertisements and no slot machines to spoil the effect, which is grand. I wish we had something like it in London. I was smoking cheerfully as we went inside the station, and a policeman—I think he was a policeman—came up to me, saluted, and murmured something quite unintelligible, from which I gathered that smoking was not allowed anywhere on the Underground. It was, even so, the only point on which the London Tubes score over the Russian Metro! When that was over we clambered back into the TRANS-SIBERIAN TRAIN!

And so we have proceeded through Russia until the thrilling moment when we crossed into Siberia, a land I had always, until recently, imagined to be covered with snow, wolves, and forests, in common, I suspect, with innumerable other people.

Actually, the scenery, except when we were about to cross the Ural mountains—which we did at night—has been dull on the whole. The most enormous plains stretch for miles and miles, as far as the eye can see. Sometimes enormous tracts of this are cultivated, and sometimes there is nothing but marsh, but never, oh never is there the faintest resemblance to a mountain. That will all change presently, I know, and we will be glad when it does. The enormous size of the country can only, I suspect, be really appreciated by travelling through it by train. What surprises us is the simply staggering amount of land under cultivation, especially as there are so few peasants to be seen. There is no doubt whatever that the Russians are making a tremendous effort agriculturally, quite apart from industry. New log houses and barns are going up everywhere along the line, huge new areas are being put into cultivation, and the impression that one gets—a true one, I think—is that there is no country in the world with such possibilities as Russia. This seems also to be the view held by those who

172

205

travel regularly through the country. As I have already said, we crossed the Ural Mountains at night, but the scenery on the foothills was very pleasant. Forests and forests of firs, with the rich red soil standing out beautifully against the green trees, made a picture that will not easily be forgotten,

It has puzzled most of us as to where the peasants live who get in the hay and the crops, and we seemed to have solved the mystery. Very often, in sidings or on portions of the double track we have passed strings of goods trucks crammed with people, all, as usual, looking very dirty and very cheerful. Apparently they live in these trucks and are moved from place to place as they are wanted in various areas. What happens in winter or where they go I don't know, but perhaps to their own villages or to the towns.

The country became better and better cultivated from yesterday morning, that is to say from about Omsk. There is great activity apparent in the villages and towns as regards building, and this morning we stopped at Krasnoyarsk, which our guide fellow said was referred to as the Chicago of Siberia. That may or may not be an exaggeration, but it is a very big place with some 300,000 inhabitants. There is a tremendous lot of building of factories, etc., going on here, and it has some impressive buildings. The large river Yenisei runs by it, and an immense amount of timber is being dealt with all along the line.

Most of to-day the scenery has been simply grand. Forests and woods of firs and silver birches, which adopt the same conical shape here as the firs, all a pleasant green, stand up beautifully on the fresh green slopes of the foothills. I'm not sure what hills we are coming to, but they are the ones round Lake Baikal. Anyway, the sight is a marvellous one, and I believe that the scene round Lake Baikal itself has to be seen to be believed, which at the present rate of progress I can well imagine.

When we arrived at Krasnoyarsk this morning the first thing that struck us was the very clean appearance of the people, especially the children. We also saw a batch of what looked like prisoners being marched off under an armed guard; they included some girls, and a very large number of the men looked very Mongolian, a common sight amongst the soldiers. Our guide told us that they were merely people who had tried to get abroad or out of the country without passports, etc., but as he puts such a very rosy appearance on anything which may be taken as being against his beloved Russia, we had our doubts, especially as the guard was very heavily armed. There are special station policemen at all the stations and all of them wear revolvers. Whenever we stop at a station we get out, and a warning bell is struck twice for us to get on again. Then comes a warning toot on the whistle and we are off.

We have discovered another fact about these travelling farm workers. Apart from living in those trucks they also erect large marquees and dwell there until their work is finished in that part. We still pass any number of these strings of trucks with their human loads. We also passed some quite large coal-mines yesterday before we got to Irkutsk. We crossed several tributaries of the Angara, which is a pretty big affair itself, and then followed the course of the Angara until we came to Lake Baikal. You must excuse me if I give you some details about these things which you doubtless already know, but other people may be as ignorant of these things as I find myself!

Lake Baikal is really a fine sight. It is supposed to be the size of Belgium, but whether it is or not I don't know. It may well be for it is enormous and charming. From the sides, steep hills, mostly wood-covered, and mountains rise up with the most delightful little valleys in which are very small villages. There are also long slopes down which huge logs are rolled, although in winter I suppose they slide them down. What happens if one happens to hit the railway I can only guess, and the answer is not pleasant for we run right along the edge of the lake for miles and !miles. We spent some two or three hours travelling round the edge of Lake Baikal yesterday and the scenery was beautiful. And all to-day it has been equally nice. I, like lots of people, could not imagine Siberia as being culti-vated at all, except in odd spots. As it is, it is the exception rather than the rule to find any area of any size whatever untilled or unoccupied by some agricultural or industrial business.

I might mention, before I go any further, that there have been several remains of smashes on this line. Nearly all of it now is double-tracked. I have only seen one smash myself and that had obviously been a pretty good one. Trucks lay about on both sides of the track after an obviously first-class collision, and some of them were hopelessy smashed and bent beyond possibility of repair. It occurs to me that I have never seen a railway smash in England and I wonder how many people have.

Lake Baikal is also getting on for a mile in depth. In the construction of the railway line round it they had to cut thirty-nine tunnels with a total length of nearly three miles. Some of the tunnels are, of course, only about twenty yards long. They also had to build fifty small bridges in forty miles of track. So you will get some idea of the sort of scenery one has round the lake as the train twists and turns for miles, always following the edge of the lake whenever possible. And this line is double tracked all the way as well, while there are as many as three and four lines in places. In places the country looks absurdly like Switzerland, which is the last place I should imagine it would have looked like. This morning and all to-day the scenery again has been ripping. A wide river flowing lazily along— this is the time when there is comparatively little water about —through pleasant meadows, winding like a snake in torment! And logs, logs everywhere. Never did I imagine there was so much wood in the world, I think.

This morning, too, we passed a very large coal-mining area, and frequently during the past three days long trains of oil tanks have passed. From Baku, or to Baku, I imagine. We seem to have passed the agricultural part of Siberia, though I should not now be surprised at anything that turned up.

I do wish Geography books and Atlases would make Russia look like any other country. All I can remember of it in maps —and I refer to Siberia especially—is a white expanse with about a town and a half in it. It never occurred to me that it was a living country with masses of towns, industries, and so on. We are all agreed on one thing on this train: that it is worth coming through Siberia to see what we have seen and to learn what we have learnt. I certainly think it is an education in itself. Yesterday, *par exemple*, we passed a huge power station being built on the Angara, and this is only one of many being built along the Angara (by the way, did you know that the Obi is nearly 3,000 miles long—or is it?). These power plants are going to equal about thirty Niagara Falls power plants, which is some going. At any rate, even if you knock off a bit for exaggeration, as I have done already, you will agree that it

is a proposition of tremendous possibilities. With the vast
quantities of electric power that will be available there should
be room for unlimited expansion, especially if the Russian is
content, or if they can keep him content, to live under his
present conditions and at his present standard.

We have just had one of our worst dinners. Caviare—we
have it all colours and I dislike them all—and soup, which is
usually the best part of the meal, and in which I found foreign
bodies of an unpleasing nature. True, that happens at times
in the best places, but it did not make me feel any better.
Then came a bird of some sort which was so high that it was
with difficulty restrained from flying at me. The rest was all
right. The track is very uneven at times and bumpy too, while
at others it is all right. You never know. The rails are
lighter; they only weigh half what ours do, so I am told, and I
should think it is true, for they seem much thinner. Anyway,
yesterday at dinner the whole train suddenly shot off to the
right—the lines went that way so that was all right; but
someone's soup and somebody else's wine shot across the table
in one magnificent dash for freedom.

As I write large herds of cattle are coming into sight with
the usual forests and woods: we never leave trees, thank
goodness.

The weather is still surprisingly cool although getting
warmer. Yesterday was the only day when it was impossible
to have the windows open owing to the dust, but, fortunately,
Mr. Tours had given me a tip about that and I pinned muslin
over the open window. Dust still came in but not so much.
It's surprising where it all comes from.

Only two more days before we reach the terminus of the
Trans-Siberian and then for Tsingtao and the future.

B. G. INGE.

SOUVENIR D'ÉTÉ.

Le ciel est bleu et clair,
L'oiseau chante pour l'oiselle,
Les fleurs émaillent toute la terre,
L'odeur en est fraiche et belle.

Les feuilles pendent immobiles des branches,
Les petites églantines sont blanches,
Que j'aime la saison estivale ;
Que j'aime la beauté rurale.

C. R. BENZECRY.

176

Appendix 6: The Japanese Invasion of Tsingtao, January 10, 1937

An eye-witness report by Dr. Margot Grzywacz in the March 1938 issue of "Oriental Affairs", a Shanghai periodical.

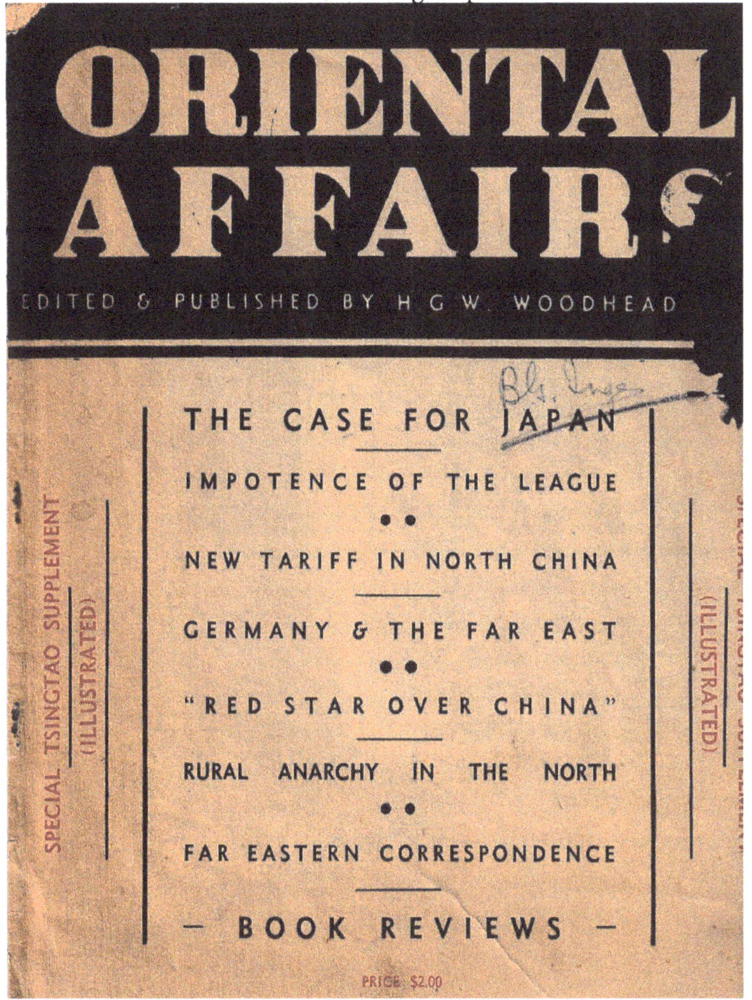

ORIENTAL AFFAIRS

A MONTHLY REVIEW

Price of this issue $2 per copy or $10 per annum

Editor and Publisher: H.G.W. WOODHEAD, C.B.E.
Office: 19, Avenue Edward VII, Shanghai, China
Telephone 84080

Postage to outports $1 per annum extra

In Europe £1 per annum, post-free   In North American, Gold $5 per annum, post-free

The Editor will be glad to consider original articles and correspondence with a view to publication.
Except where otherwise indicated, articles in this Review may be reprinted in whole or in part, with the acknowledgment of the source.

Vol. IX   March, 1938   No. 3

CONTENTS

LIST OF ADVERTISERS

Special Supplement

EVENTFUL DAYS IN TSINGTAO'S HISTORY

(December 18, 1937—January 22, 1938)

(The March issue of *Oriental Affairs* was already in the Press when the subjoined interesting and vivid narrative of events in Tsingtao reached the Editor. In his opinion the article and illustrations are of sufficient historical importance to justify a slight delay in publication, and their inclusion in a special Supplement. The Authoress, as will be seen from the narrative, was formerly a Professor of Shantung National University. She has twice previously contributed articles to this Journal, one on Ski-ing in Japan, and another on a Visit of the Chinese Science Society to Kwangsi. Shanghai has not been kept very well informed of the course of events in Tsingtao since the outbreak of hostilities. Here is the complete story.—*Ed*.)

(By Dr. Margot Grzywacz)

AFTER my short visit to Shanghai in February, 1938, where I had occasion to see the devastated areas of Chapei, Nantao, Hungjao, the Soochow creek, the Ziccawei Zone, the Civic Centre, Woosung, the many refugee centres, and thousands of destitute and homeless people, I can understand, how happy and thankful we, the residents of Tsingtao, must be that we were spared all those horrors of war. Many of us thought that we went through awful times here, but, indeed, compared with Shanghai, it was very little.

In the summer of 1937 the shadows of the Northern hostilities were thrown on the lovely summer resort: The residents, the summer guests began to become nervous. Many husbands who had sent their wives ahead of them, so that they might enjoy the cooler climate of this sea port, and who had promised to join them soon, had to postpone, postpone again, and finally cancel their trip.

Chinese residents, when they heard that the hostilities spread more and more, hurriedly left, many of the rich Chinese inviting foreigners to live in their homes, to take over their houses, free of charge, phone, water, light, servants, nice cars, gasoline, all included. Several foreigners, glad to be able to make some economy—but not very far-sighted—accepted these offers. Shops were closed, many houseboys, office employees left, too.

The situation grew tenser, when a shot was fired on a Japanese sailor in full day-light, near the Holy Ghost Convent, when at the end of August and in the early days of September all Japanese residents (officials included) were ordered to leave Tsingtao, when the Japanese Consulate closed on Sept. 9. Grave hostilities were awaited every day. And the worst of all were the rumours. "Mrs. X. says....", "Mr. Y. has heard that....", "Do you know the latest news that....?"

Preparations were made to evacuate all foreigners to a safety zone in case of danger, and the "Tsingtao International Food Committee" was formed. Many refugees from other war-stricken areas, especially Shanghai, had arrived. They were practically stranded in Tsingtao, many without funds, as communications to the southern ports were quite irregular. There was a continuous streaming in and streaming out of people. Without the rumour-mongers life might have been quite pleasant in Tsingtao during that summer. But people were worried, more and more worried every day. Many had to live separated from their families—without any news from their beloved ones. There was a general nervousness of a contagious character. Women had not enough occasions to show their new and most fashionable dresses, as the expected husbands or friends did not appear. There were not enough flirts for a summer health resort. Most of the nice motor roads around Tsingtao were closed to traffic.

Trenches were being dug everywhere, sandbags piled up, dug-outs constructed, air-raid alarms given, at first tentatively, then later seriously, though, fortunately no real air-raids occurred! All the Chinese schools, elementary and secondary ones, had been closed since summer and were never reopened. The Shantung National University in Tsingtao tried to reopen in October, but as only few of the students and professors had come back, it was closed again. Many professors had lost their jobs and travelled through the country, with much knowledge in their heads but with little food in their stomachs.

I had lost my position as Professor of the above mentioned Shantung National University, where I had been teaching for 3 years, as early as July, 1937, for the reason that—besides Chinese and several other languages—I happened to speak Japanese, too (which I started to learn 12 years ago in Germany); because I happened to have visited several times—besides many other countries on our globe— Japan, too; because I happened to have written—besides many articles about different topics in different papers and periodicals—an article in *"Oriental Affairs"* of April 1937 about "Skiing in Japan". (Skiing is my favourite winter sport). Well, mei-yu faze! So I was spared at least the strenuous experience which some of my former colleagues— who did not happen to speak Japanese, to know Nippon or to write articles about Nippon—went through in following their fleeing Universities to Anhwei, Hupeh, Szechwan, Shensi or Yünnan provinces.

Life in Tsingtao went on—rather quietly, without outstanding events—until December 18th., when a new chapter in the history of Tsingtao started.

To make history is easy, to criticize history is still easier, but to describe the true historical events is difficult, and fully to understand them, shortly after they happened, or while they are still happening, is almost impossible. So much depends on the angle under which you see the events!

SATURDAY, DECEMBER 18

I came from the movies at 5.45 p.m. A Russian gentleman stopped me in the street. I was rather angry, because I did not know what he wanted from me, but then he said: "You better go home now. Martial law at 6 o'clock." I took a ricsha, but the coolie dropped me, about 10 minutes' walk from my home. He had to hurry home, too. It was just 6 p.m. A chain of policemen stopped all down-town bound cars and passengers. All had to turn back. Only when I arrived home did I understand the meaning of all that: I found a notice of some good friends telling me that Mayor Shen had given definite orders to blow up the JAPANESE COTTON MILLS that night at 8 o'clock. Those good friends offered me shelter in their house for that critical night. Only in times of need you can find and recognize true friendship. I preferred to stay at home. And in my heart I just did not believe the rumour of the blowing up of the mills, for that had been decided so often that it could not seem true any more.

The servants in our house were white as chalk, and had put on all their clothes, one over the other. The ladies in and around my house had all packed the necessary suit-cases, ready to evacuate! How often during last summer had we all been ready to evacuate!

Then I sat down to take my dinner, and boom! boom! pom! pom! exactly at 8 p.m. the explosions started. One after the other followed. It was the first really big excite-ment Tsingtao had during all the time of the hostilities. It is always interesting to see in what different ways these incidents affect different people; some did not sleep all the night, some went on the roofs of their houses to see the big fires, others were busily engaged in storing away all their belongings in fear of the possible looters; those who were on Yin-Island on a hunting trip, on hearing the ex-plosions and seeing the flames thought that war had broken out and tried, with big difficulties, to hurry back to their homes; others who were passing the week-end in Laoshan heard the rumour that the Japanese had occupied the town and that the whole city stood in flames! I sat in my room and studied some Chinese drama harder than I had done for days. At 10 I went to bed and slept wonder-fully well, until the next morning some more explosions roused me from my slumber at 7 a.m.

SUNDAY, DECEMBER 19

More explosions, Chinese populace streaming from the city, carrying as many of their belongings as possible, and using all kinds of means of transport, even perambulators and children's tricycles. The outgoing foreign ship over-crowded with Chinese and foreigners, who had all to embark from the city bridge, as a boom had been laid in the Inner Harbour by sinking a Chinese gunboat and some other vessels. Sampans from the bridge to the ship were as ex-pensive as $10 per person. Most shops closed. Food difficult to purchase. Fathers, mothers, aunts, nephews, etc. of your servants start crowding your house to capacity. What can you do? Nothing. If you don't accept them, then your boy will leave you, too! And then? Many foreigners driving out by car to Szefang and Tsangkow to see the burning mills, the looting and fleeing populace. *Dies irae!*

MONDAY, DECEMBER 20

From the early morning hours looting in the Japanese district started. Windows and doors smashed, crowds com-ing out in plain daylight with the looted things, mostly eatables and cloth, but others carrying tables, chairs, clocks, coal, etc. In the afternoon most of the looters were checked, the Mayor having shot one of them personally. The Chin-ese marines with steel helmets bayonets and long swords patrolled the Japanese districts as well as the cotton mills. Curfew—as the days before—at 6 p.m.

Funny to say, when looting of the Japanese shops start-ed in the morning, Mr. Lee, Chief of Police, did not know nor hear anything of this looting, nor had the Police Chief of Section II (the Japanese shopping district) got the slightest notice of the looting!!?? So it happened that policemen in that section were watching and almost protecting the looters who consisted of Chinese civilians as well as of soldiers arriving in large trucks. But later, Chinese marines arrived and tried to check the crowds. When Mayor Shen heard of the inactivity of the police, he arrived in Police Headquarters, all of a sudden, delivered a very angry speech and dismissed Lee immediately. The Mayor made himself Chief of Police, and a certain Mr. Liao (who had been sent from Nanking 3 months ago) was nominated vice chief.

During Monday and the following days corpses of looters, who had been shot on the spot, were exposed to the public in some main and back streets as a warning to other prospective robbers, and so looting was gradually checked.

Japanese sea-planes were roaring overhead, some so low that you could easily distinguish the bomb-racks on both sides.

When will they be dropped??

CHRISTMAS WEEK (*From Dec. 24 to Dec. 30*)

During the Christmas days the main topic of the day was: When will Mayor Shen Hung-lieh leave? When will our town be entirely unprotected? How many houses will still be destroyed? When will the Japanese come?

More and more residents left; the crews of the H.M.S. *Suffolk* and U.S.S. *Marblehead* arranged for the transporta-tion of foreigners to the outgoing boats.

On Christmas Eve—that sad Christmas Eve of 1937 in Tsingtao—when the curfew was fixed for 7 p.m., there was a heavy explosion heard late in the night as a special Santa Claus present. That noise came from the destruc-tion of the important and very fine bridge spanning the river at Tsangkow.

The higher railway officials had left, the lower had been dismissed. So, the railway connection with the interior had been entirely interrupted.

Foreign women volunteers were helping in the Main Post Office to sort the mail, as many postal employees had left. And foreigners had to go themselves to the Post Office to ask for their letters. And thanks were due to the U.S. Navy and U.S. Consulate for the generous manner in which they allowed transport of the mail from the incoming vessels.

Much rumour was heard about forming a Volunteer Corps of special police, composed of foreign residents, but

VIEWS OF TSINGTAO

Tsangkow Pumping Station.

Tsingtao Electric Power Station.

Shanghai Cotton Mill.

Another View of Shanghai Cotton Mill.

there was no official advice yet. Chaotic circumstances were foreseen with big anxiety.

Each family was busily engaged filling all kinds of bottles, jars, tubs with fresh water every day, for fear that the other Water Works might be destroyed, as one, the main Water Works, had been demolished already. But great relief was felt, when Mr. Y. F. Lee, chief engineer of the Water Works, uttered his intention to remain at his post of duty no matter what should happen, and he thought that his staff would remain, too.

On Dec. 25, Christmas Day, curfew was extended, for one night only, to 11 p.m. What a joy!!!

During the next days Japanese warships had been sighted in the Laoshan area and on the 28th Mayor Shen published an appeal to the Chinese population advising them to leave the city and go to the countryside or to other "safer places" (where?!?), in order to avoid bloodshed.

Acting on the advice of the State Department in Washington, a large number of Americans are being evacuated to Shanghai in the American gunboat *Sacramento*.

Many Chinese Government employees, upon hearing about the fall of Tsinan, Capital of Shantung province, leave; the employees of big foreign firms and houses disappear, too. Three Chinese newspapers have to close.

On Dec. 28, in the evening, at 9.45 and at 9.57 the City trembled on account of some new explosions. Everybody thought: These are the Japanese bombs!! But "only" the cable-heads between Tsingtao, Shanghai, Chefoo and Sasebo had been destroyed, and besides the telegraph office and the wireless station badly damaged. The main electric sub-station had been dynamited, too.

On the 30th morning, by driving through the town, one could see that, though the aerials of the wireless station were still standing, the wireless building and instruments had been terribly damaged. The costly sluice gate of the recenty constructed new Naval Dry Dock had been destroyed, and the dock was full of water. The mill plant of the Towa Oil mill was completely wrecked, the offices and machinery of the Brewery were smashed, the new electric sub-Station of the Power Company at Szefang was entirely put out of working order. Its most up to date equipment had a far bigger capacity than the main station. On the 29th, in the evening, some foreigners and Chinese had tried to convince Admiral Shen that he should cancel the given order for the destruction of this sub-Station. But only a temporary postponement was reached; instead of destroying it at 10 p.m. on the 29th, it was actually done ot 5 a.m. on the 30th. That was all. It was an appalling and sad sight to see all that deliberate destruction!

The message had reached Tsingtao that the Japanese Army was bent on inflicting drastic punishment for the destruction of the many million dollars worth of Japanese owned property, the protection of which had been guaranteed by the Chinese officials in Tsingtao, when the Japanese residents evacuated in September. Of course, it is almost impossible to believe in the keeping of any guarantees or treaties in our modern world! And how can you expect it from your most bitter enemy!!?

NEW YEAR'S EVE, (*December 31*)

As the populace of Tsingtao had had a rather disturbed Christmas time, the International Club and the Tsingtao Café had made all kind of preparations to cheer up the poor minds. Invitations to the Fancy Dress Ball and following dinner at the International Club had been sent out, and the Tsingtao Café had advertised in the *Tsingtao Times*: "The Tsingtao Café, in the thought that Curfew shall still ring to-morrow night, are making arrangements for their orchestra to play until morning. Revellers can therefore make merry without the restraining fear of having to drive back home past challenging sentries. Sofa service is also being prepared for those who may find the strain too much of waiting for dawn to break."

But then there came a "Late Notice: International Club. New Year's Eve Ball. The above ball has been cancelled. Instead of the ball a Reception, ladies and men, with cold buffet will be held in the Club at 12.30 p.m. on Jan. 1st, 1938. Invitations to the ball are good for this reception. Music from 1 to 3 p.m."

The Curfew on New Year's Eve was at 7 p.m. as usual, the Tsingtao Café was deserted, sons, fiancés, fathers, brothers had to patrol in the cold night through the icy streets to check the looters and recapture some of the looted goods. The womenfolk were anxiously waiting at home, and happy when they heard the steps of their beloved ones coming back from the night patrol. And why was all that? Because in the night of December 30/31 Mayor Shen with all his staff, all Chinese troops, all the policemen, had left Tsingtao, believing that as they had destroyed most of the important factories, public institutions, etc., the city had lost its value as an industrial place for them. More public buildings, most of the remaining Japanese houses were still supposed to be destroyed, they were all filled with kerosene and dynamite, ready to be blown up.

How fate often plays an important rôle, may be seen from the following: As most of the police's cars and trucks had been confiscated by the fleeing Chinese marines, the policemen had to use horses. Mr. Liao, who had been nominated chief of police by that time, mounted one of them, but was thrown off, and, as he was unconscious, had to be carried away (later he died in Kiaochow). Now the police force had no leader! Nobody to guide them in their most responsible duties. And thus disorder started amongst them and hastened their precipitate flight in that fateful night of Dec. 30/31. Had Liao not fallen from his horse, they most probably could have been persuaded to stay at their posts.

As soon as our beloved Port had been left without any official protection, the real looting which had been kept down so long, began; and undoubtedly the whole town would have become one vast sea of flames, had not the T.S.P. (Tsingtao Special Police) protected it.

In order to throw some light on the events of the first great scale looting on that day, we may read the following article, taken from the *Tsingtao Times* of Jan. 5, page 2:

"When early on Friday (31) morning, 2 a.m., the police force of Tsingtao began to demobilize itself, the phenomenon was observed by a member of our staff, who was on all night duty. By 3 a.m. he was able to ring up Mr. A. R. Hogg, who is some kind of liaison-officer between the British Residents' Association and H.B.M. Consul General. To his so pregnant message he received the reply that the C.G. would be informed in the morning. This probably accounts for the somewhat belated appearance in the field of the British members of the Citizens' Corps on Friday morning. Apparently the German members were more on the *qui vive*, for when, about 6.30 a.m., a report came that looting had commenced in the Kwan Hsien Road and Hsi Ling districts, they were on the mark and all set to go. If those early morning mobs laboured under the impression that with the disappearance of the police from the scene, the city and all in it was at the mercy of their predatory bands, speedy disillusionment came *upon* them. The German-Russian detachment fell to with their batons, and the mobs were very soon in flight. It is our carefully considered opinion that the prompt taking up of the mob's challenge to law and order by the German-Russian detachment determined the fate of that and succeeding days. Those early morning skirmishes proved the looters' Waterloo. Had there been any delay or hesitation at that time, the mob would speedily have grown to uncontrollable dimensions, and it is possible that many of us would now be refugeeing in houses stripped entirely of those prized possessions which give them comfort and make them homes.—The thanks of all citizens, Chinese and foreigners, are due to the prompt action of the German-Russian detachment, which undoubtedly saved the day. The work so well begun was supported and maintained by the rapidly improvized system of patrolling, which was commenced immediately, in which Britons, Americans and other late-rising nationals rendered yeoman service."

The Tsingtao Special Police

It was to the T.S.P. (Tsingtao Special Police) to whom we all owe the biggest thanks, that we are still alive, that our houses are still intact. To write the history of the T.S.P.—seen from the different viewpoints—would fill a thick book, and I hope all the various reports written by different men, Mr. Hogg, Mr. Hess, Mr. Ohlwein, Mr. Antoschowitz, Dr. Ludwig etc. will be published one day.

Here I will only give a short outline which does not pretend to give a full record of the T.S.P.'s doings.

In order to prepare the possible evacuation of foreigners, a committee, the "General Concentration Committee," had been established in November, consisting of one representative of the prevailing nationalities in Tsingtao, i.e. 1 Russian, 1 Britisher, 1 American and 1 German. When the possibility of an interim period between the leaving of the Chinese and the coming of the Japanese officials—probably a period of disorder—was drawing near, there was much talk of forming a Volunteer Corps, and some nationals had made preparations and had worked out plans for a self-protection.

But it was not until Dec. 27, that definite plans for an international organization were established. Mr. Hogg, British, was elected chairman, assisted by Mr. Hess,

German, who had had much experience from his active service in the world war and from his organizing work for many years in Hankow in connection with the self protection Volunteer Corps there. The British and White-Russians sent one representative each, with war experience to "Headquarters," to assist Mr. Hess, another Russian was to be chief of staff, with Mr. Antoschowitz (who had been connected for many years with the local police) as indispensable adviser; his mere name was enough to frighten the looters.

The Consular Body, with the exception of the American Consul, had allowed the organization to be built under two conditions:

(1).—that only moral pressure should be used,

(2).—that no other weapons than sticks and clubs were allowed.

American Nationals were not allowed at that time to register for voluntary service. Some, however, when real danger came, entered all the same (an act of chivalrous courage!), and then afterwards they were officially allowed to take an active part in the Volunteers' service.

Many different plans, how to organize the whole Volunteer Corps, had been made. The main points of Mr. Hess's plan, which was carried out, were the following: The City was divided into 5 circles (sub-stations). For each circle one group of ten with their respective leader was responsible, each group had to guard their respective circle by patrolling and checking the looters:

Sub-Station I......Iltis-Brunnen (*leader*: Dr. Ludwig)
Sub-Station II.....Cafe Kurort (Mr. E. Edgar)
Sub-Station III....St. Giles British School
                (Mr. G. B. Inge)
Sub-Station IV....International Club (Mr. F. Nauert)
Sub-Station V.....German Club (Mr. H. Dohse)
Head-Quarters at the German Club.

As the number of Volunteers was rather small, the patrols had to be made by motor-car. The patrols of one circle had to meet those of the neighbouring circle at fixed times, in order to remain in close contact with each other. As big crowds of looting mobs were to be expected, two special *emergency squads*, each one consisting of specially fit persons (under the leadership of Ohlwein and Schwardtmann) were formed to assist Headquarters.

At the beginning the general rule was: 4 hours' service, 8 hours rest; as the number of volunteers later increased from 200 to 260, the time of rest was increased.

First-aid kits were procured for each station together with sufficient supplies of candles and gasoline. Armbands had all been prepared.

On December 30 this plan had been worked out in detail; and it was just in the night of December 30/31 that the last Chinese officials left town. It all fitted incredibly well together, almost like in the movies!

On December 31, in the early morning hours, the T.S.P. and the German Consul were alarmed by Mr. Antoschowitz, who had seen during his patrol thick crowds of looters in the Japanese section (See the above article taken from the *Tsingtao Times*). The intrepid advance of

Shanghai Cotton Mill, Another View.

Fengtien Cotton Mill.

Ta K'ang Cotton Mill.

Kung-Ta Cotton Mill.

Feng-Tien Cotton Mill at Szefang.

Chimney of Ta-K'ang Cotton Mill.

Tsingtao Harbour Boom

Dead Looter in Liaoning Road.

VIEWS OF TSINGTAO

Ta-K'ang Cotton Mill.

Another View of Ta-K'ang Cotton Mill.

Kung-Ta Cotton Mill.

Kung-Ta Cotton Mill.

Dec. 22. View of Waterworks

Dec. 22. Authoress among Debris of a Cotton Mill.

the first emergency squad and the following early morning "attacks" stopped the looters' rush; they had been frightened, it came all so unexpectedly for them! The courageous and fearless volunteers used sticks, pieces of wood, boards, and poles to charge the astonished and super-surprised mob.

In the later morning hours—when the whole town was alarmed—more and more volunteers registered and everybody, high or low, showed excellent discipline and willingly carried out their superiors' orders. Due to the unanimous work of all nationals together, the biggest danger was averted from the very first moment: the looting on a great scale not only of Japanese but of Chinese and foreign goods, too.

On Dec. 31, in the evening, about 100 men of the Kiaochow Railway police had come back. They were divided amongst the 5 sub-stations. The Chinese Fire-Brigade—at first one Mr. Ma, then 11, then 25, at last 35—worked day and night under the Volunteers' protection, and after some days, some policemen came back, though without firearms. So the number of the Corps changed from time to time, but it was never bigger than 260.

On the 31st. the list of Volunteers was as follows:

Russians 128; Jews 17; French 6; Germans 56; British and others 35.

This number was increased by some Americans entering later. The percentage of each nation represented you may see from the following list: On Dec. 23 there were in Tsingtao:

Russians:	200
British:	103
Germans:	82
Americans:	137

It was very fortunate that on that fateful day of Dec. 31 the Volunteers discovered just in time, that some looters were opening cases of hand grenades left in the Chinese Navy Barracks, so they threw these cases with hand grenades, together with stocks of gunpowder and dynamite, into the sea. Several machine-guns, large quantities of ammunition and navy swords were also collected, and so the looters were hindered from equipping themselves with weapons and forming armed units.

NEW YEAR'S DAY 1938

Those people who believed the previous reports that there would be a New Year's Reception in the German Club were very much disappointed to find instead of champagne and sandwiches the whole reception room full of looted things. For, as mentioned before, the German Club had been turned into the Headquarters of the T.S.P. And all nationalities were eagerly busy in taking away from the looters whatever they could. In this big room you could find shoes, tyres, silk, kimonos, yarn, sewing machines, telephone apparatus, fish skeletons and intestines in alcohol (taken from some Japanese school), bicycle parts, all kinds of useful and useless things. And more and more "booty" was unloaded in front of Headquarters. What a sight!

Some New-Year-minded spirits—however—were not so easily to be disappointed: they thought of the notice the previous day, that there would be a cold buffet at 12.30

p.m. in the International Club. Another disappointment! The International Club was used as one of the sub-stations of the T.S.P. So, all these discouraged persons had to go home and ask their cooks (if any cook had remained in their house) to prepare "k'uai-k'uai-ti" something to eat.

A five hours' extensive walk in the afternoon showed that most of the Japanese houses and shops, beginning from the area around the Japanese shrine to the Japanese market district had been thoroughly looted. Streets in the looters' district were rather empty during daylight, except that from time to time you saw some patrolling cars or trucks. But towards sunset more and more persons appeared, most of them carrying empty bags, baskets or boxes, which they hoped to fill and refill with fresh stuff in the evening. Everywhere you saw burning houses, burning shops or factories, window panes smashed on the pavement.

At 6 p.m., I as an "ordinary" person, however, had to go home, and that was the time for the T.S.P. to start their action in dispersing the incoming looters. The Volunteers' task had been made a little easier, for about 150 Chinese policemen, who had deserted their posts the previous day, had returned, as Mr. Antoschowitz had promised them food, salary and safety. They proposed that Mr. Antoschowitz become Chief of Police, but he rejected this proposal. And he proposed Mr. Tung, a former Police Inspector, for this post. Mr. Tung accepted hesitatingly.

A corps of about 200 armed Railway Police, employed by the disrupted Kiaochow-Tsinan railroad, had been definitely enlisted by the Foreign Volunteer Corps to guard the main sections of the business and residential quarters and the Szefang Electric light plants, together with other volunteers. Food had to be provided for the railway guards, policemen and fire brigade. But from where was the money to come?

Two more Japanese factories, one a dye works, had been dynamited during that day.

A group of some prominent Chinese had formed a Committee for the purpose of maintaining peace and order for the time being, they called themselves: "The Chinese Commercial Union." Their leader was a very wealthy Chinese, Mr. Lee Teh-shuen. But they did not give any actual or substantial help to those brave Chinese, who helped to protect their property as well as that of others. At least, by forming this "Chinese Commercial Union" there was a kind of official body with whom the Consular Body could discuss important questions. All together only about 50,000 Chinese had remained in the city, all others had fled.

Volunteers were guarding the premises of the Asiatic Petroleum Company, the British American Tobacco Co., the Telephone Administration, the Post Office and the Water Works; mixed squads of foreign Volunteers and Chinese Police were guarding the wireless station and the Japanese Power Plant, and patrolled the streets day and night.

SUNDAY, JANUARY 2

When I took a walk through the same Japanese district as the day before, I found that the doors and windows of more houses had been broken than the previous day, but that, on the other hand, in other parts, many of the smashed entrances and windows had been barred again. New fires at many places, but many fires of the previous days extinguished. The general impression is that T.S.P. and police have the whole situation more firmly in their hands.

During the next days, though the military situation of the town remained unchanged, many of the citizens who had left the town at the beginning of the crisis in such a big hurry, were slowly returning. As it often happens in life, and especially in times of great confusion, the best deeds are misinterpreted, and the chivalrous and very splendid work of the T.S.P. was misunderstood by some Chinese. Some could not understand the aims of that Corps, and uttered their indignation at the fact that Chinese looters of Japanese—the enemy's—property were hindered in their acts of revenge by foreigners, who had no right to check them. They overlooked, however, the fact, that the looters did not restrict themselves to Japanese goods only, but had started to rob their own compatriots, too, and would soon arrive at everyman's property, regardless of nationality. Therefore many rich Chinese had sought and found protection in foreigners' houses. Foreign flags were used where they had no right at all to be used. German flags preferably were sold and bought at high prices by unscrupulous people.

It was a period of utmost uncertainty. Nobody could foresee when the occupation of Tsingtao by the Japanese would actually happen.

Some streets had regained the outer appearance of complete normalcy. Some of the police stations, which had been emptied since December 30, were occupied again, and the policemen—raising their right or left arm, doing their traffic control duty as usual, though there was almost no traffic—gave an added sense of security. Some of the smaller shops had opened a little gap in the shutters and were doing good business. For days and days I ate cabbage and carrots, or carrots and cabbage, and again cabbage or carrots. My servant admired me openly and secretly, and perhaps despised me even a little, but I explained to him that in the world war we had eaten turnips for 2 years: dried turnips, fried turnips, boiled turnips, raw turnips, turnip soup, turnip vegetable, turnip dessert, turnip pudding, turnip pie, coffee made of turnips, juice made of turnips, cake made of turnips, and last not least bread made of turnips. So carrots and cabbage seemed most welcome to me.

On January 3 a most welcome gift of $500, was sent to Headquarters by the Salt Gabelle. Attached was a letter of thanks and appreciation for the T.S.P. work. This money was used for buying food for the Fire Brigade and Railway Guards. Later some of the remaining staff of the K.-T. Railway sent a present of 50 tins of gasoline which were most welcome and needed, too.

On January 5 heavy looting occurred in the small harbour, where the stored coal-stocks were carried away on many junks. Mr. Antoschowitz with 20 railway guards and 10 foreign Volunteers tried to hinder the looters. Here they took their booty away, there other junks, heavily loaded with the precious fire material tried to escape. Japanese

aeroplanes roared overhead and were flying so low, that their pilots and the pilots' field glasses could be easily discerned. At last 13 prisoners were taken and the looters dispersed.

The main topic of the day was the wish for a new Provisional Government of Tsingtao, to which sums due for water, light, sanitary, land taxes and motor car taxes might be paid, in order to provide for the necessary funds to pay the Police, Fire Brigade etc. Hours of waiting. The Postal Service could no more function regularly, communications and travelling facilities were quite disrupted on all roads.

Beginning from Jan. 7 all the sub-stations of the T.S.P. were dissolved, and the respective groups of Volunteers had to report for duty at the T.S.P. Headquarters. This centralization system made it easier to supervise the situation, and besides made the duty of each individual easier: 4 hours of volunteers' service were claimed in every 36 hours. The policemen were promised 40 cents per day and food.

On January 8, in the afternoon, quite a big number of Japanese warships were sighted in the outer harbour, four Destroyers and four large size Destroyers or Cruisers, and it was reported that 2 Japanese ships were anchored beyond Swallow Island and that one Destroyer was anchored in Iltis Bay. And the same day Mr. Antoschowitz had cancelled his connection with the Emergency Police Corps for the reason that some of the Police Force acted in *such a way* (it is better to omit here in what way), that Mr. A's conscience of responsibility could not agree with that behaviour. His resignation caused the Tsingtao residents (except the looters) much affliction, for all had loved him and had felt safe under his protection; only the dogs in and around town were happy, as from now on—at last!—they were allowed to stroll around at their dog-heart's content.

A meeting was held during that day with the Chinese Commercial Union and they were asked to grant a sum of $12,000 to be used amongst other important items to pay the wages of 1,000 policemen for a period of one month. But there was no satisfying result! Mr. A.'s resignation from his post caused a new desertion of the Police forces.

And so Headquarters decided, if the money needed for the payment of the police were not provided by noon, Jan. 10, the T.S.P. would protect only foreign lives and buildings. In the night of January 9-10 the hearts of most of the T.S.P. men and of their wives and families were full of sorrow: new mobs were reported gathering in the vicinities, for by this time they knew that there was only a very very small number of Volunteers to resist them. Not much help could be expected from the Foreign Navies in Tsingtao. Most of the housewives had stored their valuable belongings far far away. What will the next day bring!

The only consolation during these long sad winter days was that the ice was frozen on lotus pond in the Big Park. It is seldom so cold in Tsingtao that you can skate. This year, however, nobody took care of the icy mirror, and so those who wanted to enjoy skating (very few indeed), had to sweep and clean the ice themselves. Why not! It was a good exercise. While I was tearing

VIEWS OF TSINGTAO

Jan. 11. Japanese Landing at Long Pier.

Japanese Landed at Long Pier. (Jan. 11).

Jan. 11. Japanese Troops on Tai-p'ing Road.

Jan. 11. Japanese Troops on T'ai-p'ing Road.

Jan. 1. Holy Horse from Japanese Shrine.

Dec. 31. Holy Cow from Japanese Shrine.

VIEWS OF TSINGTAO

Japanese Forces Landing at Big Pier.

Jan. 1. Fire Brigade Extinguishing Fire in Japanese
Godown, Small Harbour.

Jan. 10. Arrival of First Japanese Units at the Hospital.

Jan. 10. First Japanese Forces Reach the German Club.

Jan. 10, Mr. Miyamoto, the First Japanese Officer to enter taking
Photos in Front of German Club.

Jan. 1. Loot in Headquarters of the Tsingtao Special Police.

hundreds and hundreds of lotus roots out of the ice, my mind was diverted from the troubles around us, though the faded flowers were angry at the unexpected and unwanted intrusion.

JAPANESE OCCUPY TSINGTAO
(Monday, January 10)

At last, the long expected day of the occupation of Tsingtao by the Nipponese had come! Early in the morning, when the sun was just rising, the whizzing and buzzing of dozens of Japanese aeroplanes awakened the slumbering population. Some people uttered a sigh of relief. Others were white as marble and thought their last minute had arrived. But instead of the expected bombs, leaflets were thrown down from the air, one bunch in Chinese, the other in English. The English text was:

"Advice to the People of Friendly and Neutral Powers!

I hereby announce that His Imperial Japanese Majesty's Forces are doing their best and greatest efforts to keep the rights and interests of third Powers in the area of operation.

However, the city is in fear of falling into confusion by battle, the people of friendly and neutral Powers are kindly advised not to approach the dangerous area, and to take means of safety of themselves, for example, taking refuge in the Edgewater Mansions and approaches to Huichuan Point.

The Highest Commanding Officer of H.I.J.M. Forces."

The proclamation in Chinese reads as follows in the English version:

"The Japanese Landing Party will come ashore to-day, to take over Tsingtao, its commercial and official centres, such as the Administration and the Police Force.

The present Government is requested to fly the White Flag of Capitulation and the Chinese remaining troops in the city are ordered to wear their uniforms, as the Police force shall do, too.

The present Administration must form a receiving Committee which will await the victors at the Main Wharf, give their welcome to the Japanese forces and proceed with them to the Japanese Shrine."

But, unfortunately, there was no actual Administration in existence at that time, who might formally surrender Tsingtao, there were no Chinese troops, not a single Chinese soldier "to wear their uniforms." What should be done?

Shortly after 8 a.m. there came the report that the Japanese were dropping bombs on villages around Iltis Hook, and that planes were machine-gunning near the waterworks.

At 9.30 a.m. Japanese were reported to have landed at Sha-tze-k'ou (one hour's drive east of Tsingtao).

At 9.40 the Consular Body ordered the concentration of women and children in Edgewater Mansions; the American Consulate ordered the evacuation to the safety zone of: women, children and men, too. A detailed concentration plan had been worked out days ago and was at hand. The protection of the refugee zone was to be carried out by the T.S.P. alone; help by the Foreign Navies in town was declined.

Much criticism has been heard and written about the inactivity of the British and American Navies in town (not to speak of their excellent horse-riding, hockey and volley-ball shows); but before criticizing one ought to gather in detail all the necessary facts from the different sources; I tried to do that, from naval and non-naval sources, and I found out to my biggest astonishment that some criticizers had overlooked some very important facts and had not the slightest idea of some very important discussions which had taken place between different Naval, Consular and other authorities. This question ought to be studied in detail, but not in this article. . . .

The Consular Body tried to inform the Commanding Japanese Admiral about the real situation in Tsingtao. Women were busily and nervously engaged in preparing the allowed suitcases, posters were pasted at the doors indicating the different nationalities (to be protected). Most of the foreign women were sad and rather unwilling to leave their homes entirely unprotected to the Chinese mob, which was prepared to take profit from this situation and loot whatever was left to be looted, and set to flames what was not yet burning. The 11 days' work of the T.S.P. would have been frustrated. There would have been robbing, burning, clashing with the incoming troops, loss of innumerable lives!

Mr. Hess, Chief of police in the T.S.P., had discussed since 9 a.m. with Mr. Hogg, Chairman of the T.S.P., and others, the idea of going over by a special launch to the Japanese warships to inform the Japanese about the actual situation, but wanted to secure the agreement of the Consular Body. While they were waiting for this consent to come, Headquarters was crowded with men of all nationalities eager to get orders what to do. The report came that many Chinese and some foreigners were rushing to Edgewater Mansions. This news mingled with the reports of bombs falling, machine-gunning, and Japanese troops landing in Sha-tze-k'ou, with the outlook of most probable bloodshed and confusion, forced the people present to quick action, to hinder—if still possible —fighting and loss of life.

And so, Mr. Hess, in his capacity as Chief of Police, decided to explain to the incoming troops that there was no more resistance to be expected in town. It is natural that he took with him some men, whom he knew personally well and upon whom he knew he could rely while undertaking his rather uncertain and dangerous drive: Mr. Ohlwein (the leader of the National Socialist Party in Tsingtao and head of one of the emergency squads of the T.S.P.), Mr. Nauert (Head of Sub-station IV of the T.S.P.), and Dr. phil. et med. Hübotter, who had been teaching in Japanese High Schools in Japan for 4 years, as interpreter in the Japanese language.

Certainly, members of other nationalities might have gone to meet the incoming Japanese Army as well, but first it was not advisable to take more than one car, secondly there was no time to discuss the matter for a long time—action was needed; and thirdly it was not a very enviable task to meet an incoming Army who resented the big loss and destruction of their nationals' property in Tsingtao. Compare the shooting of Sir Knatchbull-Hugessen, British Ambassador! Who could guarantee the safe return of the outgoing car! How many flags ought to have been on the different cars, if different nationals had driven out together to meet the Japanese troops?

Mr. Hess's car, which he drove himself, carried a small German motor-car-flag, a big German flag (to be seen from aeroplanes), and a piece of white cloth, fastened at a stick, as a peace-flag.

They went in the direction of Sha-tze-k'ou and met the vanguard, which was about 5 km ahead of the other Japanese landed troops, at a distance of about 15 km outside of Tsingtao. The Japanese troops, quite prepared and fully equipped for an attack, had been on the march for nearly one hour.

The commander of the vanguard ordered one officer and one soldier with full equipment to accompany the party farther on. As there was no more place left in the car, Ohlwein and Nauert had to stay back, and Mr. Hess and Dr. Hübotter as interpreter (equipped with his German-Japanese dictionary) proceeded to meet Admiral Shishido, Commander of the landing forces. They told the Commander that no resistance was to be expected in Tsingtao, and that a concentration of the foreigners in Edgewater Mansions would not only be unnecessary but even harmful to the safety in town.

The Admiral, who seemed quite astonished at the unexpected news, sent one of his officers, Mr. Miyamoto, who acted as interpreter, and one soldier to town, in order to convince themselves of the truth of the statement, made to him by the two German gentlemen. On the drive back, Ohlwein and Nauert (the latter had to stand in the place reserved for luggage) were picked up.

During the journey back, when the party asked Mr. Miyamoto, if and why the Japanese did not know of the real situation of Tsingtao from the newspapers and radio messages, he answered: "The papers and messages may lie." The party had the conviction that the Japanese were not at all prepared for such an easy entry into the city of Tsingtao, for otherwise they might have landed right at the long pier in town, and did not need to land so far away and start a 4 hours' walk with full fighting equipment! And they might have come much earlier.

At 11.45 a.m. Hess with his "Information Party," as I will call it, had come back to Headquarters, where Mr. Miyamoto greeted his old friend, Mr. Antoschowitz, as well as other members of the T.S.P.

In the meantime, at 10.50, the White Flag had been hoisted on Signal Hill. (As there was no big white cloth at hand, Mr. Lee Teh-shuen, head of the Chinese Commercial Union, who happened to be at Dr. Hübotter's house that morning, took, on Dr. H.'s permit, a white cloth from a big box with books which had just come from Germany. It turned out to be an old soiled cloth, that Dr. H.'s grandmother had used as bed sheet ! ! ! The old lady certainly never expected that this sheet would play such an important rôle in the Far Eastern History !)

At 12 noon two trucks and six cars went at the request of Mr. Miyamoto to bring in the Japanese Headquarters' staff. The result of Mr. Hess's "Information Party" was that foreigners had *not* to evacuate to Edgewater Mansions (the news of which was received with the feeling of great relief by all!), that not one single shot was fired, that the looting which had restarted (following the news of the probable evacuation of foreigners) near the Post Office and the Small Harbour was entirely subdued.

I have heard and read many criticisms about this "Information Party," in Chinese as well as in foreign (German included) circles, too. Many were indignant that the "Germans had surrendered Tsingtao to the Japanese" (as they said), that they did not take other nationals with them, that they did not wait and see what would happen, that they wanted to rush the events, that they did not act diplomatically enough, that they wanted to glorify their name, etc. To all these reproaches there is only one reply: The danger and high tension of the moment required quick action to do everything possible to hinder fighting and bloodshed. Whoever has been present in international or civil wars or in revolutions will know how dangerous it is if only one shot, the first shot, is fired by accident, how this one shot may roll thousands and thousands of innocent people into destruction! Anyone who was not present on the morning of January 10 in Tsingtao, who has not seen the pallid faces of women, employees and shopkeepers, who has not seen the firm but anxious expression on our menfolk's faces, when they informed us that we had to evacuate, cannot understand the true facts. Six months of waiting, fleeing, coming back, fleeing again, consoling, supporting the refugees who came and went, who went and came, food shortage, lost positions, cold rooms, curfews, bad business, sorrows heaped on sorrows, uncertainty, undecidedness, disappointment had enervated the whole population, Foreigners as well as Chinese, Chinese as well as Foreigners! So, please, Mr. and Mrs. *Critic*, make it better yourselves next time!!

At 2.30 p.m. the Japanese Flag was hoisted on the Administration building (twice the rope broke, but then a Nipponese soldier climbed the shaking flag-mast and fastened his Empire's Flag with a firm and steady hand).

At 3.30 p.m. the Japanese flag was hoisted on Signal Hill.

At 3.50 p.m. Headquarters of the T.S.P. entered the Administration Building and the Commander in Chief of Imperial Japanese Landing Forces thanked the T.S.P. for the splendid work they had done for the protection of Tsingtao.

Later in the afternoon a notice was issued discharging the T.S.P. Volunteers, however, still guarded the Litsun Waterworks until Jan. 11, when they were relieved by the Japanese marines at noon and later disbanded.

In the night of Jan. 10-11 many residents of Tsingtao slept the first really sound sleep since July 1937!

The following days more and more Japanese forces—Army and Navy—were pouring in from the Outer Harbour, the Inner Harbour (the boom was easily overcome), from Iltis Hook and from interior points. Everything went on in an orderly manner. They had brought everything with them: motor-cars, trucks, tanks, furniture, horses, food and money (everything but *Women!*)

Many Chinese shops and private houses had hoisted a white or a Japanese flag, the few Chinese you met in the streets were carrying either one or the other of the two flags, and almost everybody was carrying an armband with the names of some big foreign firm or company. The deputies of the surrounding villages arrived to pay their respects to the Japanese in the Administration building. Every strategic point in the City was strongly guarded. Curfew was still in force for some days from 7 p.m. (later from 10 p.m.) to 7 a.m. Some funny misunderstanding occurred, as the soldiers who had to enforce the Curfew law were looking at their own watches, which showed Tokyo time. So I was stopped in front of the Grand Hotel when my watch showed 6.30 p.m. and his 7.30 p.m. But as I spoke Japanese and he was an educated man, we came to the agreement, after an interesting discussion, that Einstein's "Relativitaetsgesetz" should always be remembered.

It took some days, however, before the Chinese servants ventured on the streets to buy foodstuffs, and if they did, only well equipped with flags of their masters and with nice passports written by their masters' Consulates. After a while they found out that they were not slaughtered, that no hands or noses were cut off, that they were neither scolded nor enlisted in any army, that the women's tresses were not torn off, that their bicycles were not taken away, in short that all their fear was in vain, and again I could hear our servants' falsetto voices singing long Chinese operas from olden times! The best thermometer of the population's mood! The rather oblique heels of my shoes could be repaired, and my menus started to become more variegated.

Mr. S. Ohtaka, Japanese Consul-General, reopened the Japanese Consulate, which had been closed on September 9, 1937, and Mr. M. Takahashi, who had been long connected with Tsingtao's Light and Power Station, returned, too.

The cables are repaired, the boom in the harbour is partly removed. Other well-known Japanese residents arrive. Every day new transport ships are seen in the harbour, which regains its former lively appearance.

Many Chinese-owned houses are confiscated, for where shall the returning former residents live, as their houses are destroyed!? You destroy my house, I take yours; I destroy your house, you take mine (in case I let you take it).

On Jan. 13, the Consular Body sent the following letter of thanks to Mr. A. R. Hogg, Chairman of the former T.S.P.:

TSINGTAO,
January 13th, 1938.

Sir,

We, members of the Consular Body, would be glad if you would be good enough to convey to the members of the Tsingtao Special Police, and to accept yourself, our thanks for the efficient, unselfish, and prompt way in which the volunteer force carried out their self-imposed task of keeping order and restoring confidence during a time when this place was left temporarily without any semblance of police control.

The thanks of the whole community are due for a very fine exhibition of devotion to the common duty of helping in a time of emergency, and under circumstances of peculiar difficulty and political uncertainty.

We appreciate greatly your own hard work, and that of the other leaders who with tact and patience enabled an international body—as the Tsingtao Special Police was—to work without friction, and to attain the happy ends they did without suffering or causing any casualties.

We are, Sir,
Your obedient Servants,

H. E. Handley Derry
Consul-General of Great Britain

Dr. E. Bracklo
Consul for Germany.

Samuel Sokobin
Consul of the United States of America.

A. Tatarinoff
Agent Consulaire de France

H. W. Johansen
Consul for Denmark

T. G. Schutte
Consul for Finland
Acting Consul for Norway.

A. R. Hogg, Esquire,

Chairman,

Tsingtao Special Police,

On *Monday, January 17,* in the morning, the newly established Peace Maintenance Committee was formally recognized and installed into office. The new, or better old, Five-Bar-Flag, was saluted to the strains of the Chinese National Anthem. Mr. Chao Chi was elected as Chairman of the Committee. He had been Governor and Mayor of Tsingtao from July 1925 to May 1929, when he left as a political refugee from the advancing Nationalist troops. He returned to Tsingtao, after Admiral Shen Hung-Lieh was appointed Mayor, and remained here until last September, when he went to Tientsin.

On *Wednesday, January 19,* there appeared the following invitation in the Tsingtao Times:

T. S. P.

In celebration of the successful conclusion of our work, it has been decided to hold a T.S.P. reunion dinner (men only) on Saturday, January 22nd at 7.30 p.m. at the Cafe Courort to which all members of the T.S.P. are invited to attend.

Through the courtesy of the Imperial Japanese High Command Curfew will be lifted that night until 1 a.m. for all members of the T.S.P. who must wear their Arm-bands as means of identification.

The official party will last from 7.30 p.m. to midnight, and all members are requested to be back in their homes not later than 1 a.m.

The dinner will be informal, and members are asked to wear easy dress.

Tsingtao, 18th January 1938
A. R. Hogg
Chairman.

I heard from those who were present at that memorable dinner party on January 22, that it was a very gay and successful "Last Reunion."

And with that dinner party ended a chapter in Tsingtao's history of which our menfolk can be proud: different nationals had worked and fought side by side in best harmony and comradeship against the looting mob, they had protected the common good, for they had preserved law and order, they had prevented bloodshed and death. We all, residents of Tsingtao, and especially we, the "weaker sex" offer our deepest thanks to our chivalrous protectors. May the feeling of unity and harmony which you created by unanimously defending us against the common danger continue and perpetuate the life of our beloved Tsingtao, the Pearl of the East!

Appendix 7: The Japanese Invasion, A View from St. Giles

A report from one of the staff at St. Giles' School, published in *The Thirty-Six* school magazine.

The Japanese Passing The School On The Day of Their Entry.

"ST. GILES....SPECIAL POLICE SUB-STATION NO. 3"

Christmas 1937 is in the air....the majority of Boarders are **agog** at the thought of leaving by steamer for their homes in various parts of China. The day comes—December 17th.—and we seem so quiet with only eight children in residence. We already begin to look forward to seeing them back again in a month's time——end of term always has a peculiar sadness about it.

Little did we realise when seeing "the family" off at the wharf that the morrow would see the closing of the port by ships being scuttled to form a boom. When they did ultimately return from their holidays (which is, in a way, going to the end of the story first), they were brought ashore from the steamer in the pinnace of H.M.S. Delight— in a temperature so low that the spray froze on the hood and bows !

However, Saturday the 18th. came with everyone seeming a little sad at the departures of the previous day, and as the first day of holidays, it appeared to be the portent of a very quiet month. The afternoon wore on, and apart from several Japanese Naval Units cruising close to shore, everything was peaceful. Returning with the Paper Hunt Club from our afternoon ride towards tea-time, a local resident drove out in his car to meet us. Curfew would be enforced that same evening from 6 p.m. ; its reason purported to be a desire to keep everyone indoors while the Japanese Mills (valued at about $300,000,000) were dynamited and razed.

Sitting in the Staff room at 8 o'clock, just before dinner, the silence outside was shattered by tremendous explosions which followed each other in rapid succession. Within a few seconds, the north sky was reflecting a dazzling inferno for miles—and some of the boarders even slept solidly throughout ! For several days the destruction was kept up, and of course, the poorer elements of the Chinese population, thinking they might emulate with impunity the example of their superiors, commenced looting and destroying the deserted Japanese property in the town. Shops were ransacked, soaked in petrol and fired. The Police seemed helpless to control the situation, and

231

Chinese Marines were brought out to replace them. The measures they adopted, though ruthless, were effective. Looters were shot on sight and allowed to remain where they fell as an example to others. It was a strange sight to see dead bodies littering the causeways and gutters of some of Tsingtao's principal business thoroughfares. It was obvious that the Japanese would not long delay their invasion, and as the Chinese fighting forces remaining here in control were a mere handful who could not offer any effective resistance, the foreign population sensed that Admiral Shen, his staff, and Marines would leave town at the psychological moment. If any time was to elapse between this moment and the arrival of the Japanese forces, then the whole city was going to be at the mercy of a mob of hooligans, a menace which would endanger foreign lives and property.

The foreign community began to moot the organisation of an International Police Force for their own protection; sectional meetings were organised, recruitments made, and Headquarters and Sub-stations founded. "St. Giles" became 'Sub-station 3' of the Tsingtao Special Police. Thirty men were based on it under the Divisional command of Mr. Inge.

At 3 a.m. on the morning of December 31st. telephones began to buzz—the Admiral, and powers that were, were at that moment leaving Tsingtao—the Chinese Police had deserted en bloc—looting and disturbances had commenced. The Special Police were mobilized shortly afterwards ; by 6 a.m. patrols were on the streets. A concerted effort was being made to quell a large scale disturbance in the go-down district , the successful accomplishment of which broke the morale of the mob, and made the masses realise that law and order would be maintained at all costs.

For ten days the St. Giles Police Station played its part in peace maintenance, the residential district being the principal territory under its supervision. With thirty men operating in ten cars, the amount of activity can be well imagined, as can the weariness of the commander, Mr. Inge, whose job it was to keep up telephone communication with H.Q., despatch patrols, receive and write our reports, etc. His apartments were, from first to last, full of men waiting to go on duty, or having a snooze between whiles. Hot coffee and refreshments were on tap, and as is always the case when men congregate, the room was invariably under a smoke screen. The verandah resembled a petrol depot, being piled high with five-gallon drums for the use of patrolling cars. (Filling up at two or three in the morning, using a confiscated bayonet collected from some deserted police-box or barracks to open the drum, with a biting wind blowing petrol all over one, was a decidedly unpleasant affair).

After a few days, the success of the T.S.P. induced several Chinese police to supplement the force, conditional on protection being guaranteed by the Foreign Police Chiefs when the Japanese would take the city. From this time, we had about ten of these men posted to us, and each patrol henceforth carried two of them, armed with rifles.

The duties consisted in visiting and searching various properties, apprehending looters and suspicious characters, enforcing curfew and quelling mob disturbances. These ten days of unusual activity were characterised by remarkable camaraderie and willingness, and even when an extra duty kept one away from one's bed for several hours on end on a bitterly cold night, it was done with surprising cheerfulness. The sub-stations incidentally served to bring together many men of varying nationalities who may never otherwise have met. The author remembers one very pleasant night when, from 4 a.m. to 8 a.m., while patrolling a quiet district with a German comrade, the atmosphere of the car was filled with tantalising morsels of Beethoven, Bach, Handel and Wagner—sufficiently sweet, be it added, to lull our two Chinese policemen in the back of the car, into unbroken slumber. Perhaps I should have said that they slept in spite of the music !

New Year's Eve was memorable, the whole of the School resident staff joining the twenty-odd 'specials' (who incidentally had so timed their patrols to pass the school about two minutes to midnight !) in drinking a toast to the dawning year, while the opportunity was taken to present gifts and extend good wishes to a member of the staff whose birthday was January 1st. Mr. Inge, our commander, was in the unfortunate position of having to sleep, (that is when he could get to bed) in the same room where the patrolmen foregathered to talk, smoke, read and take refreshments, while his opportunities of going out and making a tour of inspection were few and far between. Actually, his position was undoubtedly the dullest in the station, and furthermore, necessitated an almost constant wakefulness, issuing instructions, communicating with H.Q., and performing countless other miscellaneous duties. When he tried to sleep, the radio would be bringing in London, Berlin, Tokyo, Shanghai, or Manila with news-bulletins and music—(everyone spent a certain amount of leisure moments in twiddling the knobs and listening to that part of the world which constituted home for him)—and he was condemned the whole time to live in a cloud of tobacco-smoke. Small wonder that his throat and chest cracked up for a few days after St. Giles ceased to be a sub-station.

The children who remained in residence at this time took things excellently. While they certainly must have realised the seriousness of the situation, they carried on their usual activities with the utmost nonchalance, the only difference from normal times being that they were compelled to remain in the school compound for obvious reasons. Towards the end of this night-mare period, all sub-stations were incorporated at H.Q., and patrols rearranged.

We shall all remember waking on the morning of January 10th. to the drone of aeroplanes flying low overhead, and our house-boys dashing excitedly into our bedrooms with handbills they had seen fluttering from aloft. These requested us in the name of "The Highest Commanding Officer of His Imperial Majesty's Japanese Forces," to take refuge in the Edgewater Mansions on Huichuan Point in the event of military and naval action being necessary to take over the city. While the 'concentration' of neutrals was still being considered and planned, the author left with an American colleague for the Litsun Waterworks to relieve the men who had been on duty there since the previous night. He was able to keep in touch with the School by 'phone, and from time to time learned of the day's happenings. It was a relief to know that concentration was not to mater-

233

ialise, and I fear it was with a positive whoop of joy that towards 3 o'clock we heard from H.Q. that the Japanese had effected a landing. Towards 5 p.m. we were able to leave the Water works, and driving back to town past the scene of so much wanton destruction, we saw the roads dotted with tin-hatted members of the Special Naval Landing Party.

The flag of truce was flying from all Chinese buildings, to be replaced shortly by the Rising Sun or the National flag of Japan.

So ended the 'days of the T.S.P.' and when on January 17th. the Christmas holidays came to an end, "Sub-Station 3" was able to assume, once more, its normal role of "St. Giles".

F. C. W. E.

INVICTUS

(With apologies to W.E. Henley).

The Song of a Goalkeeper on the Tsingtao pitch.

Out of the dust which covers me,
Thick as a fog from Pole to Pole,
I thank whatever backs there be,
For my unviolated goal.

Stung by the blows of forwards six*
I have not failed to cry aloud,
Beneath the bludgeoning of sticks,
I urge my comrades through the cloud.

Beyond this blur of dust and sticks
Lie but the shadows of my team,
And while the centre-forward licks
His wounds, he gives off clouds of steam.

It matters not how fast the game,
How heavy is the wounded roll,
I may be battered, bruised, and lame,
DUST is the keeper of my goal !

* A quite normal Tsingtao formation—besides, it rhymes better.

MENDING A CABLE

The Patrick Stewart was a cable ship in charge of the submarine cable in the Persian Gulf. I was once lucky enough to take a trip with her when she was repairing cable. At the time she was, to say the least of it, rather ancient, and much of the deck space was given up to live stock on which the whole ship's crew would live during the trip. We had sheep, pigs and hens, and two cows accompanied by their calves.

We set out from Karachi for the vicinity of Bunder Abbas, Persia, for a fault had been detected in the cable near this town. It took three days to reach the cable ground. The ship was of course fitted with all appliances for cable mending. On deck was a special cabin in which an instrument known as the Wheatstone Bridge was housed. This machine was used for finding the position of the fault in the cable, and could locate the break to within a few yards or so.

Appendix 8: The Thirty-Six

After he arrived at St. Giles in 1935 Dad started a school magazine, named "*The Thirty Six*", and remained its editor for his entire stay there. For the reason for its name, see his Editorial for the July 1939 issue, which follows the 1937 issue below; the closing remark is classic Dad.

The following reproduction of the December 1937 issue offers an example of school life during this period. What strikes me as quite remarkable is the very matter-of-fact view of things taken by all the writers, Dad as well as the staff and pupils, considering that they were in a foreign country under occupation by invading forces, with the inevitable uncertainty regarding day-to-day activities and their safety. The Japanese – at least the Navy - seem to have treated the various foreign communities well in general, even providing a gun salute from one of their warships during the celebrations of King George VI's Coronation on May 12, 1937!

The "Trouble" Dad calmly refers to in his opening paragraph refers to the sudden worsening of the Japanese invasion of China in the summer of that year. Tsingtao had been occupied in January 1937 and stayed mostly peaceful. Japanese forces continued to advance throughout China , and by July had grown to between 7,000 and 15,000 men, mostly stationed along the railways.

On the night of July 7 they conducted military exercises outside Wanping, a walled city SW of Beijing. A Japanese soldier failed to return to his post; the Japanese commander demanded the right to search for him in the city, and the Chinese commander refused. Despite the soldier turning up quite soon (he claimed he'd been taken ill) the Japanese pressed the point. Shots were fired by both sides, tensions escalated and although a ceasefire was declared, conditions rapidly deteriorated and full-scale war between Japan and China followed in August.

Beijing fell on August 9, 1937. Shanghai fell after a bloody battle lasting from August through November; the strength of the Chinese resistance shocked the Japanese, who'd believed it would take only days. At its peak nearly a million men were involved, and the fighting had deteriorated into house-to-house battles through the city streets. An assault on Nanking, the Chinese capital, followed on December 1; the city fell on December 12. Japanese soldiers then massacred Chinese prisoners of war, murdered civilians, and committed acts of looting and rape in an event known as the Nanking Massacre.

"Trouble" indeed.

You can imagine the impact of all this on the school in Tsingtao, given that many of the pupils' parents worked and lived in these cities; it puts the School's "carry-on" attitude into stark perspective. Hong Kong, being British, was considered a safe haven at this time, although it was clearly vulnerable. Japan attacked it the day after Pearl Harbor, 8th December, 1941, and it fell on 25th December.

Despite its losses China did not surrender. Russian and, later, Allied reinforcements kept its strength up, and while the Japanese held most major cities they didn't have the manpower to control the vast countryside. The Sino-Japanese War continued for another eight years until the end of World War 2. At that point the Chinese resumed their civil war between the Nationalists and the Communists, which had been put on an uneasy hold when the Japanese invaded.

ℭ h e
Thirty-Six

BEING THE MAGAZINE
OF

ST. GILES BRITISH SCHOOL
TSINGTAO.

No. 2	December 1937.

EDITORIAL.

This magazine is definitely an unusual number. We were prepared for a summer number and most of the proofs were in our hands, when along came Trouble—it needs no further definition. Printing was held up and in view of the uncertainty existing from day to day as to future plans it was decided to abandon the magazine temporarily. Consequently this issue is in two parts—the first half of the year, and the Christmas Term. If we have repeated ourselves we apologise in advance.

It has been impossible in the Christmas Term section to put in a list of those who have left and those who have come, for the very excellent reason that we do not know who have come to stay, or who have left permanently or only "for the duration". It is all very muddling. Due to the advent of Shanghai children stranded up here we were numerically up to standard but actually, we were some fifteen boarders short and had an increased number of day-pupils under the circumstances then existing. Pupils were admitted for periods ranging from two weeks to the whole term. Meantime our lost boarders congregated chiefly in Hong Kong and we hope they will return to the fold next term.

Whatever the future may hold in store we have a great deal for which to be thankful; chiefly because all the children at school here have been spared the horrors of Shanghai, and the extremely unpleasant conditions in Hong Kong. We had three Hong Kong boarders with us all term, and every letter we have received from anyone in that port has stressed the very disagreeable conditions—to put it mildly—existing there with typhoons, cholera, and vast overcrowding.

So that is one point. Another one is that the school has not had its activities curtailed in any way whatever and has been able to carry on without a single interruption the whole term. True, there have been rumours galore, but facts are what count and that is a very solid fact. Had we been through all the troubles ascribed to us by broadcasts in Shanghai and by the Shanghai and Hong Kong newspapers at times, there would have been a different story to tell. We would not for a moment deny that there have been anxiety and worry, but we have been allowed to carry on unmolested and for the sake of the boys and girls in the school we are more grateful than we can say. We hope that these few lines will encourage the pupils of this school to pause and think of those who have not been so happily placed, and for whom Christmas will not be quite so "Merry" as it usually is.

237

SCHOOL NOTES

Staff.—We were very sorry to lose several members of the staff at the end of the term. Mrs. Napier resigned after many arduous terms here as an energetic support of the Junior School staff, while she also toiled unceasingly at the Drawing in the school. Miss Price had made up her mind definitely to return to her native land and we regret her leaving as much as the small members of her Kindergarten do. Miss Donnelly left to be married—an event upon which we congratulate her in advance—and we thank her too for her energy. and interest in the girls' games. To all of these we extend both our thanks and our regrets that they have gone. All three ladies were the recipients of very pleasant gifts from the pupils in the school.

Sunday Services.—With the departure of her sister the lot of playing the hymns on Sunday mornings fell on Stella and she filled the part very efficiently. The Girl Prefects take it in turns to take the smaller children in Bible stories, as a rule, while the older Boarders are studying the Life and Letters of St. Paul, which we have reason to believe is a popular selection.

Valete.—Sonny Utting, Bill, Biddy and Patsy Hosking, Kathleen Draper, Mary Jane Draper, Tommy Draper, Marion Love, Gladys Clarke.

Salvete. — Bill Bruce, Dick Bruce, Margaret Squires, Isabel Squires, Joan Squires, Kirsche von. Kirschbaum, Pauline Abbott, Edward Milanowsky Gordon Sayle, Leilani Lamorie, Gwyn Smith, Collum Begdon, Derek Berg, Elizabeth Ride, Edwin Ride, Dorothy Ride, Grace Bruce, Connie Bruce, George Bruce.

CHEFOO.

At the beginning of last term, the prefects entertained six pupils from the Chefoo school, who were passing through Tsingtao. Mr. Inge, accompanied by the Head girl and head boy met the guests at the wharf, where they arrived on the "Shengking".

Seeing the time was very short, we had tea but for a few minutes, we played gramophone records and talked "shop". There wasn't much in the way of conversation, because everyone was engrossed in eating.

After tea we played some kind of a card game, which was enjoyed by everyone. All the prefects with their guests packed into cars, and went down to the wharf.

H. M. S. "GRIMSBY".

One morning in Febuary, the prefects and a senior boy and girl, accompanied by Miss Teeling and Mr. Edge, were invited to H. M. S. "Grimsby". We were conducted all over the ship in parties by the officers. Then we were kindly served with refreshments and entertained by the officers in their ward-room.

The School challenged the Grimsby to a game of hockey. Both sides played exceedingly well (but unfortunately the Grimsby played better and won 3-1.-Ed.)

H. M. S. "FOLKESTONE".

The afternoon that school broke up for the Easter holidays the boarders were invited on board for tea.

The "Folkestone" challenged the School at hockey. The school team was weakened by the absence of our two best players, owing to measles. Two members of the Tsingtao club were invited to play for us, this almost doubling our strength. (This is either insulting to the school or extremely flattering to the "two members"! Anyway we won 4-1. Ed.).

TENNIS.

Tennis started during the Easter holidays and has since been very successful. Every afternoon from 3.45 to 4.45, the girls and boys play at the Race Course courts.

Seeing that we have been pressed for time, we have not been able to play any Tournaments, except for one house match which Windsor won.

O. S. G. NEWS.

We have endeavoured to gather some items of news from those who have left and the following is the result of our efforts. We would like to add that letters from Old Boys and Girls are always welcome. Of the boys we hear that **Paul Ostroumov** is going very shortly to Stanford University, California, and although he is eager to go there, he is not too keen on facing an entirely new set of surroundings and people; we can sympathise with him. **Jack Ulanovsky** is also contemplating going to a University, but we are not sure which place of learning will be favoured with Jack's lively and excellent playing on the piano. **Of Lania Brodsky** we hear little except that after leaving here he apparently showed a great and not altogether unexpected liking for his bed in the mornings!

Desmond O'Halloran is now in Australia and we have had one or two long and very interesting letters from him. He seems to be enjoying life and is apparently concentrating on Swimming. Incidentally, Congratulations to him on passing his Junior. We hope the news has reached him long before this. **Frank Hearne** has, we hear, seen something of Desmond; he himself has joined the Artillery, we understand, and we have had pleasant visions of Frank lifting howitzers out of ditches etc., with the greatest of ease and with one hand. **Brian Edgar** is at Chefoo and likes it very much although he wrote at first that "getting up so early in the mornings and having cold baths do not appeal to me". We have suffered ourselves in the same way. **Sonny Utting** left us rather suddenly on the transfer of his father to Tientsin who are the gainers of an excellent footballer and of one of our tallest members, and that at the age of 13. **Dick Croucher** is at school in England and seems as far as we can see to be having a good time. He is still very well remembered out here, especially by Captain Svane of the Daviken!

239

Of the younger generation who have left us we have continued to hear excellent reports of **Derrick Ulf-Hansen** and from the photographs we have seen of him he certainly seems happy enough. We are also delighted to hear that **Derek Hersee** is doing very well in England. He is at a Preparatory school near Reading and what especially makes us happy is to hear that he is so far recovered from his serious illnesses that he is playing Rugger. Knowing Derek, we should not be far wrong in assuming that he is doing it pretty strenuously. He certainly deserves good health for a very long time to come.

' CORONATION DAY

..The ritual for the Coronation of the Kings of England can be traced back to the Coronation Order known by the name of "Ethelred II," but it is believed to have been first used at the crowning of Harold II and William the Conqueror. May 12, 1937, twenty-six years after his father George V was crowned, George VI, by the Grace of God, of Great Britain, Ireland, and of the British Dominions beyond the Seas, King, Defender of the Faith, Emperor of India, was crowned in Westminster Abbey with his wife, Queen Elizabeth. There was great celebration in England and all over the world where there was British influence.

Tsingtao, China, had her celebrations. At the British Consulate a flag-raising ceremony was held at the hour of eight, a speech was made by H.B.M. Consul, Mr. H.F. Handley-Derry, C.B.E. on the flag of Great Britain, with a few words on the Coronation. The flag was then raised by Gladys Clarke and Bobby Miller, the head girl and boy of St. Giles British School. Medals commemorating the Coronation were passed out to all British Children.

The flag-raising ceremony was followed by attendance at the German Church. Many officials, British, American, Chinese, Japanese, were present. The congregation listened to Bishop Scott reading the actual Coronation Service as it was to take place in London. While the people were descending the steps of the Church, the British warship "Medway," and a Japanese ship fired salutes in honour of the King and Queen.

A cocktail party, held at H.B.M. Consulate, ended the morning celebrations.

In the afternoon sports were held in the Stadium, kindly loaned to the British Community by the Mayor. They began about two-thirty o'clock. Foot races started off the programme. The crowd began to increase until there was a great number of people present. The races were followed by three-legged races and other sports, such as the banana race, caterpillar race, potato races for the little ones, and three legged football. The crowd and children were highly amused by three sailors, dressed up as clowns, who cavorted between acts and "raced" against the children. Ribbons were awarded to the ones who placed first, second and third. Tea was served with delicious cakes made by Mrs. Harris. There were cakes representing crowns, and the ship "Queen Mary." Lemonade and Ginger Beer were served also. The children had their fill and showed their appreciation by not only the noise, but also by the cleaning of their plates. Everyone then assembled round the Side-Shows, and had one or two hours of enjoyment. In the stands were such things as Breaking up the

Happy Home, where we threw balls at crockery, Riding the Bronco, Bowling, Pitching Rings over Staples, Pillow Fights, and Knock His Block off, which was the most popular. One of the sailors generously offered his face as a target for tennis-balls. Ice-cream and candy were handed out. Every single one really had an enjoyable time. The crowd slowly dwindled away.

The Coronation Committee must be congratulated on their work, and the successful achievement, of the Coronation Activities.

A Ball was held at Edgewater Mansions in the evening, while fireworks were sent off by H. M. S. "Medway", situated in the middle of the bay.

And thus came to an end a memorable day. George the Sixth is now King, Long May He Reign!

Bill Bruce

QUARANTINE IN THE EASTER TERM.

By a Boarder.

St. Giles seems to be the visiting place of all epidemics. Last term chicken-box broke out, bringing down quite a number, and almost preventing some from reaching home in time for Christmas.

One Sunday, three weeks ago, one of the boys caught measles and in the evening Mr. Inge told us that we were all in quarantine until further notice; much to our disgust, as we had enough of quarantine the term before.

On Monday it was announced at prayers that the school routine would be slightly altered as Mr. Inge wanted the boarders to have as much fresh air as possible. Drill would last for a longer period, and there were to be five minutes break between each lesson.

So far, the school has run fairly smoothly, but each week brought a new list of victims. The disease spread amongst the small boys, but now it has reached the older ones. But these are expected to be the last cases, as all the other remaining boarders have had it before.

Four of the boarders who were preparing for confirmation, and who were expected to be confirmed on Palm Sunday, were not disappointed except one, who caught it four days before that event. The others, however, were all confirmed, and although we were still in quarantime, a very impressive service took place in the school house. Bishop Scott confirmed the candidates, and then announced that the absent one was to be confirmed about Coronation Day.

So although we were unable to visit the cinema, or leave the school, we have had a fairly good time. We did not have French, and we spent a long time at games and drill.—**Stella Smith.**

HOCKEY.

Last Easter Term was not productive of very much in the way of competitive hockey, as the Club were not able to raise a team as a rule, a very sad state of affairs after the previous year. However, we were able to play two games with them, one of which we won and the other we lost. The games were very keen ones, but we felt very badly, as we had anticipated, the loss of our two sterling backs, and also of our fast outside right. The games were very useful to us as they enabled us to try out promising talent. Sonny Utting proved to be a most useful back and is a player of considerable promise. Isaebal Hutchison was her indefatigable self but must still learn to hit to the right quicker; she is one of the best players we have had and is untiring in sticking to her man. Vova Ribachenko proved to be a very useful goalkeeper and has a good eye. Stella is getting faster and goes hard, but is not quick enough in centering the ball although she can hit hard. Michael Laloe is improving but he lacks ball sense and in spite of his efforts he has not yet acquired that steadiness which will improve his game so much. Nancy Cohen is an extremely hard worker but has not yet learnt to hit the ball hard enough and as a result wastes a great deal of her good tackling as she cannot get the ball away to her wings. Pauline Abbott was a new addition to the school but shows great promise. She has a good deal to learn yet but she has good ball sense, hits hard and clean, and goes very hard indeed.

Yvonne Shaw was unfortunately not too well during the Easter term at times and thus was not chosen to play for the school. As she has now we hope recovered from her troubles we trust that the loss of an appendix will make her her original self as regards hockey—she should be one of the best players in the school as she certainly has all the necessary ability.

We renewed our battles with the Navy; against H. M. S. Grimsby we found the team too much for us and went down by three goals; the match with H. M. S. Folkestone arrived with several of our team sick and so we borrowed two stalwarts from the Club. With their help we managed to win 4-1. These games with the ships are always most enjoyable and we are grateful to those who find the time to play against us during their regrettably short visits to the port.

The prospects for next season are better than they were at the beginning of the year, except that we have lost Utting to Tientsin, but we shall miss those manly and muscular backs for a while.

ARGENTINE ADVENTURE

It was very shortly after my arrival in Mendoza, that peaceful city, situated picturesquely in the foothills of the Andes at the North West corner of Argentina, that this little adventure...if I dare give it that alluring title, for the happening was hardly a thing one would care to go through more than once...befell me.

At the time, I was occupying a very large house of the Spanish Colonial type, complete with patios and imposing colonades, and all surrounded by a spacious compound fenced off with spiked railings. My servants occupied an adobe hut forty or fifty yards from the house, and as companions, I had four delightful dogs which greatly added to my sense of security. One of these... a short-legged, bushy-tailed, brown silken-coated, very affectionate animal, (of dubious parentage I fear!) I permitted to stay in my room at night, the foot of my bed being his special domain; his keen hearing was little short of uncanny, and his muffled growls or angry barking a sure indication of footsteps or other suspicious noises in the vicinity..

During my first few days' residence, I experienced an almost continual attack of 'nerves' after nightfall, due to the fact that I was the sole occupant of a large multi-roomed house in a strange part of the country, and furthermore possessed of an imagination which had full play under such circumstances. The outcome of this was that my faithful hound, who revelled in the name of "Guardian" assimilated my nerves with barely any difference in their degree of intensity, so that in the 'wee sma' hoors' he was quite as scared as myself!

Although the nights were hot, I sealed my room more or less hermetically, bolting and barring both doors and windows. (I had heard colourful stories of residents being confronted with unwelcome visitors while in bed, their visiting cards consisting of either a business-like revolver or the more gentle but equally persuasive knife, the throwing of which has been brought to a fine art in South America....and the scene of operations usually the window!). Consequently, I passed through my restless, seemingly interminable hours in exquisite discomfort. Poor old Guardian would plaintively whine his dejection and resentment, while I myself would lie awake bathed in the perspiration of awful suspense, expecting to hear padded footsteps outside, and possibly a gentle pressure at either door or window.

Came one such agonising and dreaded night, when, towards 2 a.m. I heard a distinct shaking of door and window. Immediately the dog set up first growls and then vicious barks, only to be outdone by the now quite frenzied rattle of the bolted portals and vents of my room. By this time, my heart alternately thumped heavily (my temples felt as though about to burst) or raced with sickening speed, and I had the horrid feeling of impending annihilation at the hands of an army of brigands at the very least.

Then as suddenly as it had started, the disturbance faded away; but for the space of a few seconds only. Having no means of defence, I lay practically petrified in my bed awaiting a fresh assault on the entrances; but almost at once the whole situation was to become clear to me; for, accompanied by a noise like the crescendo of rolling thunder, the room shuddered violently, throwing me on to the floor. To say that I leapt out of bed and made for the door with considerable fleetness, belittles the agility I displayed on that memorable night. I practically flew, and wrenched back the bolts and iron safety bars with feverish haste, the ground meanwhile undulating beneath my feet; the bed swung round and hurtled across the room, finally charging me with considerable force in the rear; then the ceiling came down on top of me, (fortunately laths, plaster and canvas only) and I began to wonder whether the walls would fall in or out... the latter I hoped. Just as I was about to turn the handle and bolt into the security of the open compound, the wall slewed over, putting the door out of jamb. Try as I would, I was unable to move it. The lights failed with this, and now, with the thought that I was about to be crushed to death by crumbling walls, I scrambled to the window. Fortunately, with almost superhuman exertion, I was able to wrench it free. The terrified dog was howling madly at my feet, and grasping him by his loose coat I literally hurled him out on to the patio.

It was only a five-foot drop, (all residences are only one storey high in this part of the world which lies in the earthquake belt), and I hurled myself after him without delay.

What marvellous creatures dogs are! He didn't bolt, but simply waited for me to emerge, and although the ground was still rocking and shuddering, his frightened howls ceased, and gave place to sharp barks as we dashed from the patio into the middle of the compound. Even as we were running came a shattering crash, for two of the pillars supporting the patio roof, broken with the frenzied shaking, hurtled to the ground. Outside the iron railing, pandemonium reigned in the roads, and for the first time I heard the spluttering of revolver shots by which means the vigilantes warn the populace of a 'tremblo de tierra'. After what seemed hours, the agitations of the earth stopped, and after ascertaining that the servants were safe, I was soon forcing my way through the crowds of terrified people to the nearby house of some friends. Arriving there, I found them in their night-attire (just as I was) outside their garden-entrance, showing amazing coolness. Their house, being a comparatively new one with anti-seismic foundations, had gone practically unscathed, and they being old residents, showed little signs of being perturbed.

After some speculation as to how friends and buildings had fared we ventured indoors, but there was no more sleep for us that night. We donned coats and dashed round in the car calling at our friends' homes, finding some semi-wrecked, and others intact. Unfortunately, several of the occupants had received injuries of varying degrees of severity, while the native population had suffered about fifteen deaths, and of course numerous minor casualties.

Many houses had been razed, and others of a more permanent character presented gaping cracks.

Slight quakes occurred at intervals throughout the night, but the worst had passed, and by morning, all had finished.

It was several days before the local population would even walk on the pavements again, so afraid were they that a sudden catastrophe might bring down a building on top of them.

The repairs to my dwelling lasted seven weeks, after which I took up my residence in it once more. During the remainder of my sojourn in Mendoza, I experienced innumerable shakes, and although always beset with an eerie foreboding, I gradually learned to treat them as commonplace happenings.

However, the one I have described was the most serious of them all, although in no way comparable to the calamitous quake which wiped out the city and 15,000 inhabitants on the morning of Good Friday 186-.

As a thrilling experience, it stands unique in my memory, but such thrills are not of the type that one could possibly even be curious to participate in a second time.

F. Clifford W. Edge.

NEEDLEWORK!

Yes, with an exclamation mark to express my great astonishment at the work presented for judgement on June 23rd!

It was in the autumn of 1935 that Mr. Inge, being very short-staffed on his arrival from England, suggested that one of the British Community might assist with the needlework. No needlework had as yet been included in the curriculum.

Rather fancying myself both as a needlewoman and a disciplinarian, I gaily undertook the task of organising the needlework! Task there was, with no shadow of doubt, but none of those involved could be called "gay", when once we had begun! Our early struggle with sticky needles and knotty cottons still remain in the memories of those concerned, I doubt not, and I refrain from harrowing the feelings by recalling them in detail! Likewise let us draw a veil over our achievements that term! But we all became friends, in spite of conflicting opinions on the importance of needlework in the life of today, and (silently) we all registered "Whoopee!" when the Cambridge Exams came along and sewing classes ceased!

So imagine my surprise when Miss Teeling, with well-deserved pride, introduced me to the work **accomplished since Easter!** No names were attached. That shock was to come when, the judging being over, I learnt that Yvonne Shaw was the worker of hundreds of beautiful stitches in a tapestry chair seat, and that Nancy Cohen was the creator of a fine piece of cross-stitch having counted every stitch of the pattern herself! Isaebal Hutchison's silk scarf and Stella Smith's cushion cover afforded equal surprise! If I had not looked inside Stella's work, I might have been tempted to add another to the armful of prizes she carried off! The number of stitches achieved by Jimmie Smith amazed me, Jimmie having been the class expert at finding reasons for cutting needlework! Margaret Squires' smocking on a silk blouse was excellent but the prize was lost because the plain needlework did not reach the standard of the smocking! Isabel Squires and Joan Coghill had worked well on night dress cases, and here, as throughout the class, admirable taste was shown in the selection of colour schemes for embroidery. Kirsche von Kirschbaum and Pauline Abbott had both put in some very neat work on silk scarves, Pauline's was triangular, and only those experienced in working on silk could appreciate the work involved. The prize for the Upper Division was finally awarded to Rita Toporoff for a tea cloth and set of napkins. This ambitious work was well finished and a great variety of stitches was used.

Then came the Junior Division. Mary Butts, Leilani Lamorie, and Connie Bruce will all do well if they keep on as they have begun; but sewing isn't learnt in a day and at first it does seem so slow and dull! Joan Squires will be a prize-winner some day; she was ambitious and did some hemstitching. The prize, however, went to Jacqueline Reeves who showed herself to be a very good worker with her piece completely and neatly finished. Well done, Jackie!

Rita Gordon.

MORE EXTRACTS FROM H. NAPIER'S LETTERS.

I went to two Balls during Carnival time-one at our Academy, and the other the Kunstacademie Ball in the Kuenstlerhaus. This latter was a huge affair-over 2000 people there! The place is pretty huge, usually used for exhibitions. There were 5 big ball-rooms each with an orchestra. The place was most marvellously decorated by all the famous artists of Vienna huge papier-mache masks and the walls of course, solid with mural drawings; caricatures in one room, mermaids in another, nightmares in another etc. Of course there were endless smaller rooms with tables and chairs for drinking. In one of the largest rooms with a very high ceiling was an enormous papiermache figure of Pan sitting at one end of the room, and between his knees was the orchestra. He was lit by concealed green lighting, giving him a most diabolical expression as he gloated over the crowd below. The outstretched hand alone was about 15 feet long! From certain angles he looked like a colossal Egyptian temple statue sort of brooding with a malicious smile. It was a costume ball-I went in my Sarawak costume. There were a lot of real Hindus there in their own garb. Then there were lots of people in real Arab costumes and of course simply swarms of others. I'd go crazy if I even started to describe them.

I have been delaying the writing of this till the Academy performance should be over-well now it is, Gott sei lobt, and I am free to **breathe** and work again like an ordinary citizen! It was given on two evenings as usual,-yesterday and the night before. Daddy went to both shows and said I did better the second time which was rather surprising as generally one always does better the first night what with all the excitement and knowledge that all the critics are there, not to mention the Mayor, the President's wife, Schussnigg Attaches, the President of the Academie etc. etc. The second night one usually feels flat and bored, though I didn't last night. We danced the same waltz that we did at New Year, except that it was lengthened and we were more out of breath than ever! The main piece was a fairy story and we had to act as we danced (or try to!). I was the Prince. I appear (when I first come on) on the top of the palace garden, and seeing the princess, fall in love there and then and jump down into the garden. The wall was as high as up to the top of my raised arm and hand-not frightfully high really when I come to think of some of the heights we jumped off the roofs of bathing boxes on Strand Beach, but of course that was soft sand and this was a hard unyielding stage. B. W. was awfully nervous about it always, and feared I would twist my ankle at the beginning of the dance! It was a gold wall and gate with a blue sky behind and my costume was a brilliant pinky orange and gold. My princess had red hair, but she dances far too woodenly and it was very hard to make love to such an unresponsive and shallow creature. By shallow I mean not in the ordinary sense of the word, but that she has no depth and seemed empty behind everything. The magician and old prince were geschminkt with angry ugly faces and I had my eyebrows wandering up skywards. I wanted to make myself brown, but I couldn't be brown for the waltz and there was no time to take off my original paint and start again between. As it was, C and I had simply to tear off our clothes and wriggle into the others as fast as possible and I had only time to raise the end of my eyebrows and eyes; the ends of my true eyebrows were covered up in flesh colour paint and powdered over. My costume was made by Ella Bei the best costume maker in Vienna, and she made me a headdress too, but it wasn't good and she hadn't kept to my drawing. So Dad rolled up his sleeves," spat on his hands" and got down to making a helmet crown; it turned out a peachy one, really Siamese which was the general trend of the dance. The drawing was based on a book you sent him on Angkot, and we got it from the headdress of the dancers without the spike in the middle, because with the movement I had to go through, it couldn't have stayed on.

On Easter Sunday I went to the English Church, and His Royal Highness the Duke of Windsor was there with his long tail of attache's etc. The Ambassador was also there, and they all looked as brown as berries from Ski-ing-the Duke especially, with his hair looking more bleached than ever. He read the 2nd Lesson. Someone took a photo of him from the choir gallery and sent it to the Daily Mail and got £50 if you please!!

SPEECH DAY AND PRIZEGIVING

The first Speech Day St. Giles has had took place on June 25th., 1937 in the Town Hall, kindly lent to us for the occasion by the Mayor. The entire first half of the programme had to be changed at the last minute as we found that without more time for rehearsal in the hall itself than we were able to give it was going to be a matter of extreme difficulty to ensure the audience hearing properly as we were unused to such a vast auditorium. However, the school played up very well and everything went off successfully.

To deal with the entertainment first. The opening songs were sung with considerable zest and were obviously appreciated by the audience who numbered about a hundred and fifty. Leilani Lamorie followed with a charming little piano solo; she not only played it well but deserves great credit for beginning again when she got "stuck" instead of collapsing entirely as is so often the way with small children on the platform.

The most diminutive infants in the school then had the stage to themselves. Some of them were rather awestruck but the two who feared neither friend nor foe were the two young Rides, Edwin and Dorothy, who not only did all that they were supposed to do, but lifted up their voices in the best Ride tradition.

The Junior Drill Squad then gave a really excellent display and this was so successful in its precision and smartness that a voice was heard from amongst the Governors—we refuse to give him away—murmuring in astonishment—"Talk about militarism!"

Stella Smith gave a delightful rendering of one of Chopin's more attractive Valses with a poise and assurance most pleasant to see. She was followed by the Junior Singing Class who were obviously out for a good time and who had no intention of being either "mute" or "inglorious". They rolled down to Rio and then fetched up in Dublin with cockles and mussels after paying a short trip to the Maypole in England. An enthusiastic performance well received.

The Seniors, well on their mettle after watching the Juniors gave a really grand display. The crash with which they lunged in perfect unison was worthy of the best Guards tradition, and the exercise carried out without any commands at all in complete silence was most impressive. A very good show.

Then came a most unusual performance. Kirsche, surrounded by a large group of children, as she always was when playing her accordeon, was most enthusiastically received by the audience, and especially by the German school. She really was excellent and deserved all the applause she received.

Once again the entire school burst into song, and it is worthy of note—serious or otherwise—that they enjoyed drinking songs and sea shanties more than the other songs. The closing song, "Good night, ladies," was sung with such energy and enthusiasm that it must have seemed like a terrific hint to everyone to go home!

This was supposed to be the end of this half of the programme, but at the special request of the Mayor the drill displays were repeated to a most appreciative audience.

The Consul-General-Mr. H. F. Handley-Derry, C. B. E., then opened the more serious proceedings. He spoke of his pleasure at being present on the occasion of the school's first Speech Day and of his further pleasure at seeing so many present. Mr. Handley-Derry then went on to give a brief resume of the history of the school. Founded under its present system some four years ago, St. Giles had seen many changes and passed through some very trying periods. He was, however, very happy to see the school in its present flourishing condition and congratulated the Headmaster on the excellent work that was being accomplished. What particularly impressed him was the very happy relations obviously existing between the Staff and the pupils. Difficulties there were still to face, he knew well, but he felt that with its present sound foundations these difficulties could be met by the school without undue fear.

His Excellency the Mayor of Tsingtao, Admiral Shen Hung-Lieh, D. S. O., then spoke. It was, he said, a source of extreme gratification to him that he had been asked to be present on this occasion, and he was very pleased to have the opportunity of addressing the British School. It afforded him great pleasure to have a British School in this port and he had always taken, and would continue to take, the keenest interest in its progress. He had been particularly impressed by the various performances given during the afternoon, and especially by the Drill. He was well aware of the special attention paid to games and physical development at St. Giles and he felt confident that the obvious happiness and healthiness of the children before him was due in no small measure to this. Admiral Shen went on to say that he was very pleased to see the constant use made by the school of the playing fields at the Racecourse. They had been re-arranged so that the greatest benefit might be obtained from them, and it was, he said, his most earnest wish that St. Giles British School would continue to use them whenever they wished to do so. Had the school authorities any suggestions for further improvements he would be only too willing to do everything possible to help.

His Excellency then passed on to the question of work. He considered that to have a Speech Day of this kind was an excellent stimulant for the pupils, although he was well aware that every attention was paid to having a high standard of work in the school, and he congratulated the Headmaster and Staff on the good results achieved. He regretted very much indeed that he had been unable to present prizes to the children himself. He had indeed offered to do so, but found that it was too late for this year, as all arrangements had already been made, but he expressed his firm intention of presenting some prizes next year, when he hoped to have the great pleasure of attending the school Speech Day again.

The Headmaster then rose to present the Annual Report of the school. Thanking Admiral Shen for his most kind offer, which he was very pleased to accept on behalf of St. Giles, he expressed his great appreciation of the honour paid to the school by His Excellency's presence that afternoon. He was, Mr. Inge went on, fully aware of all that had been done for the school by the Mayor and took this opportunity of thanking him most heartily for it.

The Headmaster first drew the attention of the parents and the children to the fact that the prizes had been presented by the Governors themselves to avoid the school's finances suffering and he asked the audience to record their appreciation of this most generous act.

As regards the progress of the school Mr. Inge stated that he would prefer to deal with this subject over a period of two years, since he had taken over the Headmastership. Many changes had been necessary and had been carried out. This had not been possible without the loyal co-operation of the Staff, whom he thanked very sincerely for their hard work, or without the whole-hearted support of the Board of Governors, a point on which he felt most enthusiastic. Numbers had increased, especially on the Boarding side, which would provide in his opinion the foundation of the much larger school he hoped to see one day. A wider connection was growing and children were already attending the school as Boarders from as far south as Canton and Hong Kong. As regards work, changes were contemplated which would give the pupils a greater chance of success in their examinations than they had at present in China, owing to the continual transfer from port to port or home on leave. The games, too, had improved and regular school matches provided an essential stimulant.

Continuing, Mr. Inge said that there were two more classes of people he wished to thank. The first one was the British Community for their loyal support of the school, especially financially; to the ladies he paid a special tribute for their untiring efforts. The other class were the Prefects. They seldom obtained any recognition outside the school, but it was his most sincere wish that the good work they put in inside the school should be acknowledged, and acknowledged openly. They had been splendid and especially he wished to draw the attention of the parents present to the Head Boy and Head Girl, Robert Miller and Gladys Clarke.

Finally, Mr. Inge thanked all those present for attending; it was most encouraging and would serve as an added spur to those responsible to make the next Speech Day a greater success still.

The prizes were then presented by Mrs. Handley-Derry, who expressed her very real pleasure at being present. Some amusement was caused by the very diminutive size of a few of the prizewinners, and by the way in which one or two of the older pupils came up for prize after prize with no time even to return to their places between them.

The afternoon ended with Mr. W. D. B. Miller, the Chairman of the Board of Governors, thanking Mrs. Handley-Derry for her kindness in presenting the prizes, after which the National Anthem was sung.

As the parents dispersed they took the opportunity to inspect the exhibitions of Drawing and Needlework which were in the Hall, and which were viewed with considerable congratulation to Mrs. Napier and Miss Teeling respectively.

PROGRAMME

Selection of English Songs .... The School

Piano Solo..Round and Round We Go .... Leilani Lamorie
(B. Diabelly)

Songs .... Kindergarten and First Form

Drill .... Junior Squad

Piano Solo .... Valse Brillant, A moll .... Stella Smith
(Chopin)

Song Selection .... Forms I and II

Drill .... Senior Squad

Piano-Accordion Solos .... M. L. von Kirschbaum

Further Selection of English Songs .... The School

Opening Speech by
H. F. HANDLEY-DERRY Esq., C. B. E.
H. B. M. Consul-General

Address by
His Excellency The Mayor of Tsingtao
ADMIRAL SHEN HUNG-LIEH, D. S. O.

Annual Report by B. G. INGE Esq.,
Headmaster

Presentation of Prizes by

MRS. H. F. HANDLEY-DERRY

*　*　*

GOD SAVE THE KING

The
Thirty-Six

BEING THE MAGAZINE
OF

ST. GILES BRITISH SCHOOL
TSINGTAO.

No. 4   July 1939

EDITORIAL

We were recently asked why the school magazine was called "The Thirty-Six." Without going into the merits or faults of the name, it was called this because the first number was produced in 1936. And we are beginning to think that we chose a memorable year. It is quite easy for us to imagine ourselves, old and bearded, reminiscing about the past. "Do you remember 1936?" we will ask. "Oh, yes; that was the last year in which anything approaching peace existed in China." There we are. No, perhaps that is being unduly pessimistic and we are optimists. But things happened in 1937; more things happened in 1938, still more things are happening in 1939, and as H.G. Wells might put it, "There's still Things to Come." Meanwhile, we go on and produce "Thirty-Sixes." And why not? It would be a dull world if we all sat down, did nothing, and moaned about conditions. Moaning would be a waste of energy anyway nowadays, with the air full of noises from tanks, aeroplanes and other implements of war. So we are a little pleased, slightly proud, and completely staggered at having produced this magazine again.

Looking on the cheerful side of things, we feel that we may actually miss in days to come (we said we were optimists) the present excitement of wondering whether the hockey pitch will be available or whether it is being used for cavalry charges. Then there is always the happy possibility at present (for the pupils) of not being able to get to school owing to a naval or military official of high rank inspecting Tsingtao, involving the blocking of so many roads.

We've a good deal to be thankful for at St. Giles; uninterrupted work and in actual fact very little interruption with games. And the boys and girls now at schools out here ought to be glad that they are living in such interesting times, even if they are a little too interesting now and then.

Meanwhile, is this an Editorial or an Essay? We are not quite sure, but we will proceed to make it perhaps more of an Editorial. We believe that the literary standard of this number is much higher than that of its predecessors. We draw therefore the attention of all readers to the following articles: recipes for the girls—this is a co-educational school so why not?; to all articles signed "Ian Kerr", to the essay on "Toys of my Childhood," and, in fact to the whole magazine.

In other words, here is the "Thirty-Six"; read it, and if you don't like it, say so. We could do with some lively correspondence.

251

Acknowledgements

No book was ever created by just one person, and I would like to express my heartfelt thanks to all who made this one possible.

Primarily, of course, to my father for having such a wonderful life, great stories and for writing them down for all of us, and to my mother for her lifelong love, support, and help in filling in several gaps. Various people at Dad's old schools very generously provided their time, resources and photo archives, most importantly Peter van Went of the Reading Blue Coat School and its current Headmaster Peter Thomas, but also Anne-Marie Ralph and Caroline Peacock at Downsend, and Sheena Lawrence of The Dragon School. My siblings Jill and David also contributed their own memories.

Above all, my thanks to my wife, Lindsay Geyer, for her constant support and encouragement. She never met my father, but it has been a pleasure and a privilege for me to introduce him to her through this book.

Illustration Credits*

*   BGI – Bernard Inge archives
    JI – Jon Inge
    RBCS – Reading Blue Coat School archives

About the Editor

Jon Inge is Bunny and Joyce's third child and second son. Educated at Maidenhead Grammar School (now Desborough College) and Oriel College, Oxford, he moved to the USA in 1979. Retiring in 2017 from a lifetime career in hotel technology, he now lives in Edmonds, WA with his wife Lindsay Geyer.

9 798886 927645 2